PIMLICO

289

THE SOLDIERS' TALE

Samuel Hynes was a Marine pilot from 1943 to 1946 and from 1952 to 1953, and was awarded the Distinguished Flying Cross. He has taught at Swarthmore College, Northwestern University, and most recently, Princeton University, where he is Woodrow Wilson Professor of Literature Emeritus. His many books include his memoir, *Flights of Passage: Reflections of a World War II Aviator*, *The Edwardian Turn of Mind*, *The Auden Generation*, and *A War Imagined: The First World War and English Culture*.

THE SOLDIERS' TALE

TALE

Bearing Witness to Modern War

SAMUEL HYNES

PIMLICO

Published by Pimlico 1998

2 4 6 8 10 9 7 5 3 1

Copyright © Samuel Hynes 1997

Samuel Hynes has asserted his right under the Copyright, Designs
and Patents Act 1988 to be identified as the author of this work

Pages vii–viii constitute an extension of this copyright page

First published in the United States of America by
Allen Lane/The Penguin Press 1997
Pimlico edition 1998

Pimlico
Random House, 20 Vauxhall Bridge Road,
London SW1V 2SA

Random House Australia (Pty) Limited
20 Alfred Street, Milsons Point, Sydney,
New South Wales 2061, Australia

Random House New Zealand Limited
18 Poland Road, Glenfield,
Auckland 10, New Zealand

Random House South Africa (Pty) Limited
Endulini, 5A Jubilee Road, Parktown 2193, South Africa

Random House UK Limited Reg. No. 954009

A CIP catalogue record for this book
is available from the British Library

ISBN 0–7126–6632–X

Papers used by Random House UK Limited are natural,
recyclable products made from wood grown in sustainable forests.
The manufacturing processes conform to the environmental
regulations of the country of origin

Printed and bound in Great Britain by
Mackays of Chatham PLC, Chatham, Kent

Acknowledgments

THIS BOOK has been in gestation for a long time. I might say that it really began more than fifty years ago, when I first flew into combat at Okinawa and saw that war was not what I had expected. Or perhaps it was some decades later, when I set out to write a memoir of my war, and so got to thinking about war narratives as a distinct literary kind. But it probably would not have been written if the University of Toronto had not invited me to give its Alexander Lectures in 1994. Those lectures were the first draft of *The Soldiers' Tale,* and I am grateful to the university for its invitation, and particularly to Dr. Lynd Forguson, principal of University College, and Professor Michael Kirkham for their help and hospitality.

Others, both friends and strangers, who have helped me include: Alfred Appel, Larry Bentley, Norman Blessey, John Bodley of Faber and Faber, B. B. Burkett, R. H. Cockburn, George Core, Richard Cork, Robert Cornell, Rob Cowley, Steve Ferguson, Dr. Jack Foster, C. J. Fox, A. D. Harvey, Walter Lippincott, Alex Medlicott, William Merritt, Hobie Morris, Julian Putkowski, Richard Saltus, Lt. Col. Jeffrey Smith, Alan B. Spitzer, A. P. Thornton, the late Jim Thorpe, George Virtue, Ann Waldron, David Westerberg, Frances Whistler, J. M. Winter, Robert Wohl, Jenny Wood, and Froma Zeitlin. Also, more generally, the staffs of Princeton University's Firestone Library, the British Library, the Van Pelt Library of the University of Pennsylvania, and the Imperial War Museum.

In the years during which I was writing this book, I published essays on modern war memoirs—not so much drafts as first investigations of the subject—in *The New York Times* and the *Sewanee Review*. I thank the editors of those publications for permission to quote brief passages from those essays here.

Copyright Acknowledgments

Contents

In memory of Owen Baird and Lyman Berg,
killed at Okinawa, 1945

Prologue: The Actual Killing

War always interested me: not war in the sense of maneuvers devised by great generals—my imagination refused to follow such immense movements, I did not understand them—but the reality of war, the actual killing. I was more interested to know in what way and under the influence of what feeling one soldier kills another than to know how the armies were arranged at Austerlitz and Borodino.

Those words are from one of Tolstoy's war stories. In the story, a man who is not a soldier travels to where soldiers are fighting in the Caucasus to see what war is really like, because he's interested. I understand his interest, because I share it; and so, I assume, do other ordinary, unbelligerent people. How could we not, living as we do in a world of continuous war? The historian Will Durant calculated that there have been only twenty-nine years in all of human history during which there was not a war in progress somewhere. And surely if he had looked harder he could have filled in those empty years; for the history of mankind, as the British military correspondent Colonel Repington once remarked, is the history of war. Certainly that has been true of our own century; there has not been a day since the century began when wars—many wars—were not being fought, and here at the century's end they go on as always: thirty by one count at the end of 1993, thirty-two by another at the beginning of 1994, surely at least that many as I write this preface in 1996. War is not an occasional interruption of a normality called peace; it is a climate in which we live.

So naturally we are curious about war and, more than curious, we are engaged and compelled by it. And yet when we address the actual wars of our time, the numbers overwhelm us. So many soldiers, so many battles, and so many dead—twenty-five million military dead in the two world wars alone, plus civilians beyond calculation (sixty million by one estimate, though it's only a guess; there were simply too many dead people, in too many places, to count and, in some cases, no survivors to do the counting).

Add to those numbers the living and the dead of all the other wars of our time—in Algeria, Sri Lanka, Angola, Iraq, Somalia, Lebanon, Cambodia, Afghanistan, Guatemala, Nicaragua, Ethiopia, Bosnia, Latin America—and the list goes on and on. In the presence of such multitudes the psychic defense called numbing quickly sets in; our imaginations simply can't encompass all those armies on all those battlefields. But we can and do respond to one man in his war. And so if we would understand what war is like, and how it *feels,* we must turn away from history and its numbers, and seek the reality in the personal witness of the men who were there.

Tolstoy's curious civilian located the reality of war in "the actual killing." That phrase focuses and restricts war not only to the killing but to the places where the killing is done, and ignores all the important but noncombatant business of war-making that takes place away from battlefields: the planning, the code-breaking, the quartermastering, the acts of diplomacy and government, which command the labors of so many people. These are all necessary, honorable tasks, but I too have excluded them from the tale; I too have taken the actual killing to be the center of war's compound story.

In the title of this book, *Soldiers'* is plural and *Tale* is singular. I have imagined that if all the personal recollections of all the soldiers of the world's wars were gathered together, they would tell one huge story of men at war—changing, as armies and weapons and battlefields changed, but still a whole coherent story. Such an entire tale can never exist: the men who could tell it are mostly dead, and while they lived they were inarticulate, or unlettered, or simply distracted by life, so that their wars were left unrecorded. Nevertheless, that notional tale is my subject: what happened in war, one man at a time; who the men were who told war's separate stories and what their stories tell us (and don't tell us) about war; and how the experience of war has changed in our century, as one war has followed another.

Against that notion of the soldiers' tale I set, from time to time, the myths of war. By "myth" I don't mean a fabrication or fiction; I mean rather the simplified narrative that evolves from a war, through which it is given meaning: a Good War, a Bad War, a Necessary War. Myths seem to be socially necessary, as judgments or justifications of the terrible costs of war, but they take their shape at the expense of the particularity and ordinariness of experience, and the inconsistencies and contradictions of human behavior. The myth of a war tells what is imaginable and manageable; the soldiers' tale, in its infinite variety, tells the whole story.

This book is not a history of war, or even of narratives of war, but a more personal engagement with the subject: reflections on the war stories men write, or a study of them, or maybe simply thoughts on war narratives. I have fixed my attention primarily on narratives of this century, because their wars are still our wars, present both in our historical world and in our imaginations, and also because this has been the century of personal narratives of war, for reasons that I will discuss. But even within the century's limits, I have not aimed at examining the narratives of all wars. I have nothing to say, for example, about the war in Korea, a war that came and went without glory, and left no mark on American imaginations—though nearly as many Americans

died there as in Vietnam. Rather, I have concentrated on what
seem to me the crucial points of change in our century's war
story, the myth-making conflicts that have given war the meanings it has for us. Which ones those are is clear enough: the two
world wars, which made modern war global and technological
and democratic; the war in Vietnam, which changed the way
Americans thought about their nation in the world (and the
way the world thought about America); and that other, unde-
clared war—the war that has always been waged against the
weak and the helpless, but most cruelly in our century, when
entire national populations have been potential casualties.

These are the wars that have been most remembered and
most recorded, and it is the records of these wars that I will
examine. I have adopted "personal narrative" as the generic
term for these individual accounts, defining them as first-person
writings in prose by participants in the events recorded. Of
these records there are two principal kinds, which correspond to
two quite different needs: the need to report and the need to
remember. The reporting instinct operates as war happens, and
appears in journals and diaries and letters. These accounts have
the virtues of immediacy and directness, and tend to level war
experience, reporting the ordinary days with the extraordinary
ones, the boredom as well as the excitement, and giving to their
stories the close texture, the grain of life in war. Memoirs are
another, more complex kind of personal narrative: reflective,
selective, more self-consciously constructed than the immediate
reports, an old self looking back—sometimes across half a
century—at what the young self did, what happened to him,
what changed him. I have drawn on both kinds of war narrative
in this book, though the majority of my examples are from
memoirs.

Some of these books were written by men who were, or later
became, established professional writers—men like Siegfried
Sassoon, Robert Graves, Farley Mowat, and Tim O'Brien. I consider their books here; but I also look at the one-book men,

who told their stories and then settled quietly back into their silent lives—like James Fahey, who wrote *Pacific War Diary*, his classic account of an ordinary seaman's war, and then went home to Boston to resume his career as a garbageman. The test, for me, is not how literary a book is (what does literary mean, anyway, except writing that gives a reader pleasure?), or how prominent the author became, but whether the book speaks with a voice that is stubbornly distinct, telling us what it was like, for *this* man, in *his* war.

Generally, the telling of war stories is direct and undecorated, which is the way soldiers seem to prefer it. T. E. Lawrence wrote that the airmen he knew after the First War particularly admired one war book, the anonymous *A Soldier's Diary of the Great War*. What they liked about it, Lawrence said, was that it was "sane, low-toned, and natural." Most of the personal narratives I discuss in this book are like that, though there are notable exceptions (including Lawrence's own *Seven Pillars of Wisdom*).

In all except the final chapter I have concentrated on English and American writings, though I have turned to examples from other nations and other armies when a contrast seemed illuminating. I have avoided fiction that clearly *is* fiction, though I have included narratives that are obviously factual but adopt the transparent disguise of invented names (as for example Siegfried Sassoon does in his *Memoirs of George Sherston*). I have also rejected narratives written with the help of another hand—usually some professional writer who wasn't there. Such books often contain dramatic military actions, but they fail my primary test: they lack an individual voice. And I have excluded the memoirs of generals and other senior officers, for the simple and sufficient reason that in modern wars, commanders don't usually do the fighting, or live with their troops, or get themselves shot at. I'm aware of the exceptions to this generalization: General McAuliffe at Bastogne (who, when the Germans invited him to surrender, replied, "Nuts!"), Rommel leading his tanks in

North Africa, Buckner killed at a forward observation post at
Okinawa. But as a generalization it holds: generals aren't usually
where the bullets are; they're back out of range, doing their job,
commanding. And the story of command is its own subject. The
wars considered in this book will be engaged at close range, and
for that we must look to the narratives of the junior officers and
enlisted men.

Because the soldiers' tale is told by the fighting men themselves, it is a tale of particulars: one man or a few men, in a
trench or on a beach, in a plane or a ship, acting, feeling, suffering. And because it is particular, it is the *human* tale of war.
There is a remark on the Holocaust by the Israeli writer Aharon
Appelfeld that speaks to this point. Everything in the Holocaust,
Appelfeld wrote,

> already seems so thoroughly unreal, as if it no longer
> belongs to the experience of our own generation, but to
> mythology. Thence comes the need to bring it down to the
> human realm. This is not a mechanical problem, but an
> essential one. When I say, "to bring it down," I do not
> mean to simplify, to attenuate, or to sweeten the horror,
> but to attempt to make the events speak through the indi-
> vidual and in his language, to rescue the suffering from the
> huge numbers, from dreadful anonymity.

The need Appelfeld speaks of is a moral imperative, and one
that is not peculiar to the Holocaust. If we would understand
humankind's most violent episodes, we must understand them
humanly, in the lives of individuals. That is what I have aimed to
do in this book: to bring modern war down to the human realm,
to give names and faces and feelings to the anonymous armies
and so to discover what it was really like to be there, where the
actual killing was done.

The Soldiers' Tale

CHAPTER ONE

The Man Who Was There

Take David Jones, to begin with: a gifted Anglo-Welsh painter and writer who served on the Western Front in the First World War and was wounded in the Somme offensive, and who later wrote a strange poetic war narrative, *In Parenthesis*. The subject of Jones's book is his own war, but it doesn't end on the Western Front; the last lines are from the story of a medieval battle—Roncevaux, from the *Chanson de Roland*:

> The geste says this and the man who was on the field ...
> and who wrote the book.... The man who does not know
> this has not understood anything.

Here, in the borrowed last words of his book, Jones lays a soldier's claim to authority for what he has written. The *geste* (that is, the tale) says this, and the man who was there, and who wrote the book, says it too. It is true *because* he was on the field; if you don't know that, you don't understand anything.

And that is where we must start in our consideration of war narratives, with the assertion of the authority of ordinary men's witness. About war, men who were there make absolute claims for their authority, as Jones did: war cannot be comprehended at second-hand, they say; it is not accessible to analogy or logic. "How can they judge who have not seen?" a French soldier-writer of the First World War asks; and another agrees, in a

1

sentence that seems to echo the *Roland* poet: "The man who has not understood with his flesh cannot talk to you about it." And an Englishman, from the Second War: "You have to have seen things with your own eyes before you believe them with any intimacy." And a German: "Those who haven't lived through the experience may sympathize as they read, the way one sympathizes with the hero of a novel or a play, but they certainly will never understand, as one cannot understand the unexplainable." I feel that way too. I hear a man at a dinner party say confidently of the siege of Sarajevo: "We could take those guns out with a little napalm," and I think: You have never seen napalm dropped, you don't know how it flows and spreads like a wave of fire and burns *everything*. You weren't there. It's a natural response, and I have adopted it in this book by choosing to consider only war narratives that are the testimonies of participating witnesses.

It's easy to see why men remember their wars. For most men who fight, war is their one contact with the world of great doings. Other men govern, sign treaties, invent machines, cure diseases, alter lives. But for ordinary men—the men who fight our wars—there will probably be only that one time when their lives intersect with history, one opportunity to act in great events. Not to alter those events—no single soldier affects a war, or even a battle—but simply to be there, *in* history.

So men feel a need to say, like the ubiquitous Kilroy, "I was there." Winston Churchill is supposed to have said, after the defeat of the Afrika Korps, that in years to come, when the men who were there were asked what they did in the war, they need only answer: "I marched with the Eighth Army." Everyone who fought in that war has his equivalent of that remark; he will tell you, I was on Omaha Beach, or at Anzio, or in Burma, or on Guadalcanal, or at Midway—naming the resonant names of the theaters of war and the big battles. And there will be a kind of satisfaction in his voice, that he was once a figure in an action that mattered to the world. A young British officer who was in the first wave on the first day of the Battle of the Somme later wrote: "July 1st 1916 was the most interesting day of my life." and you can see what he meant. Nothing in his life, before or after, could be so vast, or so fatal. It was the British Army's worst day; to be there, to be a witness to that huge catastrophe—of course that would be interesting, wouldn't it?

But though the old soldier, remembering, is proud of the great events he touched, it isn't their greatness that is his essential subject. He isn't concerned with the vastness of the battles of which he was a part, or the causes and consequences, or even who won. What his subject *is* Philip Caputo tells us in the Prologue to *A Rumor of War*, his memoir of the war in Vietnam:

> This book does not pretend to be history. It has nothing to do with politics, power, strategy, influence, national interests, or foreign policy.... It is simply a story about war, about the things men do in war and the things war does to them.

The two stories that war narratives tell are in that last sentence: "the things men do in war"—that's obviously essential: war is actions; but the "things war does to them" is also important. The things that are done are of two kinds: there are the inflicted sufferings of war—the wounds, the fears, the hardships, the losses—which are in the nature of war and must be accepted. Not that soldiers are merely victims—they are always to some extent agents in their lives—but much of soldiering is passive endurance: standing, not flinching, surviving. But there is also something else that is done to men by wars: no man goes through a war without being changed by it, and in fundamental ways. And though that process will not be explicit in every narrative—not all men are self-conscious or reflective enough for that—it will be there. Change—*inner* change—is the other motive for war stories: not only what happened, but what happened to *me*.

That complex story of doing and being done to has not

usually found expression immediately after the events it records: war narratives are by their nature retrospective. To per-
ceive the changes that war has made in a man requires the
passage of time and the establishment of distance from the remembered self, and it isn't surprising that most war memoirs
come late in life, that memory dawdles and delays.

There are exceptions—immediate memoirs, written while a
war was being fought, by young men who in many cases then
returned to their war and died in it (two writers of the Second
World War, Richard Hillary and Keith Douglas, are examples).
But for most men understanding comes more slowly, and imagination must wait upon memory to reveal itself. That has been
true since the beginning of written wars: Xenophon was twenty-
nine when he joined the Persian Expedition, but he didn't write
Anabasis until he was over fifty; Robert Lamb (the "Sergeant
Lamb" of Robert Graves's two historical novels) served in the
British Army during the American Revolutionary War but
waited until 1809 to publish his "original and authentic journal"
of his experiences there; Rifleman Harris published his *Recollections* nearly forty years after he fought in the Peninsula; Elisha
Stockwell was fifteen when he joined the Wisconsin Volunteers
in 1861 and eighty-one when he wrote down the story of his
battles. New memoirs of the First World War were still being
written in the 1980s, and three important accounts of the
Second War have appeared in the past two or three years. Old
men *do* remember.

The stories that men tell of war belong to a curious class of
writing. In most war narratives there is nothing to suggest that
the author is aware of any previous example: no quotations or
allusions or imitations of earlier models, and no evident knowledge of previous wars, or even of other theaters in the war that
he is recalling. War writing, it seems, is a genre without a tradition to the men who write it. Still, it has a place among established literary kinds: such writing, we might say, is something

like travel writing, something like autobiography, something like history.

It's like travel writing because wars are usually fought somewhere else, in places that are unfamiliar and odd to ordinary soldiers—on islands, in deserts, over mountains, in ruined landscapes that are nothing like what they knew back home. The teller of the story will have to give exact physical existence to those strange places and to describe his immersion in the alien, often terrible existence there and how he learned to live in it, or through it. That is what good travel books do; though one might add that it's also what *The Divine Comedy* does.

A war memoir is like autobiography in that it is the personal narrative of one man in his life; though it would be more precise to consider it a subcategory of this genre, conversion-literature, since it is a testament of a profound inner change in the teller. Most war stories begin with a nobody-in-particular young man, who lives through the experience of war, to emerge in the end defined by what has happened to him. Out of that nobody, war has forged a Self. Nobody, however young, returns from war still a boy, and in that sense, at least, war does make men.

But if it makes men, it also isolates them from other men—cuts off the men who fought from older and younger men who did not share that shaping experience, and intensifies the feeling every modern generation has anyway, that it is separate, a kind of secret society in a world of others. Here is an English soldier of the First World War reflecting on this generation sense in 1930:

Throughout Europe the phrases "before the war" and "since the war" are among the commonest on men's lips. They are used to divide the age into three periods, the world of men into three generations. Middle-aged men, strenuously as they attempt to deny it, are united by a secret bond and separated by a mental barrier from their fellows who were too old or too young to fight in the Great War. Particularly the generation of young men who were soldiers before their characters had been formed, who were under twenty-five in 1914, is conscious of the distinction, for the war made them what they are. Generally speaking, this secret army presents to the world a front of silence and bitterness.

It may be that this sense of isolation is one motive for the writing of war memoirs, that these books are communications among the members of that secret army, the men who have been there and will understand, as other generations will not and cannot.

War narratives are also something like history. Every narrative of war must move within a chronology of actual world events; the teller's battles, however minor, must have their historical locations among the great ones, and the origins of his experiences must be in the actual decisions of historical leaders. Sometimes a leader will enter the story: a general or a political man will pass by, or news of a leader will come to the teller's ears, somewhere far from the event but affected by it. (I stood outside a Quonset hut on Saipan in April 1945 and heard that Franklin Roosevelt had died, and that moment became part of my war story.) They're like history in another sense too: war narratives take the *shape* of history, they deal in causes and consequences, and in events that are ordered in real, linear time.

So war narratives are something like travel writing, something like autobiography, and something like history. But different too. They're *not* like travel writing, because a travel book makes the reader feel that he knows the place he is reading about, that he could move familiarly in the Hebrides, or the Hindu Kush, or Patagonia. War narratives don't do that; though they make war vivid, they don't make it familiar. Indeed, one motive for writing them seems to be to show how *un*familiar war is, how strange and desolate its ordinary scenes are. Here, as an example, is the German officer Rudolph Binding describing the landscape near the Somme battlefield during the German advance of April 1918:

> I can still find no word nor image to express the awfulness of that waste. There is nothing like it on earth, nor can be. A desert is always a desert; but a desert which tells you all the time that it used not to be a desert is appalling. That is the tale which is told by the dumb, black stumps of the shattered trees which still stick up where there used to be villages. They were completely flayed by the splinters of the bursting shells, and they stand there like corpses upright. Not a blade of green anywhere round. The layer of soil which once covered the loose chalk is now buried beneath it. Thousands of shells have brought the stones to the surface and smothered the earth in its own entrails. There are miles upon miles of flat, empty, broken, and tumbled stone-quarry, utterly purposeless and useless, in the middle of which stand groups of these blackened stumps of dead trees, poisoned oases, killed for ever.

I called this desolation "landscape," but it isn't that: it's *anti*-landscape, an entirely strange terrain with nothing natural left in it. It's the antithesis of the comprehensible natural world that travel writers inhabit.

War's human scenes are as grotesque as its natural ones. Private Elisha Stockwell describes the regimental camp after the Civil War battle of Corinth, Mississippi:

> When I got back to camp, they had everything loaded on the wagon, and we moved on to the east of town where they were fetching the wounded. They were laying them in rows with just room to walk between. They had tents for those that were the worst off, and where they were amputating arms and legs. There was a wash-out back of one tent that had a wagon load of arms and legs. The legs had the shoes and stockings on them.

War turns landscape into anti-landscape, and everything in that landscape into grotesque, broken, useless rubbish— including human limbs. Reading soldiers' accounts of Shiloh or Waterloo, Ladysmith or the Argonne or Hué, we see with estranged eyes. These lives are nothing like ours, and these places are like nothing we could possibly find in our familiar civilian world. War, we see, is not a place we could travel to.

War narratives aren't like autobiography, either. Auto- biographies narrate continuous lives; but a war narrative con- cerns a separate life that, however vividly it remains in the memory, is not continuous with the life the teller lives as he writes. Old soldiers, recalling themselves when young and at war, look back as though at some distant stranger: "the rather romantic tone, taken (if I read him right) by that lad who ten years ago was I" (that's from a First War memoir); "As I look upon the young man who allegedly was I in that wartime spring" (that's from the Second War). Of course that young self seems a stranger to the late rememberer: he is an innocent, on the other side of experience.

For everyone except career soldiers, military service is a kind of exile from one's own real life, a dislocation of the familiar that the mind preserves as life in another world. Farley Mowat, a young Canadian fighting on the Italian front in the Second World War, writes to someone at home:

> The damnable truth is we are in really different worlds, on totally different planes, and I don't *know* you anymore, I only know the you that was. I wish I could explain the des- perate sense of isolation, of not belonging to my own past, of being adrift in some kind of alien space.

That sense of isolation is not simply a condition of combat; it is common to the whole state of being in a war. For war is more than actions; it is a culture. Military traditions, values, and pat- terns of behavior penetrate every aspect of army life and make the most ordinary acts and feelings different.

Friendship, for example, is different there—different enough to need another name: *comradeship.* The first thing to be said of comradeship is that it is accidental. Comrades in war are not chosen: they are simply the men picked by the system to stand beside you. Because they come together so randomly, by the alphabet or by numbers, they are sure to be more different from each other, socially and geographically and psychologically, than any peacetime circle of friends could possibly be. They share no common past (which is the glue of ordinary friendship); their ties are all in the present, in the war culture they share: the daily life, the work, the skills, the hardships and dangers, the boredom, of war.

But though comradeship is accidental, it is intense beyond the likelihood of back-home life. A soldier spends virtually all his time, awake and asleep, with his mates; he is with them more continuously than most men are with their wives. And at critical moments his life may depend on their fidelity and courage. Most marriages don't come to that.

Intense, but also fragile: men die; tours of duty end; even wars end. In this sense, too, the comradeship of soldiers is all in the present. This double sense of intensity and temporariness is expressed in many narratives of war. Here is Guy Chapman, at the end of the First World War, watching his battalion march into billets:

> this body of men had become so much a part of me that its disintegration would tear away something I cared for more dearly than I could have believed.

And Alex Bowlby, a British rifleman in the Second War:

> I was afraid of anything coming between me and the Company, afraid of losing the love and support I had found there.

Add the Canadian Farley Mowat:

> Although I knew very little of the past lives and inner beings of those thirty men, I had been more firmly bound to them than many a man is to his own blood brothers.

Note the scale of the attachments: not to an army or a nation or a cause, but to a battalion, a company, a platoon. For a man adrift in alien space, his unit becomes the focus of his love and loyalty, like a family, and his feelings for it may be as strong, as complex, as family feelings are.

If affection among men is different in war, so is its opposite—hostility, and its expression in violence. There are moments in war when men become *different* men, who can do things that in their peacetime lives they would call monstrous and inhuman. We don't like to believe this—that men can change their essential natures—but it must be true, or there would be no atrocities. And there *are* atrocities, in every army, in every war. On the battlefield, in prison camps, in besieged and captured cities, the restraints of law and society lose their authority, power rules, and men are brutal and cruel. We will see examples of the cruelty of power as we consider the wars of our century.

War is another world, where men feel and act differently; and so, when they return to the other world of peace and ordinariness, they feel a need to tell their tales of the somewhere else where they have been. In memory, war seems like a dream, or the life of some other man, remembered with a kind of astonishment. Rifleman Harris retired from his soldiering to keep a shoemaker's shop in Soho, and there, forty years later, he remembered a dead Frenchman on the field at Vimiero:

> He was lying on his side amongst some burnt-up bushes; and whether the heat of the firing here had set these bushes on fire, or from whatever cause they had been ignited, I cannot take upon me to say; but certain it is (for several companions saw it as well as myself, and cracked many a joke upon the poor fellow's appearance) that this man, whom we guessed to have been French, was as completely roasted as if he had been spitted before a good kitchen-fire. He was burnt quite brown, every stitch of clothes was singed off, and he was drawn all up like a dried

frog. I called the attention of one or two men near me, and we examined him, turning him about with our rifles with no little curiosity. I remember now, with some surprise, that the miserable fate of this poor fellow called forth from us very little sympathy, but seemed only to be a subject for mirth.

Harris the middle-aged shoemaker looks back upon himself as a young soldier with surprise, as though that person were some-one else. How could he have laughed at the poor dead Frenchman? Where was his human compassion? But he did laugh: in war, even humor is different, because it is full of death; and the man who laughed was different too, in a life that was discontinuous from that of the shoemaker who remembered.

So war narratives are not quite autobiography. They're not quite history either. Historians tell the big stories, of campaigns and battles, of the great victories and the disastrous defeats; synthesizing the reports and the statistics, drawing their conclusions about strategy and tactics, assigning credit and blame, turning war's chaos into order. The men who were there tell a different story, one that is often quite ahistorical, even anti-historical. Their narratives are indifferent to the exact location of events in time (they rarely put dates to their actions) or in space (either they never knew exactly where they were or they have forgotten the names). But that seems right for the soldiers' tale they tell; exact dates and precise geography would turn personal experiences into battles, into the accounts that appear in newspapers and history books; unlocated narrative keeps it in the individual's realm. Nor do they have much to say about strategy, or about other battles, fought on other fields. They aren't even interested in victory or defeat, except as it affects them personally; survival is their happy ending.

Most of all, they are not concerned with *why*. War narratives are experience books; they are about what happened, and how it felt. *Why* is not a soldier's question: Tennyson at least got that part of the Charge of the Light Brigade right: "Theirs not to reason why." Yet the soldier assumes—*must* assume—that if he did ask that question, if he were allowed to ask it, there would be a rational answer, that what he is doing and suffering makes sense to someone farther up the chain of command. On occasions when it becomes clear that the answer isn't rational, or doesn't exist, the soldier's response is anger and bitterness (as we will see later when we come to the defense of Singapore). *Why* is the momentum behind the narratives; but it isn't the story.

The stories that soldiers tell are small-scale, detailed, and confined—"very local, limited, incoherent," as Edmund Blunden put it—and necessarily so, for that is the way they see war. Rifleman Harris has something to say about this too, as he begins his account of his actions in the battle of Roliça,

> I do not pretend to give a description of this or any other battle I have been present at. All I can do is to tell the things which happened immediately around me, and that, I think, is as much as a private soldier can be expected to do ... a soldier knows no more of his position and what is about to happen in his front, or what *has* happened (even amongst his own companions), than the very dead lying around.

That was written a century and a half ago, but it has remained true. "Shell-hole and trench have a limited horizon," a German soldier wrote after the First World War. "The range of vision extends no further than a bomb-throw; but what is seen is seen very distinctly."

Even when the range was longer, the intelligibility of what could be seen was no greater. Here is a paragraph from the journal of an infantry officer on the Somme in the third week of the offensive there:

> Today near Bazentin we watched an attack launched about a mile away on our left. It was a terrible incident of modern

war. There was suddenly a noise like the mad beating of hundreds of mighty drums, and every second or two a great crash; a rolling cloud of dust and smoke arose from the plain, and moved slowly forward, the whole inferno dying as suddenly as it began. From first to last we could distinguish no living creature, and what happened we never knew.

This is war without men, without movement, and without meaning: nothing but noise and dust and smoke. It was, it seems, the *most* you might see of that terrible battle.

The visibility was just as bad in the Second War for the men who fought; and for those who fought in machines it was worse. Here is a British tank commander in the middle of the war's most spacious battle, the Normandy invasion:

One morning ... I was told by the brigade major to report more precisely and more often what was going on. I replied that since I was shut up inside a camouflaged, stationary tank with its turret closed down I had precisely nothing, often or not, to report.... Could he tell *me* what was going on?

Men outside the machines might see more, but with no greater comprehension of what was seen. An American in the North African campaign, waiting for Rommel to attack at the Kasserine Pass, remarked that he could see for miles across the open countryside, but added: "We actually know no more, as usual, than the folks back home except about our little sector."

The view from a plane was not much better. A pilot in the First War might be close to the ground, yet he wouldn't see much and would understand less. "From the air," an American pilot wrote near the end of that war,

it is often very difficult to distinguish where the lines are or to tell just what is going on. What you do see are thousands of shell holes, the frequent flashing of guns, and a

great quantity of smoke; sometimes large heavy columns of
it, more often hundreds of little streaks of smoke.

It's no better than the infantryman's view: a warscape with no
soldiers, no fighting, no movement of any kind, only ruination
and flame and smoke, like a vision of hell, but lacking the
damned souls.

Fliers in the Second War flew higher and faster than those in
the First War, but they saw less. Read any account of the
bombing of Germany in the Second War, and see how little you
are told about the European earth below, or the large plan of
attack, and how much you learn about the inside of a B-17, what
flak looks like, how a plane falls and burns. One must conclude
that wars are fought, and remembered, by men who are un-
aware of events and meanings beyond their own vision, because
their attention is on other, closer, mortal things.

No man will see much of the battle he's in; and what he does
see he will not remember as other men who were there will. So
personal narratives will always be fallible authorities, as historians who have worked with them have found: Rudyard Kipling,
for example, who interrupted his literary career just after the
First War to write a war history of the Irish Guards. Kipling was
determined to get behind the rumors and myths, behind the
official version, to reach into the memories of the men who
fought in the Guards and find the truth there. His introduction
to his history tells us that he failed, and why;

A battalion's field is bounded by its own vision. Even
within these limits, there is large room for error. Witnesses
to phases of fights die and are dispersed; the ground over
which they fought is battered out of recognition in a few
hours; survivors confuse dates, places and personalities,
and in the trenches, the monotony of the waiting days and
the repetition-work of repairs breed mistakes and false
judgements. Men grow doubtful or oversure, and, in all

good faith, give directly opposed versions. The clear sight of a comrade so mangled that he seems to have been long dead is burnt in on one brain to the exclusion of all else that happened that day. The shock of an exploded dump, shaking down a firmament upon the landscape, dislocates memory throughout half a battalion; and so on in all matters, till the end of laborious enquiry is too often the opening of fresh confusion. When to this are added the personal prejudices and misunderstandings of men under heavy strain, carrying clouded memories of orders half given or half heard, amid scenes that pass like nightmares, the only wonder to the compiler of these records has been that any sure fact whatever should be retrieved out of the whirlpools of war.

This is an unusually personal and emotional passage to find in an official unit history—a confession of failure at truth telling, there at the beginning of the book. But Kipling had good reason to know the limitations of evidence from men at war and to empathize with those who gave it. His only son had fought with the Guards in the battle of Loos and had simply disappeared during the fighting; his body was never discovered, and though Kipling interviewed everyone he could find who was there, none had witnessed his son's death or seen his body. The one event in the history of the Irish Guards that he cared most about he could not record.

What Kipling learned about personal recollections is obviously true: as history they are unsatisfactory: restricted, biased, afflicted by emotion, and full of errors. Memoirists themselves confirm that view. Take Robert Graves, for example. His *Goodbye to All That* is one of the books from which later generations have constructed their understanding of the First World War. Yet when he considered the truthfulness of war books, he concluded that personal memoirs could not meet the test of historical accuracy:

It was practically impossible (as well as forbidden) to keep a diary in any active trench-sector, or to send letters home which would be of any great post-War documentary value; and the more efficient the soldier the less time, of course, he took from his job to write about it. Great latitude should therefore be allowed to a soldier who has since got his facts or dates mixed. I would even paradoxically say that the memoirs of a man who went through some of the worst experiences of trench warfare are not truthful if they do not contain a high proportion of falsities. High-explosive barrages will make a temporary liar or visionary of anyone; the old trench-mind is at work in all over-estimation of casualities, "unnecessary" dwelling on horrors, mixing of dates and confusion between trench rumours and scenes actually witnessed.

True but not truthful: Graves's paradox is an apt one. Per-sonal narratives are not history and can't be; they speak each with its own human voice, as history does not, and they find their own shapes, which are not the shapes of history. They are neither better nor worse, neither more nor less valuable than history; they are simply different.

If war narratives aren't travel writing, aren't autobiography, aren't history, what are they? *Stories,* first of all: responses to that primal need we all have to tell and to hear individual experi-ences, and so to understand our own lives and imagine the lives of others. Stories answer the questions that we ask of any expe-rience, whether our own or somebody else's: What happened? What was it like? How did it feel? The soldier asks those ques-tions of his war life and answers them in the telling of his story, and so discovers its meaning and gets his war straight in his mind. We, his readers, ask those questions too: they are our motive for reading.

The narratives that soldiers tell are all different, and all the same: different because armies change, weapons evolve, and battlefields shift; but the same too, because behind those variables there is always one story—the individual's journey from innocence into experience, the serial discovery of what had before been unimaginable, the reality of war. And because that is true, we must be conscious, as we contemplate the narratives of many wars, of both what changes and what is constant.

To get a sense of what has changed, consider the British soldier's existence in the early nineteenth century, at the time of the wars with Napoleon. We know what Wellington thought of his troops: "the scum of the earth," he called them,"—the mere scum of the earth." We know, too, what the authorities in those common soldiers' lives, both in the army and in society, thought of them, alive and dead. Two quotes from English newspapers of the time will make those attitudes clear:

Alive: a paragraph from the *Manchester Guardian,* August 3, 1822:

> John Furnel was tried by a court-martial for having in his possession a silver spoon, which had been stolen from the mess. He was sentenced to receive 300 lashes which punishment was inflicted. After lingering in great torture until Friday July 19 he expired.

Dead: a paragraph from the *London Observer,* November 18, same year:

> It is estimated that more than a million bushels of human and inhuman bones were imported last year from the continent of Europe into the port of Hull. The neighborhood of Leipzig, Austerlitz, Waterloo, and of all the places where, during the late bloody war, the principal battles were fought, have been swept alike of the bones of the hero and the horse which he rode. Thus collected from every quarter, they have been shipped to the port of Hull and thence forwarded to the Yorkshire bone grinders who have erected steam-engines and powerful machinery for the purpose of reducing them to a granularly state. In this condition they are sold to the farmers to manure their lands.

Brutes while alive, fertilizer when dead: both the floggings and
the abandoned dead are recorded in many soldiers' narratives
of the century.

What did such treatment do to the men who suffered it? Did
it make them less aware of their separate existences as men,
each with his own story? Did it deny them a sense of the individual value of those stories? That might be one explanation of
why so few common soldiers wrote war narratives of nineteenth-
century wars. Though the surest reason is that most of them
couldn't: they were illiterate. But then, so was Rifleman Harris:
he had to dictate his *Recollections* to an ex-officer who heard
Harris telling his stories in his cobbler's shop.

These circumstances of war—the cruel discipline, the aban-
donment of the dead, the general illiteracy of the troops—are
among the variables; all have changed since Harris's time. For
example, discipline: Field Punishment No. I in Wellington's army
meant flogging—three hundred, five hundred, even eight hundred blows—while the victim was tied spread-eagled to the wheel
of a wagon or an artillery piece By the time of Kitchener's army,
a century later, the flogging had been stopped, but not the
crucifixion on the wheel; Max Plowman, marching to battle on
the Somme, saw a man tied that way and was shocked to find
such cruelty to his own troops when death was so near at hand.
So there were changes, in modern war and in modern armies,
and those changes are part of the subject of this book; but
there were also attitudes that remained, and those, too, will concern us.

And what are the constants? Many things, beginning with the
radical strangeness of war to the new and innocent conscript.
When Harris joined his first regiment, he was put at once into a
firing squad and ordered to shoot one of his fellow soldiers
(which he obediently did). That isn't what one expects in a war,
is it? But war is like that, continually strange and unexpected.
Similar surprises occur in memoirs from other wars. When Rod

Kane arrived in Vietnam, he expected a war of ordinary violence; he didn't expect to be attacked immediately by a child
with a sack of hand grenades—but he was. Nothing in my own
experience was as startling as that, though I remember very well
my first sight of my Japanese enemy when I entered a ruined
bunker on Saipan and found a foot there—an unattached human
foot, still wearing its split-toed sandal. You don't expect war to
be composed of such odd incidents; but it is out of remembered
astonishments like these that war narratives are made.

Strangeness is the great constant in remembered wars. The
young man who goes to war enters a strange world governed by
strange rules, where everything that is not required is forbidden, a world without women or children or old people, a
violent and dangerous world where, out there in the darkness
or just over the hill, strangers wait whose job it is to kill you.

Strangest of all is the presence of death, and the ways it is
present. Most young men—certainly most young men in our century—reach adulthood without ever having confronted death face-
to-face, or not until the morticians have turned it into unreality.
Then they go to war, where death is the whole point, the truest
truth, the realest reality; and they find that death, when you see
it up close, isn't what you expected, that it's uglier, more
grotesque, less human. And so astonishing death is a recurrent
subject in the soldiers' tale. Here are some examples of how it
appears, from the three wars this book particularly examines.

From the First World War—a soldier marches through a
ruined village:

> Just past the last house on the left was a small pond,
> whence protruded the grey-clad knee of a dead German.
> The water around him was green and on his knee was
> perched a large rat making a meal.

From the Second World War—a German infantryman is
retreating on the Russian front:

We had just passed a bunker in which we noticed a body lying at the bottom. Two emaciated cats were eating one of its hands.

From the Vietnam War—a young officer remembers:

A man saw the heights and depths of human behavior in Vietnam, all manner of violence and horrors so grotesque that they evoked more fascination than disgust. Once I had seen pigs eating napalm-charred corpses—a memorable sight, pigs eating roast people.

And from that other war, the death-camp war:

Eventually there was no food at all, and I have a vivid memory of seeing somebody kneeling (as a punishment) with a human ear in his mouth. It was the beginning of cannibalism.

War is an activity in which men become the food of predatory animals, in which rats and cats and pigs eat people, even people eat people. In war every kind of monstrosity is possible. And the witness sees it more with fascination than with disgust, arrested by its strangeness. It's a simple but true proposition: in war, death is grotesque and astonishing.

So, too, are the wounds men suffer. War is men shooting at each other; but their wounds, when they occur, don't seem as straightforward or intentional as that. Thomas Hardy could write in a war poem, "I shot at him as he at me, and killed him in his place," but that was because Hardy had never been in a war. Real combat isn't man against man, someone over there shooting at you. And the man who is hit doesn't think at once: Somebody shot me! or I've just been shot in the arm! No; to be wounded, as men's narratives tell it, is a sudden explosive strangeness, more like a natural disaster or a visitation of the wrath of God than a human act. It's like this (from the first day of the Somme offensive):

What I felt was that I had been hit by a tremendous iron hammer, swung by a giant of inconceivable strength, and then twisted with a sickening sort of wrench so that my head and back banged on the ground, and my feet struggled as though they didn't belong to me. For a second or two my breath wouldn't come. I thought—if that's the right word—"This is death," and hoped it wouldn't take long.

Or like this (from an action in Tuscany during the Italian campaign in the Second World War):

The lull came. I jumped up and took my first step out of the trench, and the whole world cracked open in a sheet of flames. There was a noise like a dinner gong ringing inside my head. My face was all sticky and hot liquid streamed into my eyes. I knew that a shell had hit me, but I felt no pain. As I staggered downhill, my left arm felt numb and loose—I was quite unable to lift it when I tried to wipe my eyes.

The emotion here is not anger or fear—nothing so familiar and personal as that—but only astonishment. A serious wound hurls a man into a different existence, in which his feet don't belong to him, or a strange hot liquid runs into his eyes, and he can no longer perform an ordinary act like raising his arm. Like deaths, wounds are astonishing accidents in a war world that is entirely strange.

The strangeness of war's happenings is a constant; so is the confusion of battle; and the killing, the dying, and the dead—more dying than killing, in most men's memoirs, and more dead friends than foes. And the military virtues? The big soldierly words like "courage" and "cowardice" and "heroism": are they constants too? Certainly those terms do persist in the soldiers' tale from Rifleman Harris's time to our own, though their meanings shift. Harris believed in courage of the dashing, cavalry-charge sort and used words like "gallant" and "brave" and "hero" freely; and he despised cowardice (he once threatened to shoot a fellow soldier who turned to run from a battle). But his own war story is not about heroic courage; it is about the other, less spectacular kind, the courage of endurance by which men at war survive. That kind of courage is one of the constants in the soldiers' tale.

But perhaps the most striking constant is the feeling that is expressed in this paragraph near the end of Harris's book:

> For my own part I can only say that I enjoyed life more whilst on active service than I have ever done since; and as I sit at work in my shop in Richmond Street, Soho, I look back upon that portion of my time spent in the fields of the Peninsula as the only part worthy of remembrance.

That is the true voice of the man who was there; you find it everywhere in the personal narratives. It's not that Harris's war was particularly heroic or victorious; the stories he tells are of British disasters—the retreat to Coruna during the Peninsula campaign, the Walcheren expedition in the Netherlands. It's simply that when those things happened he was present, as soldier and as witness. Other men in other wars have said the same thing; for example, a lance corporal who was in the British attack at Suvla Bay in Gallipoli wrote: "It was a horrible and a great day. I would not have missed it for worlds." I feel that, too, about my own war, and so do other men I know who were in it. I have never met a man who fought in the Second World War—actually *fought*—who regretted having been there.

This seems to be just as much a constant in men's memories of other wars. Here, as an example, is William Merritt at the end of his memoir of the Vietnam War, having a conversation with himself on the point of it all:

> "So much noise and expense. Why did we do it?"
> "For you."
> "For me?"

"So you wouldn't have to spend your whole life selling insurance. Sorry?"

"Hell, no."

What do these testimonies amount to? Do they offer, as a constant, the conviction that war is a good, enriching thing in men's lives? Not exactly. But they do say that war expands and extends what is possible in life for an ordinary man, that for once he need not be simply a man mending shoes in Soho, or an insurance salesman. War offers experiences that men value and remember: shoes and insurance don't do that.

The subjects of war narratives are the things men do in war and the things war does to them. But not usually as those things happened. Memoirs are retrospective, filtered reality, what memory preserves. Remembering is like looking at the sun at sunset, through the earth's atmosphere; it's still the sun, but the light of midday has been turned to red. Time is like that, an atmosphere that alters what we see.

And so, though memory is the muse and source of memoirs, it is untrustworthy, not only as a source of history but as a story of a self. It selects and colors the shapes and feelings of the past that it offers us, and so may become, it seems, an obstacle to truth.

There is a passage on this point in a recently published memoir by the Italian writer Italo Calvino. Calvino fought as a partisan against the Fascists during the Second World War; some time later, in the 1960s or '70s, he wrote his recollections of that time in an essay, "Memories of a Battle," that is really a meditation on the nature of memory.

The battle was an abortive partisan attack on a village held by the Fascists; Calvino remembered it only in disconnected fragments of sense data. "What I would like to know," he wrote,

is why the broken net of the memory holds some things and not others: I remember one by one these orders that were never carried out, but now I would like to remember the faces and names of my companions in the squad, the voices, the dialect phrases, and how we managed to cut the wires without pincers. I even remember the battle plan, how it was supposed to unfold in various phases, and how it didn't unfold. But to follow the thread of my story I'll have to remember it all through my ears: the special silence of a country morning full of men moving in silence, rumblings, shots filling the sky. A silence that was expected but that lasted longer than expected. Then shots, every kind of explosion and machine-gun fire, a muddle of sound we can't make sense of because it doesn't take shape in space but only in time, a time of waiting for us stationed at the valley bottom where we can't see a damn thing.

I continue to gaze into the valley bottom of the memory. And my fear now is that as soon as a memory forms it immediately takes on the wrong light, mannered, sentimental as war and youth always are, becomes a piece of narrative written in the style of the time, which can't tell us how things really were but only how we thought we saw them, thought we said them. I don't know if I am destroying the past or saving it, the past hidden in that besieged village.

Calvino is playing a game with us, of course, using his catalogue of difficulties to invest his half-remembered story with a sharp credibility. The uncertainties, the ignorance, the muddle, are all parts of the reality; all attacks in war are like that: confusion is an essential element of battle. But he is acutely right in what he says about the operations of memory: as we remember, and write it down, the past becomes words, a *story*, a *style*. But it is all we have, all that *can* be saved from that remembered morning in the valley.

When we put Calvino's passage beside those that I quoted from Kipling and Robert Graves, we have the truth problems of war narratives spelled out: the failures of observation in the field, the confined vision of witnesses, the infidelities of memory after the events, the inevitable distortions of language. These problems are not peculiar to war narratives; they are inherent in all our relations with the past. But it seems that the circumstances of war intensify the distortions and increase the difficulties of putting events into words.

We are confronted with an apparent contradiction here: the man-who-was-there asserts his authority as the only true witness of his war; but the truth that he claims to tell is compromised by the very nature of memory and language. Compromised, too, by the cloud of witnesses, each telling his own relative truth of events. I think, though, that the contradiction is not absolute. It can be resolved if we think of the truth of war experience as being the sum of witnesses, the collective tale that soldiers tell. That tale will be an imperfect version of the everything-that-happened that is a war complete; not all the witnesses will testify. Still, that tale is the closest we will get to the reality of what men did, and what was done to them, in this war or that one. We don't need to call that convergence of witnesses historical truth, if that seems too confident; call it instead the recoverable past of war. Such recovery is possible; it is more than possible: it is imperative. What other route do we have to understanding the human experience of war—how it felt, what it was like—than the witness of the men who were there?

Calvino worried, in the passage I just quoted, that the witness of memory would fail to render the reality, that what had happened would be translated out of experience into the style of the time, into literature. That's not a problem that can be solved philosophically; memories become words when you record them, and words become literature. It is striking, though, how little the writers of personal narratives of war have been affected by the literary fashions of their time: tellers of Victorian wars have not been notably Victorian, narrators of modern wars have not been Modernists. Whatever their dates, they have nearly all been realists, adopting a common style that would come as close as language can to rendering the things of the material world as they are. Whether they were one-book amateurs or would-be men of letters doesn't seem to matter; they have reported their wars in a plain, naming vocabulary, describing objects and actions in unmetaphorical terms, appealing always to the data of the senses.

"Life is always deep in details," Boris Pasternak said, and that is certainly true of life in war, as memoirs have recorded it. War *is* details, to be put down plainly. But what odd details! Harris's roasted Frenchman, Stockwell's wagonload of legs, pigs eating people. The style in which these sights are described remains flat and uninflected; but *realism* somehow doesn't seem quite the right term for such grotesque occasions. For this kind of reality of war, perhaps we need a new term. Suppose we call such visions "Battlefield Gothic." We will come upon examples of it many times before we are done, when we observe the dead or, more precisely, when we observe soldiers observing the dead.

For the one-book memoirists, realism was no doubt an inevitable, natural style: you simply put down what happened. But for more self-conscious writers it was a choice. Here, as an example of that act of choice, is a passage from an American memoir of the First World War, Hervey Allen's *Toward the Flame:*

> I have tried to reproduce in words my experience in France during the great war. There is no plot, no climax, no happy ending to this book. It is a narrative, plain, unvarnished, without heroics, and true. It is what I saw as nearly as memory has preserved it, and I have set it down as a picture of war with no comment.

Most war memoirs are like that: everything that might be called "the style of the time" left out, only the things that the senses record and memory stores left in, because the truth is in the particulars. Maybe that's why old soldiers hang on to the things of their wars, why in my attic there are two tattered pilot's logbooks, an air-wing shoulder patch, and a yellowed plastic container that once held survival gear and now is full of old photographs. I keep them, I suppose, for their reality.

Allen chose a plain, uninflected realism for his memoir because it enabled him to tell the truths about war—the truths that a young man can't anticipate but must learn for himself in actual combat. Philip Caputo offers his version of those truths in *A Rumor of War:*

> what fear feels like and what death looks like, and the smell of death, the experience of killing, of enduring pain and inflicting it, the loss of friends and the sight of wounds ... what war was about.

How physical that all is, how entirely concerned with the senses—*seeing* and *smelling* and *feeling* war—and how emptied of abstractions. These are the lessons that are learned with the body, and they must be expressed with the body's vocabulary (remember the Frenchman I quoted at the beginning of this chapter: "The man who has not understood with his flesh cannot talk to you about it.").

Grim lessons; yet Caputo confidently asserts elsewhere in his book that "anyone who fought in Vietnam, if he is honest about himself, will have to admit he enjoyed the compelling attractiveness of combat." That sounds like a contradiction of the other passage, and certainly it goes against the conventional civilian view of war in general and that war in particular. Yet it seems true, on the evidence of many men's narratives from many wars: most men do feel war's high excitement and romance, and even its beauty (to which there are many testimonies), and not only *before* they experience war but *after*.

Some soldiers never lose that excitement. They are the war lovers, and we must acknowledge that they exist and always have. You find them in literature—Homer's Achilles is one, Othello is another—and you find them in life, in every army. In modern wars, they turn up as the adventurers, who lead the daring raids and fly the fighter planes, and sometimes as the generals (Patton was certainly one). And as the dictators: Hitler and Mussolini loved war.

What is it, exactly, that war lovers love? Not the killing and the violence, I think, but the excitement, the drama, and the danger—life lived at a high level of intensity, like a complicated, fatal game (or a Wagnerian opera). For career soldiers, there must also be a deep and abiding interest in the problems of war, in decision making, leadership, how you turn strategy into actions. Junior officers and enlisted men, the ones who do the actual killing, will become engrossed in the physical problems, the skills of soldiering; for them, war is a collection of manual arts, it's demanding, interesting work. (You learn a lot about those skills in their war narratives: how to dig a foxhole under fire, how to attack a fortified hill or shoot down an ME-110 or land a helicopter in a jungle clearing. Those lessons are part of the appeal that war memoirs have for readers who will never do any of those things.)

War is an exciting, dangerous, skillful, physical occupation, to which most men respond while they're there. Some men never lose their taste, or their need, for that excitement but go on being war lovers all their lives. They make good soldiers, but they are by and large no good for war memoirs; they stand too close to the center of war's values, and whether they mean to or not, they act out the mottoes on the flags and the slogans on the posters. What suits memory best is a war life lived close to the action but at some distance from the values, by a man who is by nature or circumstances an outsider, who can be a witness as well as a soldier, who has felt war but doesn't love it.

But even those men who return from their wars to subside willingly enough into unexciting peaceful lives retain some of war's excitement: their narratives tell us that. However terrible the actions they relate, old soldiers also bear witness to the powerful appeal war has for men, and especially for the secret army of the young who come of age in war. The excitement is there in their memoirs, a kind of energy, a momentum that moves them through their roughest days. And the most honest and self-aware of them, when they reflect on their lives as soldiers, confess to feeling nostalgia for that strange, exciting world. That nostalgia must be one reason why they write.

And us? Do we, too, feel something like nostalgia for past wars we didn't fight in? Are we, who are surely appalled by war, yet drawn to its old excitements? And if so, why? There is an answer to that question in a passage from Eric Partridge's memoir of the First War. Partridge fought at Gallipoli and on the Somme, but this part of his story is a recollection of himself *before* experience, when he was still a boy, eighteen years old, on a training-camp march in the winter of 1914–15:

> The early-winter morning was fresh and cold, yet not sharp; the air, without bite, had an invigorating tang; the sun shone clear, though weak, through the trees, merely to be alive was a joy, young legs moving freely, easily, young eyes seeing every frosted leaf aglisten, young voices singing some foolish song, young hearts astir with their entry into war, war which, next to love, has most captured the world's imagination.

There are many things worth noting in this passage: the exact physicality of the perceptions, the exuberant life, the excitement the young volunteers feel at the prospect of war, the emotional energy in young life remembered ("the war, old chap," said a French veteran to an English one, "is our youth, secret and interred"). But I quote it mainly for the sake of the phrase "war which, next to love ..." Partridge is not telling about actual experience of war here; at this point in his life he had not had any. Yet war had power to stir him even then; it existed in his mind as an idea, or as a complex emotion—a motive strong enough to take him eventually to scenes of real death and suffering. After which he would bear his witness to that reality.

The war that was in Partridge's imagination must have come from many sources: from the classic wars in Homer and Virgil (he was a classics student in Australia when he enlisted); from English history, as it was taught to schoolboys; from Victorian adventure novels of boys in battle by writers like Henty; from Tennyson and Kipling; from the recruiting posters. Every generation has such images of war; a quarter of a century after Partridge, I made my war-in-the-head out of *For Whom the Bell Tolls* and *G-8 and His Battle Aces,* and movies like *Hell's Angels* and *The Dawn Patrol,* and all the vestiges of past wars that were around me: the old men marching on Memorial Day, and the bands and the flags; the two-minute silence on Armistice Day; the rows of soldiers' graves at Fort Snelling. Vietnam veterans remember the films of John Wayne and Audie Murphy. Readers of this book, in their various generations, will have their own sources for their wars-in-the-head. We all imagine war before we know it—we can't help it. The idea of war is part of the fundamental furniture of our minds.

Those imaginary wars, however vivid and violent they may be, are romances: they are war turned into fictions, into shapely untruths. They feed our imaginations with the big abstractions of war—Heroism, Fame, Valor, Glory; they make death sentimental and battle melodramatic. Above all, they make war *familiar;* they can't not do it—the conventions of war in art are simply too expected, too established, too dictatorial to elude.

Personal narratives are not like that: they subvert the expectations of romance. They work at a level below the big words and the brave sentiments, down on the surface of the earth where men fight. They don't glorify war, or aestheticize it, or make it literary or heroic; they speak in their own voices, in their own plain language. They are not antiwar—that is, they are not polemics against war; they simply tell us what it is like. They make war actual, without making it familiar. They bear witness.

CHAPTER TWO

'Fourteen–'Eighteen:
Civilian Soldiers

A familiar British recruiting poster of the First World War shows a middle-class father sitting uneasily in his easy chair, with his little daughter on his knee. The child is asking, with a worried look: "Daddy, what did *YOU* do in the Great War?" That poster wouldn't have worked in any previous British war. Daddy wouldn't have gone to fight the Russians in the Crimea, or the Zulus at Isandlhwana, or the Dervishes at Khartoum; the regular army would have done the job. But *this* war would be different. It would be fought on such a scale that it could not be manned in the traditional way, by an army of the "scum of the earth" commanded by professional soldiers of the old officer caste. The working class and the aristocracy would provide their numbers, as they always had; but this time there would also have to be a vast recruitment of men like Daddy.

Such men volunteered in large numbers in 1914–1915. They became the junior officers of Kitchener's New Army and commanded the actions of war at the tactical level, the level of actual fighting. They were the lieutenants who cried "Follow me!" and went over the top, who led patrols into no-man's-land, who flew the planes and directed the artillery pieces, and who died in greater proportion to their numbers than any other rank.

They were also the ones who wrote the memorable war books. Think of the books from the First World War that we still read: the memoirs—*Good-bye to All That, The Memoirs of*

George Sherston, Undertones of War, Storm of Steel: and the poems—Wilfred Owen's, Siegfried Sassoon's, Edmund Blunden's; and the novels—*All Quiet on the Western Front, Under Fire, A Farewell to Arms*. All written by middle-class men who went voluntarily to war.

One might protest that a tale composed only of middle-class memories is unjust to the vast majority of working-class men who filled the ranks of every army. And so it is. T. E. Lawrence explained why, in his preface to his war book, *Seven Pillars of Wisdom*. Having first admitted that his story was unfair to many leaders and fighters in the Arab cause, he went on: "it is still less fair, of course, like all war-stories, to the unnamed rank and file: who miss their share of credits, as they must do, until they can write the despatches." And, I would add, the war narratives too. But nearly all of the millions who fought in the war fought silently as far as we are concerned, died silently or survived, but in either case left no record, because they were poor, inarticulate, unlettered, shy; or because it simply did not occur to them to write down what had happened to them.

No, the tale of the Great War didn't come from the ranks, it came from the middle-class volunteers who became the war's junior officers. That's understandable. The middle class is the great self-recording class, the class that keeps diaries and journals and considers that the preservation of one's daily life is an appropriate and interesting activity for an individual. In modern times it has also been the imagining class, out of which have come most of the novels and poems and plays that constitute Western literature. Until 1914 that recording and imagining class had not gone to war much—through the whole of the nineteenth century, for example, no major British writer had any direct experience of battle. But in 1914–18 that changed; middle-class men did go, and then wrote what they had seen. Their testimonies taken together are what we know about what the First World War was like. They are our collective memory.

The tale of the Great War doesn't begin with those volunteers, though; their stories dominate the war's later years, but they weren't there at the start. The British Expeditionary Force that crossed to France in August 1914 to meet the advancing Germans was a professional army, made up of officers and men who were already soldiers by choice or by necessity before the war began. There weren't many of them—"a contemptible little army," the Kaiser called them—but they were all that Britain had. To understand the war and its tale, we must begin with the story of those regulars.

The British troops who fought the war's opening battles included the regiments of guards, lancers, and hussars that were the army's elite corps. The officers of those regiments were soldiers in the tradition of the European officer caste, sons of the aristocracy and the gentry, for whom the army was a career, a vocation, and often the ultimate field sport. The principles on which such officers were selected are made clear in a standard textbook, Major General M. F. Rimington's *Our Cavalry*, published in 1912:

> We all know the type of officer required, but we are also aware how hard it is to get him. He has been described over and over again, and can be seen in any cavalry regiment; a man who combines an addiction to, and some knowledge of, field sports, involving horses, with sufficient intelligence to pass into Sandhurst.... The addiction to manly, and especially to rough and dangerous, field sports must be regarded as an immense asset towards efficiency for war. Time spent in the chase, "the image of war," must not be regarded as so many hours less given to his employer by the cavalry officer. We particularly want the hunting breed of man, because he goes into danger for the love of it.
>
> What, then, are the conclusions at which we arrive?
> 1. That we draw on a class who have not been used to much brain work.

2. That the young officer should be for choice country
   bred, fond of sport, a 'trier,' and must have some private
   income.

Not many war memoirs by those elite young officers exist.
You might think that is because most of them were not very
articulate or reflective, not used to much brain work, as the general said. But there is a simpler reason for their absence from the
collective tale of their war: they were the ones who went first
and fought against the greatest odds, and within a year or two
most of them were dead. They didn't have time to reflect on and
record their war; what we have of their stories are only fragments out of diaries and letters. Still, those fragments are enough
to give us some sense of what it was like to be one of them: soldiers by profession, from a tradition of soldiering, arrived at last
at the war for which they had been preparing all their lives.

Consider the young officers of the Grenfell family. There
were four of them: the twins, the Honorable Francis and the
Honorable Riverdale, and their cousins the Honorable Julian
and the Honorable Gerald William, called Billy. The Grenfells
were an old and aristocratic family (the father of Julian and
Billy was Lord Desborough) and a military one (their grand-
father had been an admiral and an uncle was a Field Marshal).
Of the seven brothers of Francis and Riverdale two had died in
imperial battles, one in the Matabele War, the other at
Omdurman; another died of illness caused by service in India. A
cousin was killed in the Boer War battle of Spion Kop. Soldiering was what Grenfells did.

In the years before the war, the twins had made reputations
as horsemen—polo players and fox hunters; Rivy had also been
a notable pig sticker in India. These activities were more than
sports; they were, as the General put it, images of war, ways by
which horse soldiers kept their skills honed until the coming of
the war that they impatiently awaited.

When the war began, Francis Grenfell was a captain in the

Ninth Lancers. Riverdale was a reservist in another regiment, but he used family influence to transfer to the Lancers, and the brothers left for France together ten days after war was declared. They went prepared to fight a cavalry war, with six horses and two grooms, and their sabers.

They found their war at the Belgian front near Mons, and here we take up the story as told by the novelist John Buchan in his memoir of the brothers:

> Francis and Rivy were much perplexed by this strange kind of battle-field. As cavalrymen they had hoped for the wide rolling downs which had been predicted as the terrain for any continental war. Instead they found themselves in a land full of little smoky villages, coal mines, railway embankments, endless wire, and a population that seemed as dense as that of a London suburb. They were puzzled to know how cavalry could operate, and they were still more puzzled to understand what was the plan of campaign.

This wasn't the war they and their kind had prepared for; *their* war was to be like a good day's hunting—headlong riding, excitement, danger. They had brought old skills to a new kind of battle. Perhaps that is the story of any war at its commencement; but it was a more acute problem here, at the start of the first war to be fought with twentieth-century technology.

On the regiment's first day of action, Francis Grenfell was ordered to lead his men in a charge on the enemy flank—a classic cavalry maneuver. They were met by fierce small-arms and artillery fire, and were blocked, like fox hunters at a fence, by the enemy's wire. In the ineffectual confusion that followed, the squadron was decimated and the survivors were forced to retire. Francis's account of the action is bitter and dismissive: "We had simply galloped about like rabbits in front of a line of guns," he wrote, "men and horses falling in all directions. Most of one's time was spent in dodging the horses." It had been a waste of men and beasts, not a proper cavalry charge at all.

The story as Buchan told it in his memorial volume was rather different:

> That charge was futile and as gallant as any other like attempt in history on unbroken infantry and guns in position. But it proved to the world that the spirit which inspired the Light Brigade at Balaclava and von Bredow's *Todtenritt* at Mars-la-Tour [in the Franco-Prussian War] was still alive in the cavalry of to-day.

Was Buchan being ironic, comparing Grenfell's attack to the charge of the Light Brigade, that classic example of British blundering and folly? Or did he really believe that one could separate the gallantry and spirit of that obsolete maneuver from its disastrous consequences? Or was he simply a romantic middle-aged civilian writing an elegy for a lost tradition in the language of that tradition, to evoke a memory of romantic war, a war-in-his-head that no longer existed?

After that failure of the charge, Grenfell was asked to save a battery of British guns that were being overrun by the advancing Germans. Here the narrative is his own, from his diary:

> It was not a very nice job, I am bound to say, and I was relieved when it was finished. It meant leaving my regiment under the embankment and riding out alone through the guns, which were now out of action and being heavily shelled all the time, to some distance behind, where I found myself out of range of the shells. It was necessary to go back through the inferno as slowly as possible, so as to pretend to the men that there was no danger and that the shells were more noisy than effective. I reported to the Battery Commander that there was an exit; he then told me that the only way to save his guns was to man-handle them out to some cover. My experience a few minutes before filled me with confidence, so I ordered the regiment to dismount in front of their horses, and then called for volun-

teers. I reminded them that the 9th Lancers had saved the
guns at Maiwand, and had gained the eternal friendship of
the gunners by always standing by the guns in South
Africa; and that we had great traditions to live up to, as the
Colonel had reminded us before we started. Every single
man and officer declared they were ready to go to what
looked like certain destruction. We ran forward and started
pushing the guns out. Providence intervened, for although
this was carried out under a very heavy fire and the guns
had to be slowly turned round before we could guide
them, we accomplished our task. We pushed out one over
dead gunners. I do not think we lost more than three or
four men, though it required more than one journey to get
everything out. It is on occasions like this that good discipline tells. The men were so wonderful and so steady that
words fail me to say what I think of them, and how much is
due to my Colonel for the high standard to which he had
raised this magnificent regiment.

This passage, so plain and exact in its language, so direct and
physical in its action, suggests that Francis might have written a
fine memoir if he had lived. It demonstrates other things as
well—about Grenfell and about the officer corps to which he belonged. There is the calm professionalism with which he surveys
the problem, and the laconic, matter-of-fact tone he uses when
he is describing his own actions—as though this was all familiar
business in familiar circumstances. There is the appeal to a regimental tradition that he clearly believed to be a moral force, and
the praise of military discipline and example, and the impersonal acceptance of casualties as part of the job. But most of all
there is in the entire passage an elation in the doing of a dangerous, necessary job of soldiering. The officer who emerges
from the account is an ideal military figure, the Happy Warrior.

Officially, Francis's work that day was heroic; for it he was
awarded the Victoria Cross—the first to be awarded in the war,

and the only one given to a man on horseback. The award cita-
tion mentions both the charge and the saving of the guns; but
when a battle picture was painted to honor him, it was the
charge that was the subject. In the painting, the Lancers have
breached the German line (which in fact they failed to do) and
are attacking the enemy with lances and sabers; the Germans try
to defend themselves with rifles and bayonets. In the fore-
ground, Francis, on his rearing horse, aims a saber blow at a
German officer, who points a pistol at him. You'd think, from
the painting, that in this engagement men armed with traditional stabbing and slashing weapons defeated men armed with
modern firearms. It is a romantic image in the tradition of heroic
battle painting; but not a true one.

Francis had twice been wounded during the cavalry charge,
and after the episode of the guns he collapsed and was evacuated from the line and sent to England for treatment. While he
was there he received word that his brother Riverdale had been
killed in action. Francis recovered from his wound and returned
to his regiment in France, where he was again wounded and
again evacuated. In the spring of 1915 he once more rejoined
the Lancers, in time for the Second Battle of Ypres, where he
was killed. His last words to his general, at the end of a battle
report, were: "What a bloody day! Hounds are fairly running!"
He had had his good day's hunting.

Of the other two Grenfells, Julian has a place in antholo-
gies of First War poetry as the author of "Into Battle," the one
memorable poem from that war by an experienced soldier that
celebrates war. Like Francis, he was a regular officer in a cavalry
regiment—the First Royal Dragoons. When the war began, the
regiment was stationed in South Africa, but it was hastily
recalled to England and by mid-October 1914 was in action in
France, dismounted then and serving as infantry.

Julian Grenfell's story, the narrative he did not live to write,
is sketched in his letters home. Here is a passage from his
account of an infantry patrol, his first experience of combat:

Then I got leave to make a dash across a field for another farm, where they were sniping at us. I could only get halfway, my sergeant was killed, and my corporal hit. We lay down; luckily it was high roots and we were out of sight. But they had fairly got our range and the bullets kept knocking the dirt into one's face and all around. We just lay doggo for about 1/2 hour, and then the firing slackened, and we crawled back to the houses and the rest of the squadron.

I *was* pleased with my troops under bad fire. They used the most filthy language, talking quite quietly and laughing all the time, even after men were knocked over within a yard of them. I longed to be able to say that I liked it, after all one has heard of being under fire for the first time. But it's bloody. I pretended to myself for a bit that I liked it; but it was no good; it only made one careless and unwatchful and self-absorbed. But when one acknowledged to oneself that it *was* bloody, one became all right again, and cool.

After the firing had slackened we advanced again a bit into the next group of houses which were the edge of the village proper. I can't tell you how *muddling* it is. We did not know what was our front: we did not know whether our own troops had come round us on the flanks or whether they had stopped behind and were firing into us. And besides, a lot of German snipers were left in the houses we had come through, and every now and then bullets came singing by from God knows where. Four of us were talking and laughing in the road when about a dozen bullets came with a whistle. We all dived for the nearest door, which happened to be a lav, and fell over each other, *yelling* with laughter. . . .

I *adore* war. It is like a big picnic without the objectlessness of a picnic. I've never been so well or so happy.

Julian sounds much like his cousin Francis. We hear the Grenfell voice, the voice of a class and a profession—excited, interested, elated by war, pleased with the way the men have performed, enjoying a soldier's work.

Enjoying the actual killing too. Julian records in his diary how he crawled out into no-man's-land on two occasions and shot German soldiers:

> I went out to the right of our lines, where the 10th were and where the Germans were nearest. I took about 30 minutes to do 30 yards. Then I saw the Hun trench, and I waited for a long time, but could see or hear nothing. It was about 10 yards from me. Then I heard some Germans talking, and saw one put his head up over some bushes about 10 yards behind the trench. I could not get a shot at him; I was too low down; and of course I couldn't get up. So I crawled on again very slowly to the parapet of their trench. It was very exciting. I was not *sure* that there might not have been someone there—or a little further along the trench. I peered through their loophole, and saw nobody in the trench. Then the German behind put his head up again. He was laughing and talking. I saw his teeth glisten against my foresight, and I pulled the trigger very steady. He just gave a grunt and crumpled up.... The next day just before dawn I crawled out there again and found the trench empty. Then a single German came through the wood towards the trench. I saw him 50 yards off. He was coming along upright carelessly, making a great noise. I let him get within 25 yards and then shot him through the heart. He never made a sound.

These anecdotes are interesting both for the feelings that are in them and for the feelings that aren't. Grenfell feels satisfaction in the skills he is using—a hunter's satisfaction, such as he might have felt at home when he bagged a brace of pheasants, or in South Africa when he stalked and killed an antelope. There is no feeling for the men he kills. Nor are there any of the inflating terms of romantic war—"glory" and "courage" and "heroism" and all that. For Grenfell, war was a field sport, and like other such sports, it gave pleasure when you did it well.

Julian Grenfell's German-hunting adventure took place in October 1914. The following spring his regiment was in the line at Ypres, near where Riverdale had died. One day as Julian stood on a hill behind the line, observing his troops in action, a shell burst near him, and a splinter entered his head. He lingered for two weeks and died. Two months later his younger brother Billy was killed on the same front while leading a charge.

Four young men from one distinguished family, dead in the war's first year: let them stand for the caste they represented, the aristocracy in its traditional role as a nation's warriors. While they were dying, that caste died too—which is itself a rather romantic way of saying that in the early twentieth century, romantic war went out of fashion (with some exceptions, which we'll look at in the next chapter). In that old tradition, war was a splendid occupation for gentlemen and a *personal* one. Men like the Grenfells (and soldiers going back to Roland at Roncesvalles, and beyond him to the heroes at Ithaca) saw the soldier as a free agent in his own war; the passages I have quoted from their writings are all about individual decisions and actions—leading, charging, encouraging, shooting, killing. In their war, at least the officers were in command of their own actions.

There would be no more of that kind of romantic war on the Western Front, no more heroic cavalry charges with lances and sabers, no more war as spectacle. Armies would change, strategies would evolve, technology would take charge of the war world. And technology is the enemy of romance, in war as in other things. The way Francis Grenfell died can be seen as a symbol of all that change: a courageous professional cavalry officer, skilled in the old ways of war, is dismounted and ordered to fight as infantry, and is shot dead at Ypres during the first attack ever made using poison gas. At that point in war's history, a new way of war began.

Were men like the Grenfells war lovers? The answer must be a little ambivalent, like that letter of Julian's that says both that war is bloody and that he adores it; but yes, I think they loved it. They loved the male world of soldiering; they loved their regiments, their commanders, their men; they loved leading their troops in the difficult and dangerous tasks that war required. War, for them was like fox hunting, or pig sticking, or polo—a sport that called for skill and courage and a bit of luck. Playing it, they fulfilled themselves and became entirely what they had been raised to be.

Looking back, across the death and ruination of two world wars and uncountable local ones, we must see those dead regulars as distant, anachronistic figures, like Crusaders' monuments on tombs. Of course they wouldn't survive the war they began; how had they survived as long as they had? Nevertheless, they are part of the First War's story; their elation at the coming of war was a part of their nation's mood in the first days. And because it was, later war stories, written after the mood had changed, by men who came after, were all in a sense revisionary. Those later stories are the ones we read. We can't read the stories of the men who fought first, because they weren't fully written. But without their voices, the version of the war that we know is incomplete. There *were* men who went to war loving it, and who served and died without disillusionment.

Those were the regulars. The New Army that followed them was different. It was a vast gathering of civilians, thrust into uniform and hastily trained, and sent to the front as the war settled into the trench stalemate, to support the Territorials (the British reserve forces) and what was left of the Old Contemptibles (the survivors of the regulars who had fought in the war's first battles, from the Kaiser's sneer at the "contemptible little army" that opposed him). To provide junior officers for these new battalions, and to replace men like the Grenfells, the army had to depart from General Rimington's principles of officer selection: there weren't enough country gentlemen with private incomes who rode and hunted and weren't too stupid to fill the need. A new principle was formulated, one that sounds like an educational standard but was really one of *class:* young men with public school and/or university backgrounds would be assumed to be officer material. This meant that the condition of "officer and gentleman" was opened to the sons of a broad band of mainly middle-class English society, including professional and commercial families as well as gentry—boys who were "gentlemen" by birth, but also boys whose families clung to the lower edge of gentility, or hoped to raise their sons to that condition. Most of these young men didn't meet Rimington's standards: Robert Graves disgraced himself by not taking leave to watch the Grand National race and not knowing how to ride; others had the wrong clothes or spoke the wrong slang. What they brought to the war was not the background of the country landowning class but the habits and tastes and values of the middle-class schoolboys they had recently been. They were football players, bird watchers, practical jokers; they carried Palgrave's *Golden Treasury* in their pockets or, if they were young intellectuals, Henry James or Homer. They were offended by obscene or vulgar speech and by what Graves called "the uncleanness of sex-life in billets" and by the bottle-a-day whiskey drinkers in the trenches. It's hard to describe them without making them seem priggish. They weren't; but they were, on the whole, what their schools had made them: decent middle-class Edwardians. They would lead the platoons and the companies, and after the war they would write the memoirs.

These young officers would feel the romance of war—their educations would make that certain—but they wouldn't share the values that the Grenfells shared. They would have no sense of the traditions of the military life, or of what the rules were, or of how to behave when they reached the fighting. They would think like civilians. And as their numbers grew, they would alter the essential character of the British forces; in the trenches, civilians would lead civilians.

The mood of that deep change is in this description, by a New-Army officer, of the battalion in which he found himself in December 1914:

> It was a new Army battalion, part of a division made up from super-numerary battalions which had existed since August 1914, but had been brought together only a month or so before being sent to France. It was almost entirely amateur. Except for our second-in-command, who had retired ten years earlier and was well over fifty, and our quartermaster, we had no regular officers. It was therefore a co-operative undertaking of amateurs in which we had to learn the hard way.

"A co-operative undertaking of amateurs": what would the Grenfells have thought of that as a description of the running of a war? And what would they have thought of the extemporized army that passage describes? This ramshackle amateurism did not prevent the battalion from fighting for three years on the Western Front, or from dying in dismaying numbers there: by the end of the war, their losses in officers and men killed in action were almost exactly equal to their initial combat strength. But even the fighting and the dying didn't make their officers into regulars or more than "temporary gentlemen," or make them think the way the Grenfells thought.

Why did those civilian soldiers go to war? There is an answer to that question in the myth of the war that we all know—the compound story that has evolved over the years and that we accept, without much thought, as the truth. The myth says that they went for high idealistic reasons: because they were patriotic; because they believed in the Big Words of war, in Honor and Glory and Heroism and, the biggest word of all, England; because they felt moral outrage at German aggression and atrocities, and compassion for poor invaded Belgium. All of these motives for enlistment were there in the war talk in England in the early months of the war, in newspaper articles, in recruiting posters, in politicians' speeches, in the patriotic poems that began to appear in the press as soon as war was declared. Of course they were: if this war was to be fought by a volunteer army (as it was by the British until 1916), then men would have to be persuaded to go.

But in the memoirs of the men who went, those high emotional motives don't figure very importantly. Instead you find enlistment narratives like this one, from Robert Graves:

> I was at Harlech when war was declared; I decided to enlist a day or two later. In the first place, though only a very short war was expected—two or three months at the very outside—I thought that it might last just long enough to delay my going to Oxford in October, which I dreaded.... In the second place, I entirely believed that France and England had been drawn into a war which they had never contemplated and for which they were entirely unprepared.

Or this one, of an Oxford undergraduate at home for the summer holidays in 1914:

> I had recently, in the Oxford OTC, gone through the necessary hoops to secure "Certificate A" which was supposed to qualify one to be granted a commission in the Territorial Army, so the natural thing for me to do when Great Britain's involvement in the war became a certainty was to bicycle to Lancaster and to offer my services to the Adjutant of the local Territorial Battalion.

Are these patriotic decisions? I suppose they are, in a reticent English way. But they don't sound much like the recruiting posters, or the sonnets of Rupert Brooke, or any of the voices of eloquent persuasion.

There is another motive, not always very well articulated, that many of those volunteers, and especially the younger ones, must have felt, because young men do: the pull of war's excitement.

You feel it, often, in the narratives of the men who were first to enlist: how they hurried to the recruiting office, afraid that the fighting would end before they got to it. It would be over by Christmas, or by Easter, or if not then, by the end of the year; always there was some imagined terminus to what might be their only chance. Chance to do what? To be what? That isn't usually very clear in what they wrote. Somewhere, in some other country, vast, historically determining events would occur, and it would be splendid to be there—not for moral reasons, but simply to be a witness and a participant in that great commotion.

The war diary of Edwin Campion Vaughan will provide us with a good example of that young excitement. Indeed, Vaughan will illustrate many typical feelings and experiences before we are finished with his war, because he was an acute and honest observer, but also because he was typical of one kind of volunteer—the nobody from nowhere. Vaughan had none of the old-army qualifications for officer and gentleman: his family was obscure (his father was a customs official in the Midlands), he had no private income, and he had gone to the wrong school (a minor Jesuit one—he was a Roman Catholic). He did not hunt; he couldn't even ride a horse. He had just left school when he enlisted at the age of eighteen; he hadn't had time for ordinary adult experience, and he wasn't clever enough to get by on his wits. As a new subaltern he was clumsy, fearful, and incompetent; he misunderstood orders and made awkward mistakes. His senior officers clearly regarded his presence in their battalion as a bad joke, as he characteristically admitted: "As I approached I heard the CO say '*who* on earth is this?' whereupon all turned and stared until Mortimore said 'It's Vaughan!' and everybody laughed."

But if he was clumsy and comical, he was also keen to get to the war, and it's that keen youth, nineteen years old and a brand-new officer, whose voice we hear as he departs from Waterloo Station on a January day in 1917, bound for war:

I had expected that on leaving for France I would be overcome by grief, for I knew that I would not see my home
again for many, many months—and possibly not again. But
when the moment came the excitement of the venture into
the dreamed of but unrealized land of war, eclipsed the
sorrow of parting, and I know now how much harder it is
for those who lose us, than for us who go.

It was an incredible moment—long dreamed of—when
the train steamed slowly out of Waterloo, a long triple row
of happy, excited faces protruding from carriage windows,
passing those which bravely tried to smile back at us—we
were wrapped in the sense of adventure to come, they
could look forward only to loneliness. We took a last long
look at the sea of faces and waving handkerchiefs—and we
had left.

When we had swept round the bend, away from the
crowded platform, ringing with farewell cheers, I sank back
into the cushions, and tried to realize that, at last, I was
actually on my way to France, to war and excitement—to
death or glory, or both.

"Excitement," "adventure," "death or glory"—those are his
reasons for going. There is no irony in his use of those romantic
terms; the romance of war was as real for him as it was for the
Grenfells. More real, in fact; for their war-in-the-head had come
out of military manuals, whereas his had come, surely, out of
romantic literature. So it was not a war but a dream of war that
drew that green boy on. There must have been many young
men like him on that troop train as it rolled toward the Channel
and France.

Vaughan doesn't say where his romantic dream of war came
from, but other memoirs do: it came from the romantic books
that such young men read. Here are three English subalterns as
they approach their first war experience. Guy Chapman, on his
first night in northern France:

By now I was growing excited. At the corner where we had turned off the main road to this place, the other finger on the signpost indicated Arras. Ghosts of Cyrano and the Duke of Marlborough flitted dimly through my memory.

And John Easton, writing in the third person as Broadchalk, on his way to the battle of Loos:

Bethune! The very word sent a thrill through Broadchalk's soul. It had always spelled ghosts to him, since the first time that he had imagined the terrible figure in a red cloak leave his house at Athos's summons....

And a British pilot on his first flight over the front, flying along the river Lys toward Armentières:

The Lys, winding like a snake, made me think of d'Artagnan and Milady.

Romantic images, out of nineteenth-century romances of seventeenth-century adventurers: Rostand's *Cyrano de Bergerac* and Dumas's *The Three Musketeers*, the sort of books that middle-class English boys would have read in the first decade of this century. Neither is, strictly speaking, a war book; but both are about soldiers—dashing, heroic, independent-minded swordsmen, for whom fighting was a personal matter.

This was the first generation that went to war with such stuff in their heads, and because they did, they went with expectations. They expected that their war would be a personal affair, like the wars in the books: that their war lives would engage them in personal decisions and adventures, that they would find occasions for personal combat, personal courage, personal killing and, if necessary, personal dying, personally chosen and accepted.

The war they expected to fight would make such actions possible. It would be a short war of movement, fought with hand weapons in brief, hard-fought battles, with cavalry charges and fierce defenses and swift, overwhelming victories. And why should they not have thought so? Wars were like that in the books they read, and had been like that in recent history—in South Africa and the Sudan, in the Crimea, in the Franco-Prussian War, in the American war with the Spaniards. European armies were trained and equipped for that sort of war: witness the Grenfell twins, with their chargers and their sabers; witness the French cuirassiers who manned the trenches at Gommecourt in 1915, wearing rusty breastplates and tall brass helmets with horsehair plumes. It still seemed possible that war, when one got to it, would be a romantic, gaudy adventure. And so one went like Vaughan, expectantly, excitedly, to death or glory, or like Sassoon, with a sense of English rectitude.

But the strongest and commonest motive for enlisting, in that war as in every other modern war, was surely neither romance, nor patriotism, nor adventure, nor glory, nor any of the high moral issues. It was simply the war itself: a young man goes to war because it is there to go to. Once a modern nation declares war—*total* war—that war becomes the only reality, and the only motive for action ("Don't you know there's a war on?"). A London journalist turned soldier, remembering what he thought on a troopship bound for France, will illustrate the point:

> I began to think that I was rather a mug for being there. I needn't have been. I had joined rather late, but still as a volunteer. Even after conscription had been brought in I might have kept out on compassionate grounds. I was not fit, from the rather high standard of the Army when I joined it, and I had only got past the doctor through influence. I had no inclination at all for soldiering, and privately knew myself to be a coward. Then what the devil was I doing in that rotten cattle-boat, probably on my way to a bloody death?
>
> Professor Freud might answer the questions. I hated

being thought a funk. I had the strongest disapproval of
young and fit civilians without dependents, but could not
very well express it while I was a civilian myself. I found it
very uncomfortable to crawl about in a lounge suit while
most men of my age were in khaki. Most of my friends who
were worth while had vanished. The three girls with whom
I had simultaneous "understandings"—although not actual engagements—were being dazzled by chronic home-
service-ites. Obviously the thing to do was to get into some
musty brown material.

On the other side of the world, at about the same time,
a classics student at the University of Queensland was having
similar problems, which he later described in a third-person
narrative:

As yet he had no thought of enlisting; there seemed to be
no urgent need of men. Through the long Vacation (end of
November to middle March) he worked at his Greek and
Latin. He began his second year without the least intention
of joining-up. But the departure of several friends for
Egypt [where Australians and New Zealanders were training for the Gallipoli campaign], the contrast of the mixed
lawn-tennis that he was playing with the strenuous life
of those friends, the gradual realisation that this was not
a war to be finished a few months ahead, that men did
take things seriously enough to offer gladly their careers,
implicitly their lives, these and other causes rendered him
dissatisfied with his present industrious but secluded existence. In times of peace the student life was all very well, in
fact it had much in its favour: in time of war it was, except
for the unfit and the indispensable, little less blameworthy
than Nero fiddling while Rome burned.

What is most interesting in these two passages is what isn't
there: no values or emotions are attached to the war at all, and
there are none of the Big Words; nor is there any mention of

adventure, or romance, or the moral rightness of the cause; there isn't even any reference to a particular war being fought somewhere that might require more soldiers. The energy that moved these two quite different men to take the same action wasn't *war* at all; it was *wartime*, the condition of emotional excitement in a nation at war, which swept them both into its current. Anyone who has been young in this century when a big war began knows the force of that current. Under its pressure men enlist for no high motives but simply because other men are enlisting, because the current is irresistible.

For recruits like these, the war was not an adventure but a duty, an obligation, or something even less voluntary than that. "People will think my being here the result of my own initiative, an act of courage," one volunteer wrote, once he was in. "On the contrary, I have been carried along on the crest of the world's event, that is all. It is weakness, the inability to resist the tide of time. No, it is not weakness; it is youth."

Those volunteers who became the New Army didn't cross to France at once—they began to reach the front in numbers only late in 1915. When they did go, it wasn't always with the dreamy excitement that the young Vaughan felt. Edmund Blunden's classic memoir, *Undertones of War*, begins:

> I was not anxious to go.... There was something about France in those days which looked to me despite all journalistic enchanters, to be dangerous.

And Guy Chapman's *Passionate Prodigality* begins in a similar vein:

> I was loath to go. I had no romantic illusions. I was not eager, or even resigned to self-sacrifice, and my heart gave back no answering throb to the thought of England. In fact, I was very much afraid.

One must remember these honest, apprehensive men as well as the excited Vaughans and the elated Grenfells. Men went to war with many motives, and some with open eyes.

The Western Front, when they reached it, was not like anything they knew or could imagine. By then the war had come to a standstill; it was fought out of ditches dug in the ruined earth by muddy, anonymous masses of men. Where in their civilian lives could those young volunteers have found such a devastated, subhuman existence? Where could they even have found it in books? It was a new world.

The commonest response of the new soldiers to this world of war, their memoirs tell us, was simply a sense of its *strangeness*. Other feelings would come later: fear, horror, grief, anger; but at first it was the unimaginable otherness of war that they felt, and later recorded. Robert Graves got that feeling into his account of his first arrival in the trenches at Cambrin:

> After a meal of bread, bacon, rum and bitter stewed tea sickly with sugar, we went up through the broken trees to the east of the village and up a long trench to battalion headquarters. The trench was cut through red clay. I had a torch with me which I kept flashed on the ground. Hundreds of field mice and frogs were in the trench. They had fallen in and had no way out. The light dazzled them and we could not help treading on them. So I put the torch back in my pocket. We had no picture of what the trenches would be like.

"We had no picture," Graves says—that is, no war-in-the-head that included those squashed creatures in the red clay under their feet. Imagination has failed before the strangeness of trench reality, in which men walk on death. Graves doesn't react to what his feet tread on; he is a soldier, or trying to be one. Or he is a writer, creating a metaphor for what it is like when you enter war's world.

In the narratives of these new soldiers, the strangeness of war is the ground bass of the story. Every memoir is a catalogue of strangenesses; how is one to enumerate it all? The noise, the stench, the mud, the rats, and the lice are all parts of the war

reality. But most of all, there is the scene that dominates the soldiers' tale of that front—the strange landscape that is not a landscape but an annihilation of what *landscape* means. Here is what
it looked like to a young English officer on the Somme battlefield in the second month of the 1916 offensive:

> The country here is stricken waste: the trees that formed an
> avenue to the road are now torn and broken stumps, some
> still holding unexploded shells in their shattered trunks,
> others looped about with useless telegraph-wire. The earth
> on both sides of the road is churned up into a crumbling
> mass, and so tossed and scarred is the ground that the
> actual line of the front trenches is hardly distinguishable.
> On the far side, in the face of a steep rise, we see the
> remains of what were deep German dug-outs; but every-
> thing needs pointing out, for the general impression is of a
> wilderness without verdure or growth of any kind.

This is surely what we visualize when we try to imagine the
Western Front: not men in action but a scene like this, in which
everything that was natural has been defaced and destroyed,
even the natural contours of the earth; a scene in which even
the landmarks of war itself—the trenches and the dugouts—must
be pointed out.

"The Western Front," our shared vision of what the war in
France was like, is the product of such battlefield descriptions.
The war, we see, was unrecognizably strange, unlike anything
we have ever known or imagined; it was life lived in conditions
of terrible absolute *difference*. That surely is a part of its appeal
to us, one reason we go on reading about it and writing about it.
Its image of total annihilation is our tragic myth of modern war.

But when you imagine war only in such high dramatic terms
you misrepresent it. War is not tragic to the men who are experiencing it—or at least it isn't *always* tragic. To soldiers in the
field it is simply life lived under strange conditions: terrible at
its worst but containing also moments of pleasure, of comedy,

even of happiness. We remember the images of annihilation and construct our understanding out of them, but we tend to forget passages like this one, from the same narrative I just quoted:

> We are marching out of Balancourt, and for the first time I am at the head of my platoon.... It is the glorious afternoon of a perfect July day. The sky is flecked with white clouds whose shadows chase across the undulating wooded country. The tall corn is ripening, and between its stalks poppies and cornflowers glow with colour. Through the valley we are descending a noisy stream finds its way, and on the hills beyond, great elm-trees stand like wise men brooding. It is a lush green country, full of beauty. The war seems far away.

This scene of the countryside behind the lines in July 1916 is neither more nor less true than the other, tragic vision of the battlefield; men were out of the lines as often as they were in. Officers on the Somme could ride back to Amiens for dinner in a restaurant with linen and silver on the table; enlisted men could find a village estaminet, get drunk on cheap wine, and talk to a French woman, or fall in line at a government brothel and go a bit further. That interweaving of ordinary, pleasurable life and life in the trenches was one of the war's strange differences.

There is another thing to be said about "the Western Front": it didn't take its totally devastated form all at once. At the beginning, the countryside was relatively unscarred, peasants worked their fields within earshot of the guns, villages were intact and occupied. But most of the soldiers' narratives we read begin later, when all that had changed; they record the torn earth and the razed villages, the maze of trenches, and the dead, unnatural space between the lines called no-man's-land. That Western Front became the reality only after a process of destruction that went on over months and years.

But even when the devastation seemed complete, the front was not all horror and ruin; there were sectors where troops led

quiet lives. Charles Carrington joined his battalion in the line
north of the Somme in January 1916, not long after the terrible
fighting at Loos; yet he felt that "the war was still a picnic, or
seemed so. The battalion was in 'cushy' trenches, that is to say,
posted in any easy position where the enemy were not too near
nor the gunfire too frequent."

Carrington isn't arguing here that in fact the Western Front
wasn't so bad; his book makes clear how terrible it was. He is
simply saying that not every day in every sector was the Inferno
that is fixed in our imaginations. That hell is the war we
remember, because we want the First World War to be the
worst, the cautionary example of war horror. And sometimes it
was; but there were also times of ordinary war, when men performed their routine duties and nobody attacked and nobody
died. Sometimes they felt moments of peace, enjoyed small plea-
sures, noticed and recorded a fine day, a sunset, as men at war
always have. They saw and felt the horrors too; of course they
did. But locally, and intermittently. Nobody lived at that pitch
continuously. What is constant in their narratives is not the
horror of war but its difference from any other imaginable existence. The narratives will tell us that, if we listen to them.

Generals recognized the war's difference too, but thought
about it differently, in military terms. Field Marshal Haig
explained his sense of the military differences in the final dis-
patch that he wrote at the end of the war, summing up the
entire enterprise and justifying his leadership as commander-in-
chief. Haig was at some pains, now that it was over, to explain
why so many men had had to die in his war. "Certain general
factors peculiar to modern war," he wrote.

> made for the inflation of losses. The great strength of
> modern field defences and the power and precision of
> modern weapons, the multiplication of machine guns,
> trench mortars and artillery of all natures, the employment
> of gas and the rapid development of the aeroplane as a

formidable agent of destruction against both men and
material, all combined to increase the price paid for victory.

It was technology that had made the war different: science
had created more powerful weapons ("mechanical contrivan-
ces," Haig called them), but it had also created stronger
defenses against them. The guns of the artillery were bigger,
and observers in airplanes made them more accurate; gas
changed the odds on infantry attacks; machine guns made
massed assaults impossibly costly in lives (though generals went
on ordering them). Haig was correct in his assessment; given
the state of military technology, which could kill more men but
could not advance armies, the war probably couldn't have been
fought on the Western Front in any other way.

But there was a more fundamental change in war during
1914–18 than the technological ones that Haig named. The
minds of the fighting men changed. The new soldiers came to
war believing that individual wills would have a role there, that
what a man did—his decisions, his actions—would affect whether
he lived or died. The new weapons of war challenged that conviction; they made death accidental. It wasn't the violence or the
power or the cruelty of those weapons that made the war different; it was the vast randomness and anonymity of their ways
of killing.

The British historian C. R. M. F. Cruttwell was in the
trenches at Ypres when the Germans first used gas, and he
wrote feelingly in his *History of the Great War* about this difference in soldiers under gas attack:

> In the face of gas, without protection, individuality was
> annihilated; the soldier in the trench became a mere pas-
> sive recipient of torture and death. A final stage seemed to
> be reached in the whole tendency of modern scientific war-
> fare to depress and make of no effect individual bravery,
> enterprise, and skill. Again, nearly every soldier is or
> becomes a fatalist on active service; it quietens his nerves

to believe that his chance will be favourable or the reverse.
But his fatalism depends on the belief that he has a chance.
If the very air which he breathes is poison, his chance is
gone: he is merely a destined victim for the slaughter.

This is more than a statement about the use of gas; it is a soldier's testimony to what happened to men's nerves and wills in
scientific war. Like so many other memories of the war, it is also
a kind of elegy for the old way of war—the Grenfells' way—in
which individual bravery might win a battle. Cruttwell knew
something about the effects of the new war on passive recipi-
ents: he was psychologically damaged by his experiences and
suffered a serious breakdown after the war. It is said that he
wrote his *History* while he was a patient in a London mental
hospital.

If this was the nature of modern war, this will-less, passive
suffering, then the men in the trenches were not agents in their
soldiering but merely victims. And if that was true, then the Big
Words of war, if they could be used at all, would have to be
redefined; and particularly the personal terms *courage* and *cowardice,* which assume meaning at the point where war and the
individual self intersect.

There were plenty of examples in the First War of courage of
the traditional soldierly kind. In the British Army, 578 soldiers
won the Victoria Cross, and we must believe that those decora-
tions were given for acts as heroic as any Victorian cavalry
charge. But the stories of those acts, when we come upon them
in personal narratives, seem displaced and dissonant, as though
they had strayed into the story from some other, earlier war, in
which men had more freedom to be brave, and bravery made a
difference. Francis Grenfell's charge is one example. Here is
another, the story of how a VC was won in the battle of Armentières in 1918:

Captain Pryce, M.C., commanded a company in this Battalion. He held out against overwhelming odds for two

days and two nights. By noon the second day he had run
out of ammunition, and his company numbered eighteen
instead of one hundred and fifty. He was entirely sur-
rounded. He had been enfiladed all day by machine-guns.
The Germans in front could no longer fire without the
risk of shooting Germans behind Pryce's position. They
thought they were being held up by at least a battalion. It
was now a question of minutes. Pryce did not surrender.
He did not even wait to be massacred. He stepped out of
his trench and led a bayonet charge against the enemy. He
was last seen being clubbed to death by Germans.

What is it that rings false in this story, set in this war? Is it the
desperation of Pryce's charge? Or its utter suicidal pointless-
ness? Or is it the sense one has that personal, defiant acts like
his were anachronisms on the Western Front?

Personal narratives of the First War don't often pay attention
to such rash acts; the courage we find in them is more commonly of another kind. The French historian Marc Bloch, then a
sergeant of infantry, reflected on that other courage in a memoir
he wrote in the spring of 1915, after fighting in the war's
opening battles in northern France:

> Military courage is certainly widespread.... I have always
> noticed that by some fortunate reflex, death ceases to
> appear very terrible the moment it seems close: it is this,
> ultimately, that explains courage. Most men dread going
> under fire, and especially returning to it. Once there, how-
> ever, they no longer tremble.

The courageous act here is not some extreme individual gesture like Captain Pryce's, but simply going back to the trenches
and standing there, enduring the shells, the misery, and the
privation, and *not trembling*. It is passive courage, a stoic endurance where there is nothing else to be done. Such courage
doesn't win medals, but it is a fine and difficult virtue, as old
soldiers know.

Many men failed that test of stoic courage. Rather than return to the front, they deserted, or did to themselves what they feared the enemy would do to them. In soldiers' narratives there are many accounts of self-inflicted wounds and many suicides; the first and the last dead soldier that Robert Graves saw during his time in the trenches were men who had shot themselves. Graves doesn't call these men cowards in *Good-bye to All That;* he simply reports the cases and speculates on the reasons for their deaths. "The misery of the weather and the knowledge of the impending attack had been too much for him," he says of one dead man, as though these factors constituted natural causes.

The army was clear enough about what cowardice was: it was being unsoldierly in the presence of the enemy, running, hiding, casting away arms. The army's ways of dealing with it were also clear: by court martial and, in the most flagrant cases, a firing squad. Eighteen British soldiers were tried for cowardice during the war and shot. But if the army was clear, the civilian soldiers in the trenches weren't. For many of them, the term was a problem they worried over. "My God!" Max Plowman wrote in his journal,

> I understand desertion. A man distraught determines that the last act of his life shall at least be one of his own volition; and who can say that what is commonly regarded as the limit of cowardice is not then heroic?

Guy Chapman reflected on the case of a soldier who had shot himself in the foot:

> Perhaps those who call this man a coward will consider the desperation to which he was driven, to place his rifle against the foot, and drive through the bones and flesh the flames of the cordite and the smashing metal. Let me hope that the court-martial's sentence was light. Not that it matters, for, in truth, the real sentence had been inflicted long ere it sat.

And Eric Partridge described cowardice from the inside, how it overwhelmed him during the battle of the Somme (Partridge wrote his memoir in the third person, calling himself Frank Honywood):

> He had gone into the Somme fiasco of July 28–29th, 1916, as bravely as any man: he had, a week later, gone into the battle of Pozières a thorough coward, although he would not for worlds have shown it nor even confessed it.... During the Bullecourt phase ... Frank's nerves were so bad, his fears so possessed him, that he often thought of deserting and planned how he would get away; but, as he bitterly admitted to himself, he had not even the courage to desert.

In the minds of all these soldiers, courage and cowardice seem to have changed places, and cowardice has lost its stigma. Cowardice is not a base act but simply fear at its most extreme, what the troops called "windiness." And fear was in every soldier who had been where battle was. A change so profound in the essential values of war was bound to have profound consequences for the war stories such soldiers told. In their narratives there would be neither heroes nor cowards but only men, and even the greatest battles would not be made glorious in the telling.

For an example of this new kind of courage, in the new kind of battle, we return to Vaughan, whom we saw a few pages back leaving Waterloo Station, dreaming of death or glory. Vaughan went to his war wondering what battle would be like and how he would behave. He learned the answers to those questions at Passchendaele. Battle there was desperate, confused movements through pounding rain and the smoke of guns, in deep, liquid mud, under relentless bombardment—movements that never advanced the line or secured any important position or accomplished anything at all except death and wounds.

Here is Vaughan leading his men in an attack on an enemy pillbox:

> Finally Wood and I led 15 men over to the tanks. The fire was still heavy, but now, in the dusk and the heavy rain, the shots were going wide. As we reached the tanks, however, the Boche hailed shrapnel upon us and we commenced rapidly to have casualties. The awful spitting "coalboxes" [a kind of high-explosive shell] terrified the troops and only by cursing and driving could my wonderful Sergeant Major Merrick and myself urge them out of the shelter of the tanks.
>
> Up the road we staggered, shells bursting around us. A man stopped dead in front of me, and exasperated I cursed him and butted him with my knee. Very gently he said "I'm blind, Sir," and turned to show me his eyes and nose torn away by a piece of shell. "Oh God! I'm sorry, sonny," I said. "Keep going on the hard part," and left him staggering back in his darkness.

If you listen closely to the voice of this passage, it's the voice of the civilian you hear, not the soldier: a man who does not judge in military terms but is astonished and appalled that battle is like *this*, that shelling can be so awful and men so terrified, and who speaks with helpless pity to the blinded boy, before leaving him to his darkness.

There is courage here—Vaughan and his men move forward as ordered—but it isn't military courage of the old, heroic kind. It isn't literary courage, either; it doesn't come out of any schoolboy's war-in-the-head. It's just dogged, blind fidelity—the only kind of courage that was possible at Passchendaele.

There is fear there too: the men are frightened, and so is Vaughan. In the battle, as he records it, fear is as much an element of the battle as the rain and the shells. All around him, as he struggles to obey orders and attack, men are behaving in

ways that the old army would have called cowardly. There is
Captain Spencer, "windy as a rabbit ... his great bespectacled
face white with fear and streaked with mud," babbling incoher-
ently in a shell hole; and Private Hancocks, shaking with fear;
and Wood, who "could not walk or even talk but lay shuddering
on a wire bed" in a bunker; and Sergeant Woodright and his
companion, who have been blown into the air by a shell and
gibber like monkeys; and Lynch, "shaking and helpless with
fear," who cries that he cannot walk but is shamed by Vaughan
into running forward, and is killed before he has gone three
yards. Vaughan records these cases sometimes with sympathy
and sometimes with contempt (he despised Captain Spencer, I
suppose, because he was an officer and should have set an
example); but he doesn't call them cowards—that term is not in
his vocabulary. They are simply frightened men.

Vaughan's cases belong not to the morality of war but to the
pathology of fear. There were many such cases through the
war, cases of men who could neither continue fighting nor run
away, but had to escape their fears in other ways—by becoming
mute, or blind, or deaf, or paralyzed, or by losing the ability to
sleep or to remember, or by developing tremors and tics and
disorders of speech, or by weeping uncontrollably. Doctors of
the Army Medical Corps had no methods for treating such
patients, since they appeared to be neither ill nor wounded.
Their solution was to label them all "shell-shocked" and
send them to a different kind of doctor—like the psychologist
W. H. R. Rivers. By doing so, they acknowledged that in this war
men suffered a new kind of injury; this would be the first psy-
chopathological war.

Rivers's writings on war psychology are still worth reading,
three-quarters of a century after he wrote them. I will take only
two points from his work that touch on the issue of cowardice:
his view of the general causes of war neurosis and his reflections
on the psychological differences between officers and men in
war.

In his study of shell shock, Rivers began with Freud but soon departed from psychoanalytical orthodoxy. "The first result of the dispassionate study of the psychoneuroses of warfare," he wrote,

> in relation to Freud's scheme, was to show that in the vast majority of cases there is no reason to suppose that factors derived from the sexual life played any essential part in causation, but that these disorders became explicable as the result of disturbance of another instinct, one even more fundamental than that of sex—the instinct of self-preservation, especially those forms of it which are adapted to protect the animal from danger. Warfare makes fierce onslaughts on an instinct or group of instincts which is rarely touched by the ordinary life of the member of a modern civilised community.

Men broke down in combat, in this war, because their lives had not prepared them to face danger, because they were *civilians*.

But their ways of breaking down were not all the same. Officers and men, Rivers found, had different neuroses. Officers suffered anxiety neuroses—the weeping and the tremors, the sleep and memory problems; common soldiers developed physical disabilities—paralysis or blindness or mutism. Why, Rivers wondered, should this be the case, when they were fighting the same war?

The answer, he concluded, must lie in what men brought to the war, and especially in their educations. Officers were on the whole better educated and lived more complex and varied mental lives. But more important, they had been educated in a particular way: most of them were public-school men.

> Fear and its expression are especially abhorrent to the moral standards of the public schools at which the majority of officers have been educated. The games and contests which make up so large a part of the school curriculum are all directed to enable the boy to meet without manifestation of

fear any occasion likely to call forth that emotion. The
public school boy enters the army with a long course of
training which enables him successfully to repress, not only
expressions of fear, but also the emotion itself.

This isn't a point about primary fear—the natural fear of death or
pain; it's about fear of fear. These young officers had been
trained to an impossible ideal of leadership and self-control; not
only must they lead their men fearlessly; they must *be* fearless.
When they weren't, when self-preservation and their public-
school ethos conflicted, the young officers often could not re-
solve the conflict and so developed anxiety neuroses that kept
them in the war but useless (like Vaughan's Captain Spencer).
The ordinary soldier, who was not burdened with old school
ideals of conduct and felt no obligations to be either a leader or
an example, could confess his fear and so survive it, or develop a
physically disabling symptom and drop out of the war.

From Rivers's study of shell shock, two conclusions can be
drawn. First, that *civilianness* itself, the experience of ordinary
life in a civilized community, is a poor preparation for modern
war and thus in an army composed of civilians there will be
mental conflicts and breakdowns. And second, that a middle-
class background—defined as a public-school education—which
had been the British army's first principle for selecting officers
from the civilian population, was in fact likely to be a liability for
an officer in the trenches, and a cause for psychoneurotic illnesses. These officers would bring to their recollections the conflict between *training*, which said: Be brave, take responsibility,
lead; and *instinct*, which said: If you do, you'll die. And a third
voice, *experience*, which said: You aren't fighting for those
public-school values anyway. Whether the writer was a man of
letters like Sassoon, or a one-book amateur like Vaughan,
whether what he wrote was a diary (Vaughan) or a retrospective
memoir (Sassoon), didn't matter; the story would rise from the
same value sources and move under the same impulsions.

And the other ranks? What about their stories? They were written, all right, and sometimes published or, if not, carefully copied out and deposited in some archive like the Imperial War Museum in London. But if you set aside a scattering of men who ought by reason of their backgrounds to have been officers—men like Frederic Manning, who wrote *Her Privates We*—there is only one English memoir by a common soldier that has achieved any kind of permanence, Frank Richards's *Old Soldiers Never Die*. Richards was a private in the Welsh Fusiliers, the regiment of Sassoon and Graves. He was more experienced than most men in the ranks—he had served eight years in the army in India and Burma before the war—and he was a good soldier; by the war's end he had won a Distinguished Conduct Medal and a Military Medal. But his story has nothing to do with courage or cowardice or leadership, or any other military virtues; it is about the unavoidable particulars of war, and the small pleasures that a soldier might enjoy, if he was cunning and lucky, and about survival. Reading Richards, you are in a different, less anxious war than the one the young officers fought—less serious, sometimes funnier, deep in common-soldier details. That war was, we must suppose, the majority war—there were more Richardses than there were Sassoons on the Western Front—but it was not much recorded, because the men who fought it weren't writers. Richards's book exists only because Graves intervened, edited it, and found a publisher.

One other point from Rivers's work is not so much a conclusion as a governing principle. Rivers took fear to be a natural and instinctive reaction to danger, and treated the failures of men to overcome their fears as a problem in psychology, not morality. If you do that, then "cowardice" ceases to be an appropriate term, and punishment for cowardly acts becomes unjust. Men in the trenches already knew this—they were notably uncensorious about desertions and self-inflicted wounds—but it took the official army a while to learn the lesson. Men continued to be court-martialed and sometimes executed for cowardice throughout the war; and afterward, when the army's legal code was changed and made more humane, "cowardice in the face of the enemy" remained a capital offense (it was abolished in 1930).

Crucial moral concepts of war—courage, cowardice, heroism—changed in the First World War. So did the meanings of another cluster of concepts, which are not, in war's vocabulary, *moral* terms: killing, the dead, and death itself.

Killing the enemy is a primary intention of war; all military heroes from the beginning have been killers, and unreluctant ones (you will remember the enthusiasm Julian Grenfell brought to this essential act of his chosen profession). But in the narratives of the amateur soldiers of the war there is a notable change: there is almost no personal killing in them. Sassoon never admits killing anyone; neither does Edmund Blunden or David Jones or Robert Graves, or the American Hervey Allen. I could go on with examples.

There is a material explanation for this in the statistical fact that most of the war's killing was done not at close range, by infantrymen (who were generally the ones who wrote the memoirs), but distantly, by artillery. But the absence of personal killing is more than a matter of statistics; war narrators seem to have felt a reluctance, a moral fastidiousness, before the act of taking a life. These civilian soldiers seem to hold back from confessing to the essential act that a soldier *must* perform but that a civilian must *not*. Here is an example of that shrinking, from Partridge's "Frank Honywood, Private." It's the early days of the Somme offensive, and Honywood/Partridge is advancing across no-man's-land, where the Germans have dug advance posts:

> On coming to one of these pits, Frank put a bullet into one who stood against the side, but even at the time he suspected that the man was already dead; looking back on that ghastly night, which seemed less real then than now,

he knows that the man must have been dead, so still he stood, or, rather, half reclined, against the back of that hole in the ground which was his own height and length and little more than his width. The only man that Honywood *knows* he shot was already dead.

But though there is little killing in the narratives, there is much dying, and there are many dead men. The dead at first were an unimaginable part of war's strangeness, for which ordinary civilian life could not possibly be a preparation. Remembering his introduction to life among the dead, the young German officer Ernst Jünger wrote:

Among other questions that occupied us was this: What does it look like when there are dead lying about? And we never for a moment dreamed that in this war the dead would be left month after month to the mercy of wind and weather, as once the bodies on the gallows were.

And now at our first glance of horror we had a feeling that is difficult to describe. Seeing and recognizing are matters, really, of habit. In the case of something quite unknown the eye alone can make nothing of it. So it was that we had to stare again and again at these things that we had never seen before, without being able to give them any meaning. It was too entirely unfamiliar. We looked at all these dead with dislocated limbs, distorted faces, and the hideous colors of decay, as though we walked in a dream through a garden full of strange plants, and we could not realize at first what we had all round us.

That first sight of the dead is a fundamental part of the soldiers' tale, being as it is the extreme case of war's unfamiliarity for civilian soldiers. Siegfried Sassoon's account of his first enemy dead, met as he moved through Mametz on the third day of the Somme offensive, makes the strangeness of death very clear:

It gave me a bit of a shock when I saw, in the glimmer
of day break, a dumpy, baggy-trousered man lying half
sideways with one elbow up as if defending his lolling
head; the face was grey and waxen, with a stiff little mous-
tache; he looked like a ghastly doll, grotesque and undignified. Beside him was a scorched and mutilated figure
whose contorted attitude revealed bristly cheeks, a grinning blood-smeared mouth and clenched teeth. These
dead were unlike our own; perhaps it was the strange uniform, perhaps their look of butchered hostility. Anyhow
they were one with the little trench direction boards whose
unfamiliar lettering seemed to epitomize that queer feeling
I used to have when I stared across No Man's Land, ignorant of the humanity which was on the other side.

There the dead are, grotesque and undignified—another bit of
Battlefield Gothic. But the subject of the passage is not really
the two corpses, it is Sassoon's reaction to them, his shock, his
sense of their unfamiliarity; not the dead, but the civilian soldier
looking at a phenomenon that was new to him—what had been
men, now robbed of dignity and reduced to "butchered hostility." If these objects were human, then humanity meant something different from what he had thought it meant. It's this
reaction that makes Battlefield Gothic *Gothic:* not the sight, but
the horror.

At first, Jünger said, the dead were too unfamiliar to be recognized. But that passed. Because the war on the Western Front
was stationary most of the time, the dead were densely and continuously present on the front lines; troops lived in a world of
corpses, walked over them in the trenches, watched them
decompose on the barbed wire, exhumed last year's dead when
they dug this year's trench, until eventually, as Jünger put it,

we were so accustomed to the horrible that if we came on a
dead body anywhere on a fire step or in a ditch we gave it

no more than a passing thought and recognized it as we would a stone or a tree.

Like stones and trees, the dead became one of the materials of the earth, to be walked over or around, and even used, when necessary, in the construction projects of war. Frank Richards describes a trench:

> Some parts of the parapet had been built up with dead men, and here and there arms and legs were protruding. In one bay only the heads of two men could be seen; their teeth were showing so that they seemed to be grinning horribly down on us. Some of our chaps that had survived the attack on the 20th July [on the Somme, in 1916] told me that when they were digging themselves in, the ground being hardened by the sun and difficult to dig away quickly, if a man was killed near them he was used as head cover and earth was thrown over him. No doubt in many cases this saved the lives of the men that were digging themselves in.

Those corpses weren't stones, though; each of them was a memento mori, a grim reminder of the enormity of the losses on both sides, and the insignificance of the gains. Reminder, too, that a death in the trenches was rarely a clean one—not the quick bullet in heart or brain, but more likely a shrapnel fragment that left a corpse without a leg, or a face, or a head, or an exploding shell that dismembered and buried the men it killed. It's the hideousness of death on the Western Front that the memoirs tell; histories, even military histories, don't usually go into that.

In the world of ordinary civilians, the dead are given the ritual attentions that we agree they deserve: a decent burial, the formalities of grief, a monument. On the Western Front those attentions were often impossible, and the dead were left where they fell, like Elpenor in the *Odyssey*, unburied and unknown.

Soldiers' narratives tell many stories of those dead—left in the shell holes of no-man's-land or on the wire—and of dying men abandoned; Vaughan, moving up the line at Passchendaele, heard men drowning in flooded shell holes and went on walking, and Carrington remembered how he saw a man with a bleeding wound in his throat, speechless and helpless and dying, and passed by.

And there were the other deaths, the annihilated, lost men— blown to unrecognizable bits in a shell explosion, or buried in earth or mud. And the pilots, who took off and simply disappeared; flew off the earth, as it seemed. Altogether, half a million of the British dead were never found, plus God knows how many Germans, Russians, Austrians, Frenchmen. The European earth was manured with the nameless dead. It has always been like that in war—look at the story of the Waterloo bones that I quoted in Chapter 1. This war was no different, except that the bones weren't harvested.

Death is different from the dead, another kind of presence, unseen but always there. At any moment, in any sector of the front, a shell or a bullet might be in the air, on its way to kill you. "In this sunshine," Max Plowman wrote, "it seems impossible to believe that at any minute we in this trench, and they in that, may be blown to bits by shells fired from guns at invisible distances." But he *did* believe it; it was part of his trench consciousness. To Vaughan, crouched in a mud-filled shell hole, "terror and death coming from far away seemed much more ghastly than a hail of fire from people who we could see and with whom we could come to grips." But that is how death did come in the trenches—not man-to-man, but out of the air, from a distance, random and anonymous. Death in war was no longer a fate you chose, for your cause or your country, or because it was your job; it was something done to you, an accident, as impersonal as the plague.

It was surely that war experience, that sense of life as an endless series of possible last moments, that worked on men's minds on the Western Front and made the state of their nerves more important than the state of their bodies. "My nerves are under control," an officer wrote in his diary in 1916, "and I can do my job all right, but I am feeling the strain in a way I used not to do." And Wilfred Owen, who had been one of Rivers's "shell-shock" patients, wrote to his mother, after he had returned to the Front, "my nerves are in perfect order," and went out to be killed in one of the last attacks of the war. Not *nerve*, but *nerves*, a one-letter vocabulary change that marks a fundamental change in soldierly values. *Nerve*, traditionally, is the inner source of brave actions; *nerves* "under control" or "in perfect order" means only the control of fear, a man's ability to stand and not tremble. Marc Bloch's redefinition of courage had become the war's definition. It's there in the narratives of the war on the Western Front.

If death was an accident that was in the air, so were wounds, and there, too, there was a redefinition. In earlier wars, a serious wound led commonly to slow death from infection. Chances improved in the First War: military medicine was better, first aid was quicker and more efficient, trench hygiene improved; and so the wounded lived. But there was another and more profound change, which had nothing to do with hygiene: a serious wound, if it didn't kill you, gave you a ticket back to England to convalesce—it was an escape from death's continual presence. The troops had words for such a wound, words the old army had brought back from India: it was a "Blighty," from the Hindi word for *home*, or a "cushy" one, from a word meaning *pleasant*. "To get a cushy one," Graves wrote in *Good-bye to All That*,

> is all that the old hands think of.... They look forward to a
> battle because a battle gives more chances of a cushy one,
> in the legs or arms, than trench warfare. In trench warfare
> the proportion of head wounds is much greater.

It seems monstrous for healthy men to desire injury and to rejoice in damage to their bodies. But it was true on the

Western Front. Edward Liveing was an infantry subaltern who
went over the top with his regiment on the first day of the
Somme offensive, and was wounded, and managed to make his
way back out of the battle to a first aid station. This is the scene
there, as he recorded it:

> After about five or ten minutes an orderly slit up my
> breeches.
> "The wound's in the front of the hip," I said.
> "Yes, but there's a larger wound where the bullet's come
> out, sir."
> I looked and saw a gaping hole two inches in diameter.
> "I think that's a Blighty one, isn't it?" I remarked.
> "I should just think so, sir," he replied.
> "Thank God! At last!" I murmured vehemently, conjuring
> up visions of the good old homeland.

Feelings like Liveing's are outside the range of courage and
cowardice; this is a young man who had done what patriotism,
duty, soldiership, all those words and concepts, required and
had been released from further encounters with death. For him,
his wound was not a misfortune but a gift of life. No other war
and no other front that I know of drove its troops to desire
wounds, or to wound themselves, or even to kill themselves, on
the scale that was true on the Western Front in the First War.
One must take these wounds as evidence that, whatever amelio-
rating circumstances there might have been, however one might
want to qualify the vision of that war as hell, it was what our
myth says it was—the worst war in the world.

Redefinition: you could say that every war narrative is that,
that every young man who goes to war finds the experience
strange and disorienting beyond his expectations, and so must
redefine his war terms and turn the imagined war-in-his-head
into another, stranger story. But I think the narratives of the
Western Front had particularly to be acts of redefinition,

because of the young men who wrote them and because of the radical, terrible differences in the war they found there.

In the most memorable of those narratives, the story is not simply the record of one man's war but a process, a movement through strangeness to comprehension. An Irish Guardsman in Carroll Carstairs's *A Generation Missing* sets out the framework of that story:

> In the beginning war is adventure. Then comes war weariness, a period of adjustment. You stick it or give up. The third phase is an acceptance, a resignation, a surrender to faith. The brave man is the man who gets through to the third phase.

This flat résumé of war endured omits the big words of romantic war (weariness and resignation are scarcely martial values in the old tradition), and though it keeps a place for the brave man, his bravery is of another sort, redefined, like Bloch's, as patient endurance of the unendurable.

That Guardsman seems to be speaking of war in general; but what he is really describing is the changes that occurred in *his* war, there on the Western Front, to young men like himself and Carstairs, who came to war out of their middle-class civilian lives and had to learn, in the trenches, how to be soldiers in this, the Great War of Endurance.

CHAPTER THREE

'Fourteen–'Eighteen:
The War Elsewhere

For most of us, the soldiers' tale of the First World War is the story of four years of fighting along a narrow band of earth that stretched across northern France from the Channel to the Swiss border. Along that band two lines of trenches faced each other across a dead space that was called no-man's-land. From time to time through those long years men rose out of one trench or the other to attack across that dead space and were cut down by artillery and machine gun fire, in battles whose names for us are weighted with pointless death: Ypres, Loos, Arras, Verdun, the Somme, Passchendaele. Eventually, the tale goes, the Germans were forced by hunger and attrition to retreat, and the war ended.

This is the story that the most memorable personal narratives tell; so do the poems and novels we have read and the war films we have seen—even recent books and films, created by people who are the grandchildren of the men who were there. Accepting that compound story, we create our own war-in-our-heads, in which the Western Front is the entire war. Think of all the campaigns, all the battles and the dying, that that story leaves out: the actions in Italy, Gallipoli, Salonika; the Eastern Front; the African campaigns; Mesopotamia, Palestine, and Syria; the sea battles at Coronel and Jutland; the submarine war. All these battles were, in the phrase of the time, "sideshows" to the main conflict, like the strong man and the freak show at a

74

fair. And so we neglect them: the Big Show, we agree, was in Europe.

A reader's defense of this parochial view of the war might be that the literary soldiers, the real writers, weren't in those other battles, that the poets and novelists somehow all went to France. And that does seem to be nearly, though not entirely, true: Graves, Sassoon, Blunden, Jones, Max Plowman, Charles Carrington, Cecil Lewis—all men who later became serious writers of many books—were all at the battle of the Somme, for example; so of course we know that battle more vividly than any other of that war. For we know other men's wars from the books we read, and we are most likely to read the war books of literary men.

There is another reason, I think. It is that the stalled trench war on the Western Front is a paradigm of modern war as we conceive it, or *feel* it: war as total unwilled destruction, with neither advantage nor victory, only annihilation of men. If you want the purest embodiment in history of that vision of war in all its cruelty and stupidity and power, the Western Front is the place to go. It is a tragic vision, on a vast scale; compared to the Western Front, other wars are only wars.

It's partly the scale that gives the Western Front its power to move and overwhelm us; not the geographical scale (though that war was fought in the world's longest ditches), but the scale of human damage and destruction. Large casualty figures are not unique to the First War: other battles have cost armies appalling losses: thirty thousand at Austerlitz, seventy thousand at Borodino, nearly all of an army of half a million men in Napoleon's assault on Moscow and subsequent retreat (Napoleon was the greatest of the casualty makers). Yet even set against those numbers from the past, the casualties on the Western Front are monstrous: one-third of all French combatants in the first five months of the war, nearly three million men killed or wounded; a million casualties—British, French, and German—in the Somme offensive; a total, for the entire war on all fronts, Allies and Central Powers together, of nearly forty million casualties. Perhaps "tragic" is the wrong word for such mass-produced carnage; can forty million dead and wounded men be tragic, collectively? Probably not. Nor can they be romantic, individually or collectively. Perhaps there is no adequate vocabulary for suffering on that scale, but only the huge numbers.

The romance of war died on the Western Front, or so it seemed. Romance is adventurous, dashing, and personal, and moves swiftly to its brave conclusion; but the new weapons by which Field Marshal Haig defined his war made that kind of fighting impossible. This war, it was clear, would be nasty, brutish, and long. But there were other fields of the Great War, and other kinds of fighting, where a personal war could still be fought. Narratives from those fields tell their own stories; and because of them the possibility that war could be romantic survived.

One narrative in particular, from what its author called "a side-show of a side-show," remains a towering classic. T. E. Lawrence's *Seven Pillars of Wisdom* is so different from the Western Front canon that one might easily forget that it came out of the same world war. Everything about Lawrence's war was anachronistic: the men, the numbers, the weapons, the fighting. It was, in its dramatic phases, a cavalry war, fought across open, empty deserts by bands of irregulars mounted on camels, against a modern army and its lines of communication, fought in a campaign of swift guerrilla raids and deft ambushes, without much help from the powerful new weapons of war—no heavy artillery, few airplanes, no poison gas. (And, one might add, only one middle-class witness to make a memorable record of it— Lawrence.) It was costume-drama war; it was *romance*.

Lawrence's narrative of the Arabs' war tells of long marches across desert spaces that tested men's endurance, of hunger and thirst and cruel acts of discipline, and then of sudden swooping charges on Turkish positions, like this one:

Nasir screamed at me, "Come on," with his bloody mouth;
and we plunged our camels madly over the hill, and down
towards the head of the fleeing enemy. The slope was not
too steep for a camel-gallop, but steep enough to make
their pace terrific, and their course uncontrollable: yet the
Arabs were able to extend to right and left and to shoot
into the Turkish brown. The Turks had been too bound up
in the terror of Auda's furious charge against their rear
to notice us as we came over the eastward slope: so we
also took them by surprise and in the flank; and a charge
of ridden camels going nearly thirty miles an hour was
irresistible.

A swift, galloping, shooting victory won by a few courageous
men: of course that's romantic.

There was more to the romance of the Arab war, as Lawrence told it, than the cavalry charges; the men who charged
were romantic too. Lawrence's Arabs are like Homer's Greeks
and Trojans: brave, proud, quarrelsome men, each with a name
and a personal history, aware of his skills and his honor; they
were men who lived by the bold gesture and the blow struck
against the odds, who endured hardship stoically and killed
ruthlessly and with evident pleasure.

These men fought for a cause that never changed, never
went sour or faded in disillusionment—the cause of Arab nation-
alism. Like many men on the Western Front, they were volunteers, but with this difference, that they fought only when they
wished, and left when conviction failed them. As Lawrence
wryly remarked, many armies had been voluntarily enlisted, but
few served voluntarily. His Arabs did. So when they fought, it
was in a war that each man personally chose to fight and in
which every violent act was willed and significant.

The fierceness and meaning of their violence is illustrated in
an incident that occurs late in the book, near the end of the war.
The Turks have just retreated through an Arab village that is the

home of one of Lawrence's lieutenants, whose name is Tallal. The Arabs enter the devastated village, passing the sacked and burned-out houses, the heaps of slaughtered villagers, a dying child, a violated woman—a long, terrible scene that is the only Battlefield Gothic in the book. Lawrence tells us Tallal's reaction:

> Tallal had seen what we had seen. He gave one moan like a hurt animal; then rode to the upper ground and sat there awhile on his mare, shivering and looking fixedly after the Turks. I moved near to speak to him, but Auda caught my rein and stayed me. Very slowly Tallal drew his head-cloth about his face; and then he seemed suddenly to take hold of himself, for he dashed his stirrups into the mare's flanks and galloped headlong, bending low and swaying in the saddle, right at the main body of the enemy.
>
> It was a long ride down a gentle slope and across a hollow. We sat there like stone while he rushed forward, the drumming of his hoofs unnaturally loud in our ears, for we had stopped shooting, and the Turks had stopped. Both armies waited for him; and he rocked on in the hushed evening till only a few lengths from the enemy. Then he sat up in the saddle and cried his war-cry, "Tallal, Tallal," twice in a tremendous shout. Instantly their rifles and machine-guns crashed out, and he and his mare, riddled through and through with bullets, fell dead among the lance points.

Compare that solitary ride to death with Captain Pryce's bayonet charge in the last chapter. Pryce's act was a gesture of suicidal despair that meant nothing; Tallal's is a ritual of grief. His friends understand its meaning—"God give him mercy," one says, "we will take his price"—and so does Lawrence: he orders, for the only time in the war, that no prisoners shall be taken. In the Arabs' war, wild, tragic gestures like Tallal's could be brave, significant acts. On the Western Front they could not; the trenches offered the violent death but not the meaning.

The Arabs' campaign against the Turks was not the whole of the Middle East war; standard histories tend to mention it only parenthetically, between more central military matters (Cruttwell's *History of the Great War*, for example, gives Lawrence one paragraph). Yet Lawrence made that desert sideshow into an epic narrative—the only one to come out of the war. Like other epics, it is a great adventure story, full of action and excitement and brave individual deeds, told—as epics usually are—with a kind of nostalgia for that world of action, the heroic past. One can see how a man like Lawrence, so modern, so civilized, and so English, would feel that nostalgia, and why we, the later readers of his story, might feel it too. For *Seven Pillars* speaks to our desire, our need, perhaps, for one romantic story from the Great War in which brave men hazard their lives for a good cause and are triumphant; one field where the heroic age still lived.

There is another story in *Seven Pillars*, which is not heroic. It is the story of the teller himself, an introspective, self-doubting intellectual, thrust by accident into the role of man of action, like Hamlet compelled against his will to play Henry the Fifth. In this unwilling role, Lawrence could see in the situation what the Arabs couldn't—the inevitable conflict between their simple goals and values and the complex and devious motives of the English authorities. The Arabs believed what their English allies told them, and accepted their promises of Arab independence; but Lawrence perceived that the promises would not be kept, that the English would betray the Arabs, as modern always betrays primitive. So while the war ended gloriously for the Arabs with their triumphal entry into liberated Damascus, it ended for Lawrence in bitter self-reproach.

> Among the Arabs I was the disillusioned, the sceptic, who envied their cheap belief. The unperceived sham looked so well-fitting and becoming a dress for shoddy man. The ignorant, the superficial, the deceived were the happy

among us. By our swindle they were glorified. We paid for them our self-respect, and they gained the deepest feelings of their lives.

That's the *modern* story in the book. Lawrence confesses that he has dressed himself up in the romance of the Arabs and so has helped his English masters to gain what they wanted from the war, but at the price of his self-respect and theirs; whereas the Arabs have been swindled of the independence for which they fought but have gained the deep feelings that come with a brave fight for a lost cause. Lost causes are always romantic, and so there is still romance in war. Only not for *us*.

If the Arabian sideshow was romantic, why wasn't the one in Mesopotamia? Or in Persia? Or Africa? The fighting in those places resembled the Arab war in many ways—it was small-scale and mobile, it was fought with hand weapons, and it included indigenous troops; yet those engagements have no place at all in our collective memory of the First War. It's not that they weren't written about—they were; but not by the right men, or not at the right time. Joyce Cary—who would become a distinguished English novelist—was in the Cameroons campaign and might have written memorably about it, but didn't; Francis Brett Young, also a novelist, was in East Africa and wrote about operations there in *Marching on Tanga*, but he wrote too soon, perhaps, while the war was still being fought in France, and he was not much noticed. And there were other memoirs by serving soldiers out of Africa, Persia, and Palestine. But there was no romance in them.

Indeed, those wars seemed so unromantic to the men who fought in them that some even envied the troops on the Western Front. "Ah," one East Africa campaigner lamented, "I wish to hell I was in France! There one lives like a gentleman and dies like a man, here one lives like a pig and dies like a dog."

*   *   *

There was another romantic war, though; it was the one that was fought in the air. In some ways it was the opposite of Lawrence's. The desert war was an anachronism that faced backward to tribal battles, cavalry charges, and traditional hand weapons, whereas the air war faced the future and a new weaponry. But they had this in common, that they offered to the combatant the possibility of a personal war, and to the public the possibility of heroes.

The air war was romantic from the beginning because flying was. In the years before the war, European and American imaginations were caught by the excitement of aviation. Fathers took their families to see airmen fly, schoolboys built airplane models, and flying novels like H. G. Wells's *War in the Air* were enormously popular. Flying was an adventure, a conquest, a miracle. So it is not surprising, when the war began, that Wells should write in a London newspaper that flying was "The Most Splendid Fighting in the World":

> One talks and reads of the heroic age and how the world
> has degenerated. But indeed this is the heroic age, sud-
> denly come again. No legendary feats of the past, no battle
> with dragons or monstrous beasts, no quest or feat that
> man has hitherto attempted can compare with this adven-
> ture, in terror, danger and splendor.

Already, in the second month of the war, Wells was acknowledging that there would be no heroes in the land war in France; but he thought that flying would restore romantic war and bring back the heroic age.

The romance of the air wasn't only a journalist's or a layman's emotion; it is in the diaries and memoirs of the men who flew. Everything about flying was exciting to them, everything was interesting, because it was all new: the feeling of taking off into a new dimension, the things a plane does in the air, the experience of simply being up there where men had not been before and seeing the world from above, as God sees it.

D. H. Bell, an infantryman turned airman, wrote during his flight
training:

> I begin to realize the real romance of flying here, in this
> cloudy gusty October weather, over the seashore and cliffs
> and the sprawling and castled heights of Dover, over the
> green fields and purplish-brown woods of Kent.

And he went on, as though embarrassed by his poeticizing:

> We fly Avros, beautiful machines, but they are fitted with
> an 80-h.p. engine, which has a terrifying habit of blowing
> out an inlet valve, and, if you are not quick at switching off
> ignition and petrol, of catching fire.

These elements—the excitement, the weather, and the technical
details—are constants in the fliers' writings (as they are in pilots'
conversations still): excitement, because flying is a stimulant, in
a way that other modes of fighting aren't; weather, because
weather is the geography of the air, and because it can kill you;
technical details, because they connect the flier to the sources of
his excitement and because, like the weather, they can be instruments of death.

All that is the excitement of flying itself—anytime, anywhere.
There was a different and particular excitement when the pilot
flew in France, above a war in progress. What was it like there,
over the Western Front? The first and most fundamental answer
is that it was altogether different from the war that went on
down below: separated, isolated, lifted above the dark, cramped
dying of the trenches. Pilots felt at once that they were in
another war. Here is young Cecil Lewis, just arrived in France,
taking off alone from Saint-Omer to observe his new war world:

> I turned south towards Boulogne, climbing, always climb-
> ing. Already I was two miles above the earth, a tiny lonely
> speck in the vast rotunda of the evening sky. The sun was
> sinking solemnly in a black Atlantic cloud-belt. To the east,

night crept up: a lofty shade drawn steadily over the war-
ring earth. The earth, so far below! A patchwork of fields,
browns and greys, here and there dappled with the green
of spring woods, intersecting ribbons of straight roads,
minute houses, invisible men.... Men! Standing, walking,
talking, fighting there beneath me! I saw them for the first
time with detachment, dispassionately: a strange, pitiable,
crawling race, to us who strode the sky.

This is Lewis in his middle age, speaking for his eighteen-year-
old self and being a bit grandiose and rhetorical (I doubt if
many pilots thought of themselves as striding the sky, then or
any other time). But the emotions are true ones: the sense of
solitude, the feeling of being not *in* a war but *above* one, of
being not so much a combatant as a floating, solitary witness;
the awareness of the beauty of space and the exhilaration of
flight. These are any ordinary pilot's feelings, impossible for
men on the ground to share. They mark a radical break in the
unity of men at war; from here on, fighting men would be
divided into *above* and *below,* those who fly and those who fight
on the surface of the earth.

The excitement of flying didn't make those young pilots war
lovers; most of them, I'm sure, were simply *flight* lovers—in love
with their new machines and with what they could do with
them. Most of them were very young—Cecil Lewis was seventeen when he enlisted, and eighteen when he began to fly over
the Somme; the French ace Georges Guynemer was only twenty
when he was killed; Richthofen was twenty-two when the war
began, twenty-five when he died.

Many of the new pilots came to war straight out of their
games-playing schools and found in the air a new kind of game,
played with elaborate new toys. It was a game that they had to
learn to play as they went along: there were no instruction books
for doing an Immelmann turn, or getting out of a right-hand

spin, or making a dead-stick landing. You just had to do it. You can hear the spirit of that game-playing in this exchange between two new pilots on an airfield near Armentières in 1915:

> Wilhelm grabbed my arm and drew me into his cabin.
> "I've done it!" he exclaimed in an excited whisper.
> "Done what?" I asked, catching some of his excitement.
> "Looped! This afternoon—well away from the lines, behind Armentières."
> "Good work—what was it like?"
> "Frightful! I was scared stiff."

A loop isn't a combat maneuver; it's an act of skill and nerve that you perform in the air, like a swan dive from the high board. Young men do it because they're afraid to.

Those new toys had two military roles in the early months of the war: either they were Intelligence, observing and reporting on enemy positions, or they were Artillery, dropping projectiles on enemy troops—petrol bombs at first, and hand grenades, and eventually bombs. They couldn't attack each other, because they weren't armed. Until they were, until planes could fight each other with their own weapons, air war wouldn't really be serious and there would be no exciting, romantic air narratives. It wasn't enough that pilots had learned to fly; they would have to learn how to kill in the air.

Pilots' accounts of the early days tell of their groping attempts to arm their planes effectively—attempts that often sound more like the fancies of some comic artist, a Rube Goldberg or a Heath Robinson, than of a proper ordnance man at work. One pilot attached a hand grenade to a length of control cable and swung it at his enemy's propeller; another secured a rifleman to the upper wing of his plane, so that he could fire at enemy planes without falling out; another flew close to a German plane and fired thirty rounds from his revolver at his opponent; a British and a German pilot met in the air and fired everything they had—rifles, revolvers, even Very pistols—and flew away unharmed. "There must have been many such comedies in the early days," one pilot wrote wryly.

The serious war in the air—the one we know from books and films—began in 1915, when first the Germans and then the Allies equipped their planes with machine guns that could fire forward through the propeller without hitting the blades. This made the entire plane a weapon to be aimed at its target, and made mortal single combat in the air possible. Once that happened, a new romantic figure appeared—the fighter ace—and the war, which had been so anonymous and indiscriminate in its killing, had its truly modern heroes. And they remain its heroes: of all the men who fought on the Western Front, the aces are the ones whose names we remember: Guynemer, Richthofen, Bishop, Rickenbacker, Ball. No soldier in the trenches was a hero in the way they were, or ever had such glamour.

Once aces entered the flying scene, the war above the earth changed, and the actions and feelings of war there—the killing, the dying, the courage, and the fear—became different. We can define the nature of that difference by considering a problem of nomenclature that the new air forces faced: once you have a certain number of single-seated airplanes with fixed forward-firing machine guns under one command, what do you call them collectively? The British and French borrowed terms from the cavalry and called the planes scouts and the groups squadrons; but the Germans, perceiving perhaps that this new kind of flying required a new term, called their groups *Jagdstaffeln:* hunting units. It wasn't a term that could possibly have been used for any other military unit on the Western Front: only fighter pilots *hunted.*

Hunters was certainly the way the pilots who became aces thought of themselves. The Frenchman Georges Guynemer called himself a "Boche hunter" and recorded his hunts on page after page of his diary:

May 2nd, 1917.—On hunting circuit. One fight. Two hours, fifteen minutes, 5,000 meters.

Hunting. Four fights, one jamming, but I brought down one Albatross of a group of four, on fire. Two hours, ten minutes.

May 3rd, 1917.—Hunting circuit. Wounded an Albatross seriously to the north of the Malmaison front. One hour.

Richthofen, too, thought of himself as a hunter, and a competitive one; it would be fine, he said to be "*der Spitze der Jagdflieger*"—literally the first of the hunters who flew, and he referred to planes shot down as pilots' "bags," as though they were all together at some country-house shooting party, out after grouse or pheasants. (Note that Guynemer also saw the planes he hunted as living creatures, which could be "wounded.")

When aces fought, they often met in public combat, above the trenches, where thousands of men might witness it. It might be like this, from the diary of the British ace "Mick" Mannock:

Had a splendid fight with a single-seater Albatross Scout last week on our side of the lines and got him down.... The scrap took place at two thousand feet up, well within view of the whole front. And the cheers! It took me five minutes to get him to go down, and I had to shoot him before he would land.... I went up to the trenches to salve the "bus" later, and had a great ovation from everyone. Even Generals congratulated me. He didn't hit me once.

How long had it been since two men fought while armies watched and cheered?

That kind of flying—so heroic and so individual—quickly became the goal of would-be pilots. When Cecil Lewis enlisted in 1915, he already knew what he wanted:

... from the first, the light fast single-seater scout was my ambition. To be alone, to have your life in your own hands, to use your own skill, single-handed, against the enemy. It was like the lists of the Middle Ages, the only sphere in modern warfare where a man saw his adversary and faced him in mortal combat, the only sphere where there was still chivalry and honour. If you won, it was your own bravery and skill; if you lost, it was because you had met a better man.

You did not sit in a muddy trench while some one who had no personal enmity against you loosed off a gun, five miles away, and blew you to smithereens—and did not know he had done it! That was not fighting; it was murder. Senseless, brutal, ignoble. We were spared that.

The vision of war Lewis describes here is the new "heroic age" that Wells had imagined in 1914. It seems an archaic and ridiculous fantasy for a modern battle of machines, but men who flew, in both world wars, felt it; it's in their narratives. In the First War, aces were like chivalric knights: when they were victorious, kings and generals sent congratulations and invited them to tea; when they were killed, their opponents provided military funerals or flew over the dead pilots' airfields and dropped flowers. And when they drank together they praised their enemies' skills and lifted sentimental toasts to them, like the one that James McCudden reported:

> he asked us all to rise to drink to "Von Richthofen, our most worthy enemy," which toast we all drank with the exception of one non-flying officer who remained seated, and said, "No, I won't drink to the health of that devil."

Some of the famous aces wrote accounts of their flying wars— diaries or journals or hastily written memoirs—and because they were heroes, these records got published, some of them while the war was still being fought. But they don't tell us much, or answer our primary question: What was it like? One could explain that by saying that the aces were like General Rimington's ideal cavalry officer, not used to much brain work, and that does seem to have been true: certainly there was no literary intellectual among them, no T. E. Lawrence. But there is more to it than that, I think. The aces were entirely engrossed in their vocation: the planes they flew, the enemy planes they met in the air, the maneuvers and the gunfire and the victories. They're like professional athletes: they tell us how they did it, and they report their scores. But there is no place in those stories for the private self, the man within who feels and suffers and is changed by war. They don't acknowledge fear, they don't seem to feel comradeship, or deep grief when a comrade dies. They have no earth-bound lives: they pay little attention to the ordinary plea-sures of squadron life—the parties, the drinking, the girls, the leaves in London or Paris or Berlin. They concentrate on their job: which is no doubt why they were so good at it.

Captain James McCudden is an example, less remembered now than the Red Baron or Billy Bishop, but famous in his time. McCudden's flying career was an unusually long one: he joined the Royal Flying Corps in 1913 and flew, first as an observer and then as a pilot, until the summer of 1918, when he died in a careless flying accident. By then he had shot down fifty-four German planes.

In the months before he died, McCudden wrote *Five Years in the Royal Flying Corps*, a classic ace's narrative—plain and con-vincing about what it tells, which is how he flew, and how he became an ace, and nothing else. In that telling his reader will learn some interesting things, if he is interested in how men learned to kill in the air in that first aerial war: how before the machine gun days McCudden armed a Bristol Scout with two rifles set at forty-five degrees to the fuselage, how cold it was in a D.H.2, where the pilot sat in front of the engine—the sort of technical details fliers think about. The reader will also learn some things about the mind of an ace: his pleasure in the hunt, for example, what "very good fun" it is to shoot Huns, and what "fine sport" a patrol could be. And that it is the enemy *plane* he fights, and not the man in it:

It seems all very strange to me, but whilst fighting Germans
I have always looked upon a German aeroplane as a
machine that has got to be destroyed, and at times when I
have passed quite close to a Hun machine and have had a
good look at the occupant, the thought has often struck
me: "By Jove! there is a man in it."

And his British sportsman's sense of fair play (a term, I was once
told, for which there is no German equivalent):

I hate to shoot a Hun down without him seeing me, for
although this method is in accordance with my doctrine, it
is against what little sporting instincts I have left.

Hunting, and the pleasure of demonstrating hunting skills,
connects the aces with old-army regular officers like the Grenfells, and with Lawrence's Arabs. Personal killing, whether of a
bird, or a Turkish soldier, or a plane, is a craft; it's what hunters
and soldiers and fighter pilots do; it's why they exist. And there
is some interest in entering the minds of such men and sharing
that hunter's condition, for a while.

Still, theirs are not the great memoirs of wartime flying. They
tell us about the job they did so superlatively well; but we want
something deeper, more human and more intimate. Tell us, we
say: what was it like? And for the answers to that question we
must turn to the ordinary, everyday fliers, the ones who don't
kill, or not very often and not with great enthusiasm, but who
record the dailiness of a life in which one flies, and looks around
at the sky and the earth and the war, but also lives, feels fear
and ordinary grief. They were the ones who flew the humdrum
flights, artillery spotting and patrolling the lines, who were shot
at both from the air and from the earth, and did it every day,
and without glory.

This is what that daily life was like:

We were always at the mercy of the fragility of the machine
and the unreliability of the engine. One chance bullet from

the ground might cut a thin wire, put the machine out of
control, and send us, perfectly whole, plunging to a crash
we were powerless to prevent. So, in the later stages, we
had to win victories over ourselves long before we won any
over the enemy, for it was not impossible to turn back, to
tell a lie—not always easy to verify—of faulty engine, bad
visibility, jammed guns, and so stave off the inevitable for
one day more. We came in for some admiration at that
time, just because we were pilots, just because we flew. But
flying is pleasurable enough, in short doses, and was even
in those days reasonably safe. Truthfully, there was little
admirable in that. But to fly on a straight line, taking
photos of the enemy trenches, an easy Archie [antiaircraft]
target, within range of the ground machine guns, bumped
by eddies of passing shells and pestered by enemy scouts,
that required nerve. And it would have to be done twice a
day, day after day, until you were hit or went home.

To fly those flights took a special courage, like the courage
that Marc Bloch described in the trenches—standing without
trembling—but more: the courage to take off and fly toward
danger and not turn back. It took

> a sort of plodding fatalism, a determination, a cold-
> blooded effort of will. And always alone! No friends right
> and left, no crowd morale. The lot of the P.B.I. [Poor
> Bloody Infantry] was hopeless enough; but each in his
> extremity had at least some one at hand, some one to cheer
> and to succour.

That special courage was a part of daily flying. So was a special
fear. Fear, like excitement, is present somewhere down in the
sludge of the unconscious whenever a pilot leaves the ground.
It's in the awareness that you have left security, and that
beneath you now there is a mile or two of empty space, and
that gravity *wants* you (the Icarus complex, you might call it).
Add to that the fallibility of the planes themselves, which

weren't really tested but were simply rushed to the front and tried out in action, so that there was always the chance that the engine might fail, or a wing might collapse in a dive, or a bullet from your own machine gun might hit a propeller blade and cause a vibration that would shake the plane apart (that's how Immelmann died).

Add to that the fear of being shot down, of which there were continual reminders in the air: antiaircraft shells that burst and left puffs of smoke to tell the pilot he was being shot at; artillery shells that rose to the level of patrolling planes, and could be seen at the top of their trajectory, and sometimes hit planes; machine guns that sent up tracers from the ground.

And add the hunters, unseen and then suddenly there. One forgets how near those fighting planes got to each other and how slowly they flew, so that the man who fired the bullets that set his enemy afire could see the enemy gunner's stricken face, the slumped pilot in his cockpit, the flames spreading along the fuselage; and the men in the hunted plane could look across a narrow space and see the blinking guns. Even McCudden, the unflinching ace, was troubled when he hit a German plane from a range of fifty yards:

> At once a little trickle of flame came out of his fuselage, which became larger and larger until the whole fuselage and tailplane was enveloped in flames. The Albatross at once went down in a vertical dive, and I zoomed upwards and felt quite sick. I don't think I have ever been so conscience-stricken as at that time, and I watched the V-strutter until he hit the ground in a smother of flame in a small copse north-east of Polygon Wood, and caused a fire which was still burning when we flew home.

That's how it felt to be McCudden, the hunter, over Polygon Wood; but how did it feel to be the pilot in the Albatross?

A burning plane like that one would die spectacularly and leave a signature of smoke down the sky, and the man in it,

having no parachute, would burn with his plane or jump and
sprawl down the air and die apart. Pilots' narratives describe
those deaths of planes and men; seeing them, other fliers must
have thought: Next time it will be me. And gone on thinking it,
after their flights. "I can't prevent myself from flying in imagination when I am in my hut at night," one ordinary pilot wrote in
his diary, "however much I try to force myself to read. Sometimes I imagine myself going down in flames." Aces in their tales
don't talk about either the daily courage or the daily fear. That's
why the narratives of the ordinary pilots are more satisfactory;
they reach further into the reality cf war in the air.

    Like the war in the desert, the air war was not at the center
of the First World War: nothing that airplanes did turned the
tide of any offensive, and there were no great air battles; it was
at best a supplementary belligerency, a sideshow. Yet it is
important to the story of the war; it made war for the first time
three dimensional, and it added a vast new battlefield where
fighting would be unimaginably different and where the
romance that earth-bound war had lost would still be possible.
In that new war scene there would be heroes, remembered long
after most of them had been killed. They would survive most
vividly not in their own stories but in the narratives of less brilliant fliers, who would remember them the way soldiers have
always remembered their dead heroes, since Nestor in the
Odyssey mourned for his lost comrades, in a litany of names:
"Mannock is dead, the greatest pilot of the war"; "McCudden
the great has been killed." So perhaps Wells was right after all
about war in the air.

    T. E. Lawrence emerged from the war as its most romantic
figure, to be cherished especially by later writers, as evidence
that a literary, modern heroism was possible. The flying aces
found a different audience: their romantic lives and deaths
entered the popular imagination through pulp fiction and films
and so became the next generation's war-in-the-head, the myth
that drew young men (I was one) to flying in the next war, and

affected the way they thought about their air war, and the way they wrote about it too.

One might expect that stories of the First World War would end at the same point in time, the moment when the last shot was fired and the war was over. When I was a boy in the Thirties, we all knew when that moment had occurred: it was at eleven o'clock in the morning on November eleventh. Every year, on the anniversary of the Armistice, we stood in our classrooms for two minutes then, to commemorate the end of the war, and all the dead. But endings impose meanings on narratives, and not all meanings of that war were the same. We must look, here at the chapter's end, at endings, to find the various and conflicting meanings there.

To Marshal Haig, it was perfectly clear when the war ended, and why: it ended on that November day in 1918, because on that day the enemy was capable "neither of accepting or refusing battle." When an army can no longer choose either to fight or not to fight, it has lost its war—it's a definition out of military handbooks, a general's definition. That end was the culmination, Haig wrote, of a process that began when the British stopped the last German offensive in the spring of 1918 and moved to the attack. "The annals of war," he wrote,

> hold record of no more wonderful recovery than that which, three months after the tremendous blows showered upon them on the Somme and on the Lys, saw the undefeated British Armies advancing from victory to victory, driving their erstwhile triumphant enemy back to and far beyond the line from which he started, and finally forcing him to acknowledge unconditional defeat.

"Victory" and "unconditional defeat": for a field marshal, those were the proper words for the end of a war, those were what ending meant.

But not for the men who fought. Their narratives have little to say about winning or losing, and they almost never end at the Armistice. One might argue that that is simply a matter of chance, that the men who wrote the memorable accounts weren't there in the lines in November 1918. But those scattered and indecisive endings seem to me more than accidents: they seem a way of saying that there was no Victory on the Western Front; or that the important questions were not who won and who lost, but who fought? who suffered? who survived?

There are two basic kinds of soldiers' endings: those that come while the war goes on and those that stretch on after the Armistice. The wartime endings make one grim point: the only way out of a war while it is being fought is through death, or wounds, or some other loss of the capacity to go on fighting, to accept or refuse battle. Of the soldiers of the First War whose narratives I have mentioned in these chapters, Sassoon ended his story in an English hospital, Plowman on the way back to England (and Dr. Rivers's mental hospital) with shell shock, "Private X" in hospital with trench foot, Bell on a hospital ship in the Channel. Of the flying aces, Mannock, McCudden, Richthofen, Immelmann, and Guynemer were dead.

Two important memoirs are exceptions to this generalization, in that they end with the narrator alive and unwounded and on the battlefield, while the war continues. One is Vaughan's. We last saw him at Passchendaele, leading his men through the rain and the shellfire. His narrative continues for a few pages, and then stops. It isn't the end of the war, or even of the battle of Passchendaele: that fighting went on for another two months, cost 600,000 casualties on each side, and accomplished nothing. Nor is it the end of Vaughan's personal war: he went on to fight in Italy, and then again in France, won a Military Cross, and was alive and at the front when the Armistice was signed.

But at his *story's* end, he is still at Passchendaele. So many of his senior officers have been killed by then that he has been made a company commander, and in his last entry he goes wearily out to take muster of his company.

> Standing near the cookers were four small groups of bedraggled, unshaven men from whom the quartermaster sergeants were gathering information concerning any of their pals they had seen killed or wounded. It was a terrible list. Poor old Pepper had gone—hit in the back by a chunk of shell; twice buried as he lay dying in a hole, his dead body blown up and lost after Willis had carried it back to Vanheule Farm. Ewing hit by machine gun bullets had lain beside him for a while and taken messages for his girl at home.
>
> Chalk, our little treasure, had been seen to fall riddled with bullets; then he too had been hit by a shell. Sergeant Wheeldon, DCM and bar, MM and bar, was killed and Foster. Also Corporals Harrison, Oldham, Mucklow and the imperturbable McKay. My black sheep—Dawson and Taylor—had died together, and out of our happy little band of 90, only 15 remained....
>
> So this was the end of "D" Company. Feeling sick and lonely I returned to my tent to write my casualty report; but instead I sat on the floor and drank whisky after whisky as I gazed into a black and empty future.

There's an ending here, but it's the company that is ended, not the war. And if that is the case, then what does Vaughan's story mean? That war kills individual men (and how real they are, as Vaughan mourns them, how vivid and actual their deaths); that war is black and empty, and creates blackness and emptiness; and that it goes on. Here at the end of his story, the awkward, ignorant boy that was Vaughan has become a soldier and a leader. But there is no one to lead, and nowhere to lead them. And no victory.

The other example is by an American. I have not mentioned many American books in this account of First War narratives

because, though a considerable number were written, few are
memorable. Why should that be the case, when other American
wars produced many excellent soldiers' stories? Perhaps the
answer is that the Americans fought a different, less terrible war.
The essence of the war on the Western Front, for the armies that
were there from the beginning, was its grim continuousness—
the way the war dug into the French countryside and became a
trench war, the long purgatory of the static front, the endless
cycles of movement into the lines, out to rest, and then back
again into the trenches, where the same lives, the same fears,
and the same deaths waited. It was these elements that gave to
British, French, and German narratives their grim authority.

The war the Americans fought wasn't like that. American
troops didn't reach France in substantial numbers until the
spring of 1918, and went on the offensive only in the war's final
months. Their war, once it began, was hard-fought, but by
Western Front standards it was brief, mobile, and light in casualties (of the four and a half million Americans in uniform in
1918, only about a third of a million were killed or wounded,
fewer than the British losses in the Somme offensive alone).
Because it was brief, American soldiers don't seem to have lost
their recruiting-office feeling that this war would be an
American adventure, to be entered into for the goodwill of the
thing, because Europe needed help. It didn't generate disillusionment among the American troops, or any change of national
feelings about leaders and values; it was moral at the beginning
and moral at the end.

The American war was different in another way too. An
impressive number of British, French, and German writers
fought in the trenches and wrote about what they had seen and
felt there: Sassoon, Graves, Blunden, Apollinaire, Péguy,
Jünger—one could make a long list. But though many young
Americans volunteered for one service or another, almost none
of those who would later become famous writers reached the
front and actually fought there. William Faulkner, F. Scott

Fitzgerald, John Dos Passos, e. e. cummings, Ernest Hemingway were all in uniform of some kind; think what a soldiers' tale the United States would have if they had been in the war in the combatant sense. But they weren't.

There was one American writer who was. Hervey Allen was later to make his reputation as the author of the best-selling *Anthony Adverse*, but before that novel he wrote a war narrative of exceptional interest: *Toward the Flame*. Allen's story covers only a few weeks in the summer of 1918, during which American troops attacked German positions in a village near Château Thierry and were virtually annihilated. It wasn't a crucial action—the Germans gained nothing by their momentary victory—and it shed no particular glory on the Americans who fought in it. But it is a convincing picture of the American war—the new, untried troops moving anxiously through country they don't know, uncertain of where the enemy is, where their supporting troops are, or even what they are expected to do. Troops move, bivouac, move again, attack and are attacked, without ever knowing quite what is happening. What they do know is the immediate physical scene in which they live and fight and die: the village, its river and bridge, a stone wall, a hill. Allen's narrative has the virtue that all good battle memoirs have: it makes real the part of a war that one man, fighting, sees.

I have introduced Allen's book here mainly for the sense of its ending. In the last episode, Allen and his men are sheltering from the German shells and gas in a dugout in the village. The shelling stops, and Allen realizes that an enemy attack is about to begin, and tries to marshal his men to cover the hilltop over which the Germans will come. This is his final paragraph:

Suddenly along the top of the hill there was a puff, a rolling cloud of smoke, and then a great burst of dirty, yellow flame. By its glare I could see Gerald [a fellow officer] standing halfway up the hill with his pistol drawn. It was the *Flammenwerfer*, the flame throwers; the men

along the crest curled up like leaves to save themselves as
the flame and smoke rolled clear over them. There was
another flash between the houses. One of the men stood
up, turning around outlined against the flame—"Oh! my
God!" he cried. "Oh! God!"

Here ends this narrative.

Allen could have gone on, to tell how this attack was beaten
off, how he was sent next day to a hospital, gassed and
exhausted, how he returned to duty in October for the Argonne
offensive and collapsed when a shell burst in the dugout to
which he had just reported, and how he was then relieved of
active duty. He might even have continued the story for another
few weeks, to the end of the war.

Instead he chose to end his narrative in the uncertain middle
of the attack, with the arrival of the *Flammenwerfer*. Why there?
Allen's own explanation, in his preface, is this: his book is "a
moving picture of war, broken off when the film burned out."
Which means, I gather, that his capacity to record stopped in
that terrifying moment when the weapon of fire appeared. But
the ending means more than that. More than a flamethrower
comes over the hill in that final paragraph: a new kind of war
appears, toward which the whole narrative (and perhaps the
whole war) has been moving—or why is the book titled *Toward
the Flame*? It is Apocalypse that crests the hill that August
morning—the end of the world, the fire next time. The end of
Allen's war is here, not at the Armistice.

Many narratives of the First War continue past the war's end,
most of them in uneventful deceleration, like runners who have
passed the finish line but can't stop running. Chapman's *Passionate Prodigality* ends in 1919, as his regiment marches into
Germany to become occupation troops; Carrington, who ended
his war in a training battalion in England, tells how he was
demobilized and went to Oxford, "to be not a man of action but
a mere purveyor of criticisms"—that is, a professor; Cecil Lewis

found a flying job in China and ends his story with his last landing there, in Peking in 1921. None of these endings is exciting, or even very interesting, but you can see what they are doing: they're demonstrating how, after war's terror and excitement, the men who were there reentered ordinary, unexciting life, which was all there was, now that the war was over.

For some men, that return was more difficult and took longer. Robert Graves continued his war story through an entire decade after the war, because the war went on in his head. He came out of the army, he said, in a state of shell shock (which would now be called post-traumatic stress disorder). His symptoms were many and disabling: he couldn't use a telephone, he was sick when he traveled by train, if he saw more than two people in a single day he couldn't sleep, and the war recurred in his mind in vivid flashbacks of trench scenes and sounds. He and his friend Edmund Blunden agreed that they would not be right until they got their wars onto paper, and at the end of the Twenties both did. Apparently the horrors ended then.

One other thing to note about these run-over narratives is the way they record the actual end of the war, November 11, 1918. Let me quote a couple of examples:

A pilot:

> So it was over. I confess to a feeling of anti-climax, even to a momentary sense of regret.... When you have been living a certain kind of life for four years, living as part of a single-minded and united effort, its sudden cessation leaves your roots in the air, baffled and, for the moment, disgruntled.

An infantryman:

> To throw so powerful a machine out of high gear into neutral, neither stops its progress nor makes it easy to control. Life was pointless, and very few soldiers were lucky enough to know in what direction their lives would tend.

Millions of young men had known no other career, no
other destiny than battle.

The greatest war in history was over, and their side had won!
But where was the triumph, where was the rejoicing? In the
streets of London and Paris and New York people danced and
cheered, but the end of the war didn't feel like that at the front.
For the soldiers there, the end was an unraveling of order in
their lives and the beginning of a life that most of them had not
known—the civilian adult's life of decisions and obligations. For
four years, war had given their lives meaning and direction; now
that it was over, *who were they?* Every young soldier must feel
that at the end of his war. Life will never be so simple again, or
so exciting.

This sense of loss at the end is an uncomfortable feeling for
men who know that they *ought* to rejoice, and we find that discomfort in their narratives. Duncan Grinnell-Milne ends his with
this little scene with a fellow pilot as they watch the dismantling
of their airfield in France. The other man says:

"Funny, after a rotten war like this, how hard it is to leave."
He sighed. And then smiled quickly to hide his feelings.
"War's all wrong, I guess, but—ah well, them *was* the happy
days, them was! Goodbye, G.-M."
        The lorries rumbled away down the long straight road
to Cambrai. I watched them go, I, the only one left of all
the men in that once powerful squadron; for the acting-
adjutant had been posted to England with the records, the
last men had travelled down to the base, even the orderly-
room clerk had gone. And with the final break-up of the
squadron everything that had given zest to life seemed to
have gone too. The deep rumble of the lorries died away,
and in the wintry silence which then fell, the only sound I
could hear was the faint humming of telegraph wires—
feeble echo of past endeavour.

The nostalgia of old soldiers begins here.

War memoirs rarely end dramatically; more often they simply stop. The final chapter of *Good-bye to All That* begins: "The story trails off here," and that is true of most soldiers' narratives: old soldiers never die, they just fade away. For the wars of individuals are personal and local, and are subject, like anything personal, to the contingencies of existence and so are not likely to have much dramatic shape. A war as a whole will be an action in Aristotle's sense—it will have a beginning, a middle, and an end—but the wars of individuals start and stop with the arbitrariness of military orders, and even if their endings coincide with the firing of the last shot, they are not likely to close dramatically; wars aren't operas, for the spear carriers.

For the men who fought, the First World War ended in bitterness and disappointment—we all know that, because we've read Remarque's *All Quiet* and Barbusse's *Le Feu* and the poems of Owen and Sassoon, and have taken their story into our imaginations and made it our myth of the war. I once summarized that myth like this:

> a generation of innocent young men, their heads full of high abstractions like Honour, Glory, and England, went off to war to make the world safe for democracy. They were slaughtered in stupid battles planned by stupid generals. Those who survived were shocked, disillusioned and embittered by their war experiences, and saw that their real enemies were not the Germans, but the old men at home who had lied to them. They rejected the values of the society that had sent them to war, and in doing so separated their own generation from the past and from their cultural inheritance.

The principal theme of this bitter version of the war is betrayal: of the young by the old, of soldiers by politicians, of idealism

by cynicism. Certainly you can find that theme in the personal
narratives of men who were there; but not in the most immediate accounts, not at the war's end. It enters the story later, in
the mid-Twenties, and increases over the next decade or so. It
appears, I think, partly as the product of an emerging awareness,
as the postwar years passed, that the war had brought nothing
about; and partly as a kind of leakage from war poetry and fiction, the more emotive forms for re-creating experience.

Here are four examples of that retrospective bitterness, two
from the Twenties and two from the Thirties:

From a suppressed introduction by T. E. Lawrence to *Seven
Pillars of Wisdom*:

> ... when we achieved and the new world dawned, the old
> men came out again and took our victory to re-make in the
> likeness of the former world they knew. Youth could win,
> but had not learned to keep: and was pitiably weak against
> age. We stammered that we had worked for a new heaven
> and a new earth, and they thanked us kindly and made
> their peace.

From *War Birds* (1926), ostensibly the diary of John
McGavock Grider, an American pilot with a British squadron
who was killed on the Western Front, but actually written by
another American flier, Elliott White Springs:

> War is a horrible thing, a grotesque comedy. And it is so
> useless. This war won't prove anything. All we'll do when
> we win is to substitute one sort of Dictator for another. In
> the meantime we have destroyed our best resources.
> Human life, the most precious thing in the world, has
> become the cheapest. After we've won this war by
> drowning the Hun in our own blood, in five years' time the
> sentimental fools at home will be taking up a collection for
> these same Huns that are killing us now and our fool
> politicians will be cooking up another good war.

From V. M. Yeates, *Winged Victory* (1934); Yeates was a British pilot who was encouraged by his friend the novelist Henry Williamson to write a memoir; he wrote it in the third person, as though it were a novel, but it is clearly very close to his experiences and to his feelings in 1934:

England, my England; precious isle set in the silver sea; tongue that Shakespeare spake; and all the rest of it, was all very well: he could quite well appreciate the splendours of English literature, the beauty of some of the unindustrialized parts of England, and the glories of fox-hunting, cricket, and the Lord Mayor's show: but everything was vitiated by the consideration that the war was a profitable gambit for a minority of speculators. Every aeroplane that was crashed, every bomb that exploded, was adding to someone's private fortune, and helping a munition-worker to acquire a ridiculous grand piano. This war, declaring itself godly, righteous, a crusade, was tainted and suspect, and the disgusting ignoble civilization that supported it deserved eclipse.

From Siegfried Sassoon, *Sherston's Progress* (1936):

My knight-errantry about the war had fizzled out in more ways than one, and I couldn't go back to being the same as I was before it started. The "good old days" had been pleasant enough in their way, but what could a repetition of them possibly lead to?

How could I begin my life all over again when I had no conviction about anything except that the war was a dirty trick which had been played on me and my generation?

That collective story of disillusionment has had significant consequences not only in the ways we understand the First World War but in the ways we think about war generally. The theme of betrayal has made that war (and in some minds *all* wars) seem an avoidable folly, caused by the blindness of statesmen and prolonged by the stupidity of generals. War ceased to be a human institution and became simply a perversion of peace.

Some old soldiers resented that version of their experience, and wrote against it. Carrington ended his *Subaltern's War* with an epilogue in which he spoke for the generation of young men like himself, the secret army "who were soldiers before their characters had been formed, who were under twenty-five in 1914."

> Loath to speak of their experience, if they speak, it is with a sort of rough cynicism which it has become fashionable to describe as disillusion, disenchantment. A legend has grown up ... that these men who went gaily to fight in the mood of Rupert Brooke and Julian Grenfell, lost their faith amid the horrors of the trenches and returned in a mood of anger and despair. To calculate the effect of mental and bodily suffering, not on a man but on a whole generation of men, may seem an impossible task, but it can at least be affirmed that the legend of disenchantment is false.

There must have been many men like Carrington, who fought in the First War and returned home with their beliefs intact, or who changed in ways that were different from what the myth of the war asserts. And men like Graves too, who told their story and found it turned into legend in the minds of reviewers who came to it with expectations of disillusionment. "I was surprised," he wrote,

> at being acclaimed in the headlines of daily papers as the author of a violent treatise against war. For I had tried not to show any bias for or against war as a human institution, but merely to describe what happened to me during a particular and not at all typical one in which I took part. Much of this experience was painful, even shameful, but by no means all. I did record that about half-way through the war

I began to have doubts as to whether its continuance was justified or not. But that was only after two years of attrition, so this might easily have been construed as a plea for short modern wars fought in a somewhat more gentlemanly way. As it happens, it wasn't; but I left the matter open.

Is Graves being ironic? Yes, he is, at the expense of the myth, which told the tale of war too simply.

But it was the myth that prevailed. It was the story the public wanted, and books in which it appeared—or seemed to appear—were the popular war books. It spoke with a strong, compelling voice that set the tone of the whole decade of the twenties, affecting the spirit of the time like a ten-year hangover, and lingers still, as the right ironic attitude to take toward war. We may think we know the First War's story, but it is the hangover we remember.

The case for reading soldiers' narratives of the First World War, and not only the canonical ones but those that are outside the canon and are forgotten, is simply this, that they tell us that the war wasn't what the myth says it was, or not entirely: that not all young men went to war in a mood of exalted self-sacrifice; that not all of them suffered endlessly and passively; that they were not all victims; that they did not all fight on the Western Front; that not all of them returned at the war's end bitter and disillusioned. The soldiers' tale that emerges from the reading of many narratives will not be less grim than what the myth says: it will tell us how the dead looked, and about the mud, and the smell of cordite and corruption, and about fear. But it will also tell us about other things: comradeship, and the courage to stand without trembling, and the resilience of the human spirit. Later generations have seized on the myth because it offers a clear and correct moral view of a terrible, destructive episode in history. But the men who were there say that it was not that simple. They went to war, they fought, and because they fought they were changed; but not like *that*, not always.

The First World War remains our favorite war—the one we most want to know about, the one that most moves us. Why is that? Is it that we all have an appetite for passive suffering and for stories of betrayal? Or for the witness of men's capacities to endure the unendurable? Or is it perhaps that we have come to see that war as the end of something that was worthy to survive in the world and didn't?

What that something was we can find in a poem by Philip Larkin, written long after the war and titled "MCMXIV":

> Never such innocence,
> Never before or since,
> As changed itself to past
> Without a word—the men
> Leaving the gardens tidy,
> The thousands of marriages
> Lasting a little while longer:
> Never such innocence again.

This is a poem both about the innocent world before the war— and about the innocent army that left that world to fight the war. An *innocent* army? What could that mean? It isn't an adjective that anyone would have thought of applying to the troops who fought in the Peninsula or the Crimea. But this war was different. This time the middle classes sent their own civilian sons, and so both families and sons, whose lives until then had been innocent of war, learned what war meant.

"Never such innocence again": not for that generation, and not for any later one. "Innocent" means "unacquainted with evil," and Larkin wrote his poem as though he looked back from the other side of some lapsarian experience, from an acquaintance with evil that the men and women of 1914 didn't and couldn't have. What he knew was what the narratives of those innocent soldiers tell us. For them, it was all new, all strange and irrational, and we feel the newness in their narratives—the scale of it all, the anonymous muddy armies, the long-range killing and the new machines. It isn't new for us, and it never will be again, because in their war an army of literate men wrote their stories, to instruct us in the true nature of war, as men who are there see it and feel it, and so to prepare us for other wars ahead. For their war was, after all, only the *First* World War.

CHAPTER FOUR

Everybody's War

By the time the Second World War began, the canonical literature of the First War had been written and read: *All Quiet on the Western Front* was first an international best-seller and then a successful film; the memoirs of Sassoon and Graves sold like popular novels; literary people knew the poems of Wilfred Owen and quoted "the poetry is in the pity" to each other. Modern, technological war would not come to the young men of the 1930s generation as something new and strange, as it had to their fathers in 1914; they had been there before, in their imaginations. The war-in-their-heads, when war came, would not be the romantic fancies of nineteenth-century writers but the antiwar myth of the Western Front.

Such an imaginative change should have affected the ways people, and especially young people, confronted the prospect of another war—and it did. During the decade of the Thirties a Second World War began to enter imaginations, first as a fearful possibility, and then as a certainty. In 1933 Hitler came to power in Germany and began to re-arm the nation; in 1935 Mussolini declared war on Ethiopia; in 1936 a civil war began in Spain that was widely regarded as the prologue to the inevitable world war that was coming. Some people in the western democracies responded by becoming pacifists; in England men and women signed the Peace Pledge and vowed never to fight for their country; in the United States college students joined the

Veterans of Future Wars and demonstrated against militarism. Never before had opposition to war been so organized and so widespread—and at a time when war was not yet a reality, but only a threat in the future. Some of that emotional opposition must have come from the feelings that the First War left behind—the horror of war, the disillusionment, the sense of waste, the Long Hangover of the Twenties.

Even after the prediction had come true, and the nations of Europe were once more at war, the myth of the Great War still affected young minds. The English writer Edward Blishen recalls how he felt in 1940, just out of school and facing conscription:

> If war began—I'd been very clear about this, in my last year of school—one would be tempted, the flood would seek to carry one with it; but only by intolerable betrayal of all those haggard men of the first war, I thought, only by turning one's back on Barbusse and Remarque and Sassoon, could one give in.

Blishen was faithful to the myth makers and registered as a conscientious objector—an example of a man dissuaded from war by literature.

The antiwar myth worked for him, but not many responded as he did; for every Blishen there were a thousand who volunteered to fight. For us (I speak in the first person here, because this was my generation), the myth had not dispelled the excitement we felt at the prospect of actually being in a war of our own. We had learned what the war books and the war movies had to tell us about the First World War—we knew about the muddy trenches and the corpses on the wire, the shells exploding and the burning planes; but all those terrible particulars became somehow part of the excitement. There is testimony to that transformation in the memoir of a member of this generation, Philip Toynbee. Looking back, after the Second War, on himself and his friends in the Thirties, Toynbee wrote:

It seems to me now that our picture of war was as falsely romantic, in its different way, as anything which had stirred the minds of Edwardian boys, brought up on Henty and the heroics of minor imperial campaigns. The desolate No-Man's-Land pictures of Paul Nash; Bernard Partridge cartoons of the Kaiser; songs from *Cavalcade* and the compassionate poems of Wilfred Owen had made a powerful, complex and stimulating impression on us, so that we felt less pity than envy of a generation which had experienced so much. Even in our Anti-War campaigns of the early thirties we were half in love with the horrors which we cried out against, and, as a boy, I can remember murmuring the name "Passchendaele" in an ecstasy of excitement and regret.

Passchendaele—yes, that was one of the resonant words; and Verdun, and the Somme. I in America thought of the Argonne Forest, and Belleau Wood, and of the names of planes—Spads, Fokkers, Nieuports—and their pilots—Rickenbacker, Immelmann, the Red Baron. For our generation, the cautionary tale of the First War writers had become romance. We had our war-in-the-head.

What we knew and felt about war was not made only of books and films. By the end of the Thirties the First War had been translated into monuments and ceremonies, and those remembrances told a different story from the soldiers' narratives—and still do. At the Cenotaph in London on any November 11, the flags, the bands, and the old men with their medals, marching, are not a demonstration against war; they testify to pride and sacrifice, and say that though war may be terrible, it is also great, the greatest experience most men will have. Other ceremonies do the same: the two-minute silence kept at 11:00 A.M. on Armistice Day when I was a schoolboy was full of awe; something had happened at that time that was worthy of our reverence.

And so, when our war came, we enlisted. The conclusion is

obvious: in matters of war, cautionary literature and the evidence of experience do not change many minds or alter many romantic expectations. Every new generation will respond anew to war's great seduction—not to the uniforms and the parades but to the chance to be where danger is, where men are fighting. War brings to any society its electric, exhilarating atmosphere, and young men rush to join in it, however grim the stories of war they have read and accepted as the truth. Every generation, it seems, must learn its own lessons from its own war, because every war is different and is fought by different ignorant young men.

Some of the differences between the two world wars are obvious. One is the long run-up to war in the decade of the Thirties. The First War surprised most Europeans; the Second War didn't—it was part of European reality and consciousness before it started. British and European boys grew up in those years expecting to have to fight, sooner or later; and that expectation affected both their experiences and the stories they told about them. That wasn't true in the United States, or at least not in the Middle West, where I was growing up. We thought that Europe was none of our business, and it took the Pearl Harbor attack to engage our attentions—and to engage them westward. (New Yorkers probably felt differently, and faced east.)

There was also a difference in moral authority. The First War began in idealism but lost its moral certainty as the fighting ground on. The Second War began with a clearer sense of moral necessity and never lost it. Most people accepted that Nazism was evil and, to a lesser degree and later, that the men who ran Japan were evil too. A war against those enemies was a "Good War"—a phrase that never became an oxymoron, not even at the end, though by then sixty million human beings had died.

Not that you'll find the men who were there remembering their war in good-and-evil terms; you won't. Soldiers never have much to say about why they fight, and even this Good War was no exception. If you look in the personal narratives—British or

American, it doesn't matter which—for explanations of why men went to that war, you'll find remarks like these:

> We knew that war was imminent. There was nothing we could do about it. We were depressed by a sense of its inevitability but we were not patriotic. (Richard Hillary, English)
>
> Like the rites of initiation of primitives, joining the army at eighteen was a shedding of adolescence for manhood. (Patrick Davis, English)
>
> I never lost the certainty that the experience of battle was something I must have. (Keith Douglas, English)
>
> ... prompted by a deep feeling of uneasiness that the war might end before I could get overseas into combat, I wanted to enlist in the Marine Corps as soon as possible. (Eugene Sledge, American)
>
> Seventeen years old, a few months out of high school, no job, there was only one thing I knew to do, what all inland mountain boys do, go to sea. (Alvin Kernan, American)

The causes here are personal and contingent, not moral: the eagerness young men feel for excitement, change, and admission to the world of adults; but also the feeling that young men in wartime have no real choices, that the future has already been decided by the world's elders.

But though "war between good and evil" doesn't appear explicitly in the narratives, it is there, *behind* the telling—an unexpressed conviction, so certain that it doesn't need to be said, that this was a war worth fighting. That assumption, the Good War principle, amounts to a war myth of sorts, one that preceded events and didn't need to be revised. John Updike, who was a child when the war ended, wrote his version of the myth forty years later, in these terms:

> This war, at least for Europeans and North Americans, has become the century's central myth, a vast imaging of a

primal time when good and evil contended for the planet, a
tale of Troy whose angles are infinite and whose central
figures never fail to amaze us with their size, their theatri-
cality, their sweep.

This is a romanticized and aestheticized version of the war,
putting it into literary and theatrical terms in a way that
obscures complex issues; but it seems to be the way many
people imagined it and still do. And the drama was there all
right; there *were* heroes and villains. What is more important,
they never changed; at the end of it all, the armies went home
still certain that the same goods were good, the same evils evil.

There was, I think, one other basis for the shared conviction
that the war was morally right: that is the perception that the
Second War was the most democratic war ever fought. Some
readers will remember the Vietnam antiwar slogan "What if
there was a war and nobody went?" Well, in 1939–45 there was
a war and *everybody* went, or nearly everybody: all classes, all
races, both sexes. Civilians, too, worked, suffered, sometimes
fought, died. For once in human history, a war was fought that
was everybody's war. That sense of a shared struggle got the
British through the Blitz and the Germans and Japanese
through the bombing of their cities; it made conscription toler-
able and rationing endurable. It defeated all military efforts to
win the war by attacking the morale of enemy civilians, and
defused the tension between fighting men and the people back
home—the Old Men and the profiteers and the ignorant
women—that had divided the English and embittered the troops
in the First War. And it strengthened the capacities of armies to
endure. Even Fascist states were democratic in this sense, or so
it seems to an outside observer.

The Second World War was a Good War, but it wasn't an
idealized one. The men who were there accepted the causes
they fought for, but they were skeptical and mocking about the
operations of armies—the strategies, the commanders, officers of

all ranks, the food, the weapons, the propaganda language their
governments uttered. I remember an officers' club on some
Pacific island—was it Eniwetok?—where there was an enormous
brassiere mounted on a board above the bar like a stuffed
tarpon, with this slogan burned into the wood: REMEMBER PEARL
OLSON. A typical military joke, you might say; Americans are a
wisecracking people. But a joke about *Pearl Harbor*? In wartime?
It's significant, I think, that servicemen's irony had reached that
far that soon.

You find that tone, too, in the way First War phrases were
turned to Second War uses. General Patton, for example, drew
on the familiar British recruiting poster to encourage his troops
as they prepared for the Normandy invasion:

> When it's all over and you're at home once more, you can
> thank God that twenty years from now, when you're sitting
> around the fireside with your grandson on your knee and
> he asks you what you did in the war, you won't have to
> shift him to the other knee, cough, and say, "I shoveled shit
> in Louisiana."

There's more in that speech than the salty character of Patton;
there's the tone of the war—coarse and skeptical, but nonetheless belligerent. It wasn't only the Americans who adopted it;
you find it in British and Canadian memoirs as well. It's not the
style of a nation but the style of a war.

That skeptical tone was the product, surely, of the First War
narratives. Men went into the Second War expecting to find discomfort, confusion, and the company of fools because they had
been there before, in the books, or had assimilated the story at
second hand from films or simply out of the postwar culture.
They knew they should distrust the Big Words, the recruiting
slogans, the speeches, and the high emotions of war. And later,
when they told their tale, they did so with a wary knowingness.
It was the legacy of the writers of the *other* war, who had among
them created an appropriate tone for modern war.

Some writers have called that tone disillusionment and have suggested that Americans in the Second War somehow inherited it from the British experience in the First. When Robert Sherwood remarked, in 1948, that the Second World War was "the first in American history in which the general disillusionment preceded the firing of the first shot," that must be what he meant—that the bitter English reaction to the First War had entered the general American consciousness as the right way of responding to modern war, even before the new war began.

In a sense, Sherwood was right: the tone *had* been defined. But "disillusionment" was the wrong word for it. Disillusionment is a loss of belief in a cause; you can't inherit it: it has to happen to a person or a nation as a present cause fails. That didn't happen to Americans in the Second War (or to the British, for that matter, though it did happen to the French and to some Germans and Japanese, or so some memoirs tell us). "Irony" is a better term, and perhaps that is what Sherwood meant. Irony was a serum that inoculated Americans against the disillusionment that had caused England its long hangover. Americans would come out of their war without disillusionment; that would come later, and most bitterly, in the Vietnam War.

I've been talking about differences between the two world wars, but I haven't mentioned differences in scale. The Second War was perceived as being vastly bigger than the First: more men, more theaters of war, mightier battles, more dead. That isn't exactly accurate. In total numbers of combatants, for instance, there isn't much difference between the two wars (though the figures are slippery): the Allies in both wars mobilized forces in the forty millions of men; the Central Powers in the First War and the Axis in the Second managed roughly half that number. Yet with virtually the same number of men in the field, the Second War killed more than twice as many as the First: something like twenty million, as against about eight million. As for battles, the scale varied: the Somme was a smaller battlefield than Normandy, but more men were engaged there on the first day of the great Somme offensive than in Normandy on D-day, and by the end of the day far more of them were dead.

What about geographical scale? It's a common notion that the Second War was *really* a worldwide war, while the First wasn't. As I've said, that is partly a failure of perception. The First War was fought in Africa and the Pacific and the Middle East, just as the Second War was; it's only that those engagements haven't entered the myth of the war. Still, there is a crucial difference: the Second War took the form of two vast geographical expansions and contractions, the Germans and Italians in Europe and North Africa, the Japanese in the Pacific and Southeast Asia. There was no such tidal process, so systematic and so extensive, in the First War.

Instead of numbers and geography, we might consider two other terms by which to define the Second War: *space* and *movement*. The two great expansions of the war spread troops over the surface of the earth as no other war had done before or will probably ever do again. Technology made it possible for them to fight at great distances, across immense empty spaces (as in the Pacific naval battles and the European air wars), and the emptiness and the space worked upon men's imaginations and so entered into their soldiers' and sailors' tales. And because the war involved two different surges of imperial conquest, of seizing nations and islands and seas and then losing them, it was also a war of extraordinary movement, and that, too, affected the stories that the men of those fleets and armies told. Their tales would have giant narrative energy and direction; they would be spared the First War experience of living out a war in the same place, among the ruination of old battles and the corpses of old casualties. There would be dead men enough, and ruin enough this time, but they would be objects a man saw as he passed, not the fixed and permanent constituents of his life.

As an example of how mobile this war could be, consider the military career of a young Englishman, Christopher Seton-

Watson. An Oxford undergraduate in 1939 when the war began, he enlisted immediately in the Royal Horse Artillery. By the end of the year he was with the British Expeditionary Force in France, where he fought in the hopeless delaying action against the advancing Germans, retreated to Dunkirk, and was evacuated with other survivors. In November 1940 his regiment was sent around the Cape to Egypt, and then on to Greece for the brief, ill-fated campaign there, and another retreat. Moved to the Western Desert, he was in yet another retreat when the British fell back from Tobruk in July 1942. That autumn the victories began with Alamein, and in the following spring the conquest of Tunisia, and Seton-Watson was in those battles. He and his regiment were then moved up to Italy, where for the next year they fought their way slowly north. On V-E Day, May 5, 1945, Seton-Watson was still in line, near Bologna, after nearly six years of soldiering—and how many miles of traveling to and through his wars?

Seton-Watson's account of those travels, *Dunkirk–Alamein–Bologna*, is made up of his diaries and letters written at the time, and it gives a sharp immediate sense of what it was like, in that most mobile war. Here are two passages, one from a retreat, the other from an advance:

Dunkirk, May 29, 1940 (the battery has been ordered to destroy its guns):

> The dismal work of destruction was completed by first light, and I set off on foot with H Troop, Battery HQ and B Echelon, a party of about seventy, for Dunkirk, about 25 miles distant. For about five miles we had to walk in single file through the solid block of British and French vehicles. We passed through one village which had been completely flattened by bombing and was littered with charred corpses.... German planes were busy overhead as soon as it was light. About 0800 contact was made with I Troop, which still had some vehicles: so our party was able to ride

for about another ten miles, very slowly and along side roads, the main roads being more likely to attract the enemy's attention. We crossed a small salient of Belgian territory and only with difficulty found our way round Watou, which had been made impassable by bombing. At Westhoek we had finally to abandon our vehicles and continue on foot. It was very hot. On reaching the canal which ran in a semi-circle round Dunkirk, we rested for an hour in a barn and ate. There was a mass of burning vehicles on the canal bank and all the pitiful signs of a rout.

Alamein, November 4, 1942 (from a retrospective account written in a letter the following summer):

In the early stages of the battle we were firing almost every hour of the day on Kidney Ridge; and on the day of the breakthrough, November 4th, our guns followed the tanks over Aqaqir, truly "the grave of the Panzers," as the official account has called it. That scrub-covered, sandy ridge was a terrible sight—littered with tanks and lorries and guns, still smouldering as we drove through, scattered graves in twos and threes, slit trenches filled with machine-guns and ammunition, papers and documents blowing in the wind, still unburied corpses, clothes and equipment lying in confused heaps and huddles, just as they had been abandoned a few hours ago in the panic of that first retreat.

These passages contain all the by now familiar signs of war—the rubbish and ruins, the abandoned weapons and vehicles, the corpses, charred, unburied. But in both, such things are seen in passing, in brief, snapshot-like glimpses, as the witness moves on, retreating or advancing, through his war.

And that is the Second War story in general: always movement, always a new scene. That scene might be simply another desert, or another mountain to cross, or another Pacific island to storm; but it would be a new one—war would mark its accom-

plishments by its scene changes, and all those scenes would be
parts of the story. Marshal Haig said that the First War was a
single continuous campaign, and our imaginations hold it as
such—one long clash of armies on the Western Front. But the
Second War would be many campaigns, each a different story,
all of them necessary to the telling of the whole tale.

Those huge movements of armies and navies across vast
spaces—the Russian plains, the North African desert, the wide
Pacific—give the Second War the epic scale that it has in our
imaginations. But there was at the same time another kind of
war being fought which was nearly the opposite of that—a small-
scale war that is also part of the story. It was fought by small
groups of men, in high-risk operations against small-scale targets: the commando raid on Dieppe, Wingate's Burmese expedition, the Doolittle raid on Tokyo, the kidnapping of a German
general in Crete, Special Force parachute drops into France, an
attack on a German airfield in Sardinia. Militarily, these attacks
accomplished very little, and some were disastrously expensive
in lives. They seem to have been dropped into the war story like
pebbles into a pond, for the sake of the ripples. It was as though
the planners at their desks in London and Washington regretted
that the First War had lacked romantic adventures and were
determined to get some into the Second. (One of the London
planners was Ian Fleming, who would later create the ultimate
romantic adventurer, James Bond.)

These small-scale escapades produced some of the most
vivid personal narratives of the war, and that's not surprising. In
war, small *is* vivid: six men parachuting onto an enemy island
make a good story; 170,000 men landing in Normandy don't—
they scatter into incoherence. But good stories are not necessarily good tactics, and many conventional commanders disliked
and distrusted the irregulars. John Verney, who went on the
Sardinian raid with a group that he calls Bomfrey's Boys, quotes
a general's judgment of their kind of war:

A general in the War Office, one of the rugged sort ... once told me that in his opinion all irregular formations and private armies like Bomfrey's Boys contributed precisely nothing to Allied victory. All they did was to offer a too-easy, because romanticised, form of gallantry to a few anti-social irresponsible individualists, who sought a more personal satisfaction from the war than that of standing their chance, like proper soldiers, of being bayoneted in a slit-trench or burnt alive in tank. He went so far as to hint that Bomfrey's Boys in particular had caused more dislocation to its own side than it ever had to the enemy.

In the general's professional-soldier view, escapades like the Sardinian fiasco (in which nothing was destroyed and the entire raiding party was captured by the Italians) happened because the wartime army was full of useless amateurs; regulars—"proper soldiers"—would have known better. And in the case of Verney and Bomfrey's Boys (and many others who were like them), he seems to have been right. For Verney was the essential civilian soldier, the temporary man-at-arms who acts as a soldier but also stands back and observes and judges (and sometimes mocks) his soldier's acts. In his memoir there is a sense, which Verney consciously develops, that war is an extemporized game and military uniform a masquerade.

But not all the adventurers were amateurs. Orde Wingate was a professional soldier, and so were many of the men who went into Burma in the adventure that made him famous. Bernard Fergusson, for example, who commanded one of Wingate's columns and wrote a book about the campaign, was a captain in the Black Watch and went on to a long and brilliant army career. Fergusson's assessment's of what Wingate's Raiders' actually achieved is professionally severe:

What did we accomplish? Not much that was tangible. What there was became distorted in the glare of publicity soon after our return. We blew up bits of a railway, which did not take long to repair; we gathered some useful intelligence; we distracted the Japanese from some minor operations, and possibly from some bigger ones; we killed a few hundreds of an enemy which numbers eighty millions; we proved that it was feasible to maintain a force by supply dropping alone.

In the course of those small accomplishments men were abandoned, men drowned, men starved; in all, a third of the invading force did not return. It was an expensive demonstration.

The Wingate raid, like many other small, irregular operations, had another function. Fergusson's angry reference to the glare of publicity reminds us that this was a democratic war that depended on the support of the people, and that men died in these operations partly for public relations reasons, to keep civilian morale high. This was particularly necessary to the British in the early years of the war, when they stood alone and won no battles. If real victories were not possible, then the spirit of the people would have to be propped with dramatic, aggressive gestures; better a disaster at Dieppe than nothing. That, surely, is why the small-scale-war story is primarily a British product. Even after the tide had turned, though, the irregular actions went on: Alamein was fought in late 1942; Wingate's forces entered Burma in early 1943; and the German general was kidnapped in the spring of 1944. It must have seemed to the morale shapers a good idea to keep the war stories coming; or perhaps by then irregular war had become a British habit.

The raising of morale may explain why the small-scale actions were thought necessary, but it doesn't explain why men volunteered for them. Why did they go? Fergusson, the regular officer, said he joined the Wingate expedition "to exorcise the thought that I had spent almost all the war in safe places," and that must have been a motive for many men who sought action when they didn't have to do so. And not only the professional soldiers: in war, too-great safety may be an embarrassment even to the amateurs. But there is another reason why men went so enthusiastically into danger, a reason that Verney, the civilian soldier, explained:

> If we were eager, light-heartedly enough, to undertake Operation Swann [the code name for the Sardinian raid] it was for the adventure itself rather than for its military significance. To keep our self-respect we had to do something and Sardinia sounded as nice a place as another to do it in. Let it be Sardinia.

They went off to their small-scale wars—by parachute, by rubber boat, or on foot through the jungle—because this time, in this war, adventure was possible. Perhaps it was the war's great spaciousness that made it seem so; among all those theaters of war, so broad and so various, surely there must be room for even the most individual and unorthodox soldier.

Not even the most senior regular officers were immune to that feeling. Field Marshal Wavell, for one, admired the eccentric, independent Wingate—he called him a genius—and praised the spirit of British irregulars generally. In a foreword to *The Jungle Is Neutral*, he wrote:

> We have been inclined to believe that our armed forces are excessively professional and regular. This war has shown, as others have before it, that the British make the best fighters in the world for irregular and independent enterprises. Our submarines, commandos and air-borne forces ... have proved that where daring, initiative, and ingenuity are required in unusual conditions, unrivalled commanders and men can be found both from professional and unprofessional fighting men of the British race. The spirit which found its most renowned expression in the Elizabethan adventurers lived before them and still lives.

Wavell compared the author, Colonel F. Spencer Chapman, to another famous colonel—T. E. Lawrence. And understandably, to what Wavell was claiming for the British soldiery was the quality Lawrence exemplified: romance. Lawrence in his war was a uniquely romantic figure; in the Second War there were many such figures, and many romantic narratives of their adventures have been written.

From those narratives a whimsical reader could construct a version of the Second War that would demonstrate that it had all been fun. And so, it seems, it had been for the adventurers. It had been, in their terms, a Good War: not in the sense that it was morally defensible (that question doesn't arise in their stories), but that it had been entertaining, enjoyable, exciting beyond anything peace was likely to offer, that it made a good story. In the middle of the attempt to kidnap the German general from Crete, one British irregular sent a note to another, beginning: "All my very rosiest and sincerest and completest congratulations on presenting everyone with quite the best war story yet!" As though wars existed so young men could have adventures that would make good war stories. It's a frame of mind that is present in many narratives of the Second War, and particularly those by British writers; you won't find it in First War stories.

Beyond all the differences between the wars that I've been noting, there was another that made the Second War unlike any that had gone before and unimaginable in the past's terms: it was a war in which machines fought machines. Put like that, such fighting sounds automatic and dehumanizing, like some futuristic battle in H. G. Wells. But the opposite was in fact the case; it was in the battles of the machines that individual freedom of action and individual skill—those soldierly values that the Western Front had seemed to make obsolete—were restored to war. In machines, men could once more take pleasure in the dangers they faced, because they could choose what actions they took against them. The man who is attracted to war, the war lover, is drawn by just these opportunities—to choose and to act skillfully in conditions of danger. It's more than a

matter of adrenaline, I think; it's proving oneself in action,
which is different from that other, passive courage of standing
still under fire. In a fighter plane over the Channel, or a tank in
the desert, a young man could feel that he controlled his fate, or
at least contributed to it. He might be wrong; but he could feel
that way. Is this romantic? Of course it is; that's the point:
machines renewed the romance of war.

Consider the Battle of Britain: a unique event, the only major
battle in military history fought entirely by airplanes, a battle
watched from the ground, it seemed, by half the population of
southern England, and made into myth by the Prime Minister
before it was over: "Never in the field of human conflict was so
much owed by so many to so few." It was the ultimate romantic
battle, a back-to-the-wall defense of the home island against
superior forces, fought one against one, like the fighting in the
Iliad (or so it seemed, as the myth grew).

The story of the Battle of Britain began to be told almost as
soon as the battle ended, in narratives with titles like *Spitfire!*
and *Spitfire Pilot*, written by young pilots in the periods between
one stretch of combat flying and another. So they are brief and
marked by haste; but they are honest books, and to my ear very
English—laconic, modest, and filled with the particulars of the
flying life. They tell the reader what happened there over the
Channel, the actions of air fighting, how planes and men behave
in space. At their best they make that high excitement clear and
immediate, as in this passage from D. M. Crook's *Spitfire Pilot*,
describing an attack on a Stuka:

> I was in an ideal position to attack and opened fire and put
> the remainder of my ammunition—about 2,000 rounds—
> into him at very close range. Even in the heat of the
> moment I well remember my amazement at the shattering
> effect of my fire. Pieces flew off his fuselage and cockpit
> covering, a stream of smoke appeared from the engine, and
> a moment later a great sheet of flame licked out from the

engine cowling and he dived down vertically. The flames enveloped the whole machine and he went straight down, apparently quite slowly, for about five thousand feet, till he was just a shapeless burning mass of wreckage.

It's deep in details, like all good war narratives; but more than that, it's mythic, like the fall of Icarus—a towering death from the sky that the sea receives. The essential fighter pilot's story is there: the rush of the attack, the fascination with the kill, the invisible dead. And as so often in those stories, the thing that dies, the "he" of the passage, is not the German pilot but the plane. In the wars between machines, it's the machines that are mortal. Mortal, and heroic too. The Spitfire in particular became more than a machine in the Battle of Britain; it became an animate, courageous combatant. When fighter pilots wrote their memoirs of that battle, it wasn't their own names they put into their titles, it was *Spitfire*.

Early wartime narratives like *Spitfire Pilot* tell that story, and in the telling make the excitement and romance of combat flying palpable. The excitement comes from the twentieth century's love affair with machines: to be up there, in control of a beautiful, powerful airplane, is in itself a joyful thing. The romance is the inheritance of the First War's flying story, for these young men were the second generation of fighter pilots, and they knew their ancestors. They had read about Bishop and Guynemer and the Red Baron, and they went on reading about them. An old RAF pilot I know remembers how during the war he and his friends hunted in bookshops for copies of V. M. Yeates's *Winged Victory* and shared them with their squadron mates, as though by reading a pilot's story of the first flying war they could discover some secret of the romance they shared.

If there is nonetheless something lacking in these first narratives of the air war, it is that time did not allow them to be reflective. The pilots who wrote them paused only long enough to set down the actions and the excitement of their stories, and returned to their war, and sometimes died there (the author of *Spitfire Pilot* was dead in a crash before his book could be published). Of course they didn't reflect on their experiences—how could they? Nor did any of them find a distinctive voice, or a complex self within the story, or reach beyond action to meaning.

Except one, whose book became the best-known narrative of that part of the war in the air—Richard Hillary, who wrote *The Last Enemy*. When the war began, Hillary was a student at Oxford and a member of the University Air Squadron. He joined the RAF at once and eagerly, for reasons that he explains early in his book, in a remembered conversation with a pacifist friend:

> In a fighter plane, I believe, we have found a way to return to war as it ought to be, war which is individual combat between two people, in which one either kills or is killed. It's exciting, it's individual, and it's disinterested. I shan't be sitting behind a long-range gun working out how to kill people sixty miles away. I shan't get maimed: either I shall get killed or I shall get a few pleasant putty medals and enjoy being stared at in a night club.

How romantic and adolescent that seems—a mass war that will be individual and exciting; and how unreal his notion of the killing and the dying is.

That's at the beginning, of course, before he had killed anyone; later it would surely be different. Only it wasn't. When he shot down his first plane, his feelings, he recalled, were these:

> My first emotion was one of satisfaction.... And then I had a feeling of the essential rightness of it all. He was dead and I was alive; it could easily have been the other way round; and that would somehow have been right too. I realized in that moment how lucky a fighter pilot is. He has none of the personalized emotions of the soldier, handed a

rifle and a bayonet and told to charge. He does not even have to share the dangerous emotions of the bomber pilot who night after night must experience that childhood longing for smashing things. The fighter pilot's emotions are those of the duellist—cool, precise, impersonal. He is privileged to kill well. For if one must either kill or be killed, as now one must, it should, I feel, be done with dignity.

Hillary was right about one thing—in a fighter pilot's war, death is impersonal; as we saw in the *Spitfire Pilot* passage, it's not a man you kill but a machine. But the rest of his reflection on dignified dying is just as romantic and ignorant of death as before he killed. Hillary knew that was the case when he wrote this paragraph; he was setting up himself and his reader for the ironic change that shapes his book. A few days later he would be shot down by a German plane that he never saw, and not killed with dignity but burned and horribly disfigured.

The Last Enemy is not primarily a narrative of combat flying. It's about learning to fly and the joy of mastering a difficult, beautiful skill, about the comradeship of young men doing the same thing and the ignorant excitement they felt about the war ahead. And then it's about what happened afterward: the burning plane, the hospitals, the skin grafts, and the change in the man who endured it all. For of course he changed: how could he not? War had turned him from a handsome, almost beautiful young man into a damaged *other*, with a remade face that his friends said could no longer express emotion, and hands like claws—a person so grotesque that when he was sent to America to speak in support of the war, the United States government forbade him to do so, for fear he would frighten American mothers and stall the recruiting program.

The latter part of Hillary's book belongs to a subcategory of war literature that is new in the twentieth century—the literature of wounds. Wounds have always been a part of war, of course, but two factors in modern war combined to bring them forward in the story. First, the technology of armaments spread the capacity to wound behind the fighting line and made more men vulnerable; and second, the greater sophistication of military medicine meant that more men who were cruelly injured survived. In the First War, one-third of the men under arms were wounded, and inevitably many of the men who wrote memoirs were among those casualties: Sassoon was, so was Graves (so seriously injured that he was reported dead); so were most of the other soldiers and pilots whose narratives I quoted in the last chapter. Some of them describe wounds and the treatment of them in some detail—Graves does, for example—but most seem to regard a wound as an interruption of the real war story, or as an embarrassment, and return their stories to the front as soon as possible. You don't find that reticence so often in Second War narratives. In cases like Hillary's, the will to survive great injury and pain is a long act of courage, as great as courage in battle, and the story of his wounds is the heart of his story.

Why should that story have been a wartime best-seller? Not for its account of the Battle of Britain—other books have told that story more fully—but for its suffering. Hillary recorded his own pain, but he did something more: through his suffering he reached out to the pain of others, to all the soldiers and sailors and airmen who had been hurt by the war; and to the civilians too, who had been bombed and burned for two years by the time Hillary's book appeared in 1942, and who knew that in this war anyone could be both a combatant and a victim. This blurring of the line between the fighting man and the helpless victim of war is a major change in the conception of war in our century. It isn't only that more civilians became casualties in technological war; it's that a sense of helplessness spread until even soldiers began to think of themselves as victims, and passive suffering became a military experience. ("I'm not going off to die," Antoine de Saint-Exupéry wrote when he entered the French Air Force. "I'm going off to suffer." In fact he did both.)

This point about common suffering is made explicitly in the final episode of *The Last Enemy*, where Hillary, released from a convalescent home, helps to dig a woman from the rubble of her bombed house. She looks up at his ruined face and says: "I see they got you, too," and Hillary builds on her sentence to make his peroration on war, humanity, and civilization. Evidence from his letters suggests that in fact the digging episode didn't happen, that Hillary invented it to complete and close his book, and critics have scolded him for faking the scene, and so breaking faith with his readers. But to me it seems a venial sin, given the circumstances: a young, scarred pilot, in the middle of his war, tries to find the moral meaning of his suffering and to write it down before he returns to flying. And so he creates a little parable, a meeting of two war-damaged souls. Perhaps an older, wiser, more reflective man would have found another way; but time wouldn't wait for wisdom then.

There is another point to be noted in Hillary's scene with the dying woman. Not only are soldier and civilian united but class lines disappear. Hillary is Oxford educated, upper class, and an officer, the woman is working class; but in that moment of recognition, their class differences are dissolved by their shared suffering. This idea that war's tribulations had transformed class-ridden England into a classless society was a powerful part of the special English myth of the war. You see it also in the story of the Blitz, in the little boats at Dunkirk, in Churchill's "we shall fight them on the beaches" speech. In the myth, a democratic war had created a truly democratic nation. Perhaps it had, while the war lasted.

Hillary made shared suffering into a moral parable and a justification for the war: the sufferers were humanity, and the war was for them. He expressed no bitterness and no sense of disillusionment with the war that had so scarred him; the English cause did not become hollow, politicians and journalists were not to blame, and his friend the pacifist was still wrong. This certainty, in a man who had suffered in battle, that the suffering was *for* something, that it had meaning, must have encouraged a people whose lives were full of hardship to continue in their trial. Perhaps it seems naive and forced now, a moral that was necessary in 1942 but is no longer vital to the book. If we read *The Last Enemy* still, it is for a different reason: for its cruel irony, contrasting the expectations of the beautiful youth who flew so romantically into combat and the things war did to him. We read it for its ignorance.

Perhaps we also read it sentimentally, for its story of loss. Hillary was one of the privileged young men who came from Oxford into the RAF at the war's beginning. By the time he wrote his book, two years later, all the others were dead: he was, he said, "the last of the long-haired boys." Other fliers tell similar stories. D. M. Crook observes, halfway through *Spitfire Pilot*, that of the men from his school who had joined his squadron, "I was the only one left now." In peacetime this last-survivor talk would be the conversation of the very old; in wartime it is the soliloquy of the young. It's another tale of a Lost Generation—of the price that privilege pays for its amenities. The same assumptions about class and leadership that made public school boys into platoon commanders in the First War put university students into Spitfires in the Second, and with similar results.

That story seems to appeal to all of us, whether we're English or not. There is a sad romantic pleasure to be had in reading about the lost and the last: the lost battalion, the last survivor, the "Only I" who remains to tell the tale. What is it in that story of implacable diminishment that so attracts us? The death of youth and promise, the wasted, unlived lives—it seems too cruel to be endured. But the evidence of war stories is clear: we *like* it.

War in a small machine could be romantic; war in a big one couldn't. For the men in the heavy bombers, the Lancasters and Liberators and Flying Fortresses that put the concept of strategic bombing into practice, flying was more fearful than exciting. Their stories do not tell of the pleasure of simply being up there, or of the satisfaction that lies in the pure skill of flying, or of the adrenal rush that an attack on an enemy plane gives. The acts of war in which they engage are not personal.

These differences are inherent in the kind of war that the bombers waged: many men in a crew, only one of whom has control over the machine that carries them; many planes in a formation that is itself like a huge machine, fixed and symmetrical, each plane maintaining its position in the pattern, opening its bomb doors when the plane ahead does, dropping its bombs when the leader drops, returning home still in formation. In such circumstances there must have seemed little that a man could do that would be his own significant act. The gunners might fire at attacking fighters and even shoot one down, but there would be others; the pilot might take evasive action against the antiaircraft barrage around him, but other shells would burst in his new path. And there were the other possible misfortunes: the engines that might fail, the navigational errors, the weather over rainy England, the German-held lands below—Belgium, the Netherlands, Romania, Yugoslavia—the Channel or the Adriatic to be crossed. And those flights had to be made again and again—twenty-five times, or fifty times (the required number for a complete tour of duty changed as the war changed), so that a man was always aware both of the missions completed and of the number still to be flown before he would be finished, and safe.

It's not surprising that the men who were there in the bombers didn't feel the exhilaration of battle or think, as Hillary did, about killing well. To judge from their narratives, they flew in a spirit of tense waiting, maintaining it through the long hours of those flights until the burst of action over the target, when the flak and the ME-109s came up.

You might think that these waiting men would spend their time observing the earth below them and would tell in their memoirs what a bombed world looked like. They don't. That failure has partly to do with weather, no doubt—above a solid cloud cover there is nothing to see—and partly to do with

altitude: on a clear day the earth seen from thirty thousand feet
loses its particularities, its hills and valleys and villages, and
becomes abstract, like a colored map. But it's more than that: in
a bomber on a combat mission, only two things were worth a
man's attention: doing his job and staying alive. And so, though
you don't learn much about northwest Europe or the Balkans or
the Japanese islands from the bombers' stories, you learn a lot
about the insides of airplanes, and what flak looks like and how
it rattles against the fuselage, and the way a fighter's guns wink
as it attacks, and how a hit plane disintegrates and falls. The
"world" becomes the air around the plane, where the fighting
and the dying are happening. The close observation of airmen is
focused there.

Here is what a Fifteenth Air Force pilot saw as he headed
into an attack on Ploesti—arguably the worst enemy target in
Europe:

> Far ahead of us, the sky looked different. There was a band
> of brown haze from eighteen thousand feet up to about
> twenty-three thousand. It was not easy to see; you had to
> know what you were looking for. I knew what it was; I had
> seen it before. Flak. The dirty strings from a flak barrage
> drifted in the cold wind. Less than five minutes ago a
> group had gone through it, and now the shreds of smoke
> were fading and were barely visible. A black column was
> rising from the ground in the southeast. Someone had hit
> something big, something that had violently blown.... We
> were beginning our run.
>
> There was not a daub of black in the sky; for a blessed
> moment we made our slow, inexorable passage across it
> unchallenged. Seconds passed. When it came, it came like a
> mighty shout, a malediction hurling up at us through four
> miles of twisting wind. They were everywhere; the dark
> flowers of flak were everywhere. Four successive shells
> exploded in front of my right wing, and I felt the wheel
> tremble in my hands. An orange core glared out of a

shroud of smoke in front of me. Our plane shuddered against the concussion of two bursts underneath us.... My left wing dropped away from me, and I drove my foot hard against the right rudder to bring it up. I didn't pray. I didn't curse. I didn't think. I crouched in my cave of instruments, tubes, and wires.

That's a pilot's story—threatened but active, he flies his plane through dangerous space, not thinking about the earth below, not thinking at all.

And what about the other men in the bombers, the ones who didn't fly but only navigated, or aimed the bomb, or fought off attacking planes? What did they see and remember? Elmer Bendiner's *The Fall of Fortresses* offers answers. Bendiner was the navigator on *Tondelayo,* a B-17 of the American Eighth Air Force, flying out of England against German targets. His narrative is vividly written and full of details, but there is almost no earth in it, no Germany, no views of the target cities; there is only the immediate space through which *Tondelayo* moves, and the interior of the plane. And when he looks below him, it is not landscape he sees. This passage is from his account of a raid on Schweinfurt:

We were somewhere between Antwerp and Aachen when I was aware of the first rocket attack. It seemed to come in from seven o'clock over *Tondelayo*'s left wing. I remember seeing a brownish object tumbling and then bursting into an orange-yellow flash and an enormous black cloud. *Tondelayo* reared like a frightened horse.

I do not recall seeing a rocket actually hit a B-17. I remember only the fireworks and the gust of wind. The smell and sight of battle are still with me—the acrid gunpowder and the disordered plexiglass cabin—but I cannot recall a sound of battle except the clump and clatter of our own guns....

I do remember looking down somewhere after Eupen

and counting the fitful yellow-orange flares I saw on the
ground. At first—so dense am I—I did not understand them.
Here were no cities burning. No haystack could make a fire
visible in broad daylight 23,000 feet up. Then it came to
me as it came to others—for I remember my headset crack-
ling with the news—that these were B-17s blazing on the
ground.

The story here, as in every bomber story I've read, is not the
bombing mission itself—not, that is, the successful destruction
of the target—but the damage and loss suffered by the attackers,
the planes that fall. (Note how often the word "fall" occurs in
the titles of bomber narratives: *The Fall of Fortresses, A Thousand
Must Fall, Those Who Fall.*)

All men who fight are interested in violent death—their kind
of dying, in their kind of war. Soldiers remember and retell the
deaths of their comrades with a terrible exactness—where a man
was hit, how he fell, the bloody details of spilled brains and dismembered limbs. Fliers don't do that, exactly: they remember
the deaths of planes. In a battle of machines, it's the machines
that are hit, stagger, fall to earth; it's their deaths that are visible
and dramatic. The men who are in them die invisibly, and
because machines die in flames, they leave no corpses. The pilot
who witnesses the fall of another plane sees not personal death
but the fate of a plane that could next time be his if he is careless, or unlucky, or just not good enough. That's why pilots read
accident reports the way old men read obituaries—to identify
the mortal element in flight that has overlooked them this time.
Crewmen no doubt see it differently, with a more helpless
fatalism.

In narratives of air war it's the dead machines that provide
the Battlefield Gothic. Here is Bendiner's account of his first
dying plane (he is en route to an attack on Bremen):

I saw death long before I saw pain, and I could not believe
it. I balanced my gun in one hand and stared beyond it at

Carlson's left-wing man. Was it Johnson? Was it Ashley? I
no longer remember. There was a yellow flare on the out-
board engine nearest me. The great silver ship banked
sharply and turned its belly to the sun, which paled the
yellow flames. There were no screams. The plane lost
speed, slipped back and spiralled gently down. I saw a
piece of wing shatter and fly off like a target in skeet
shooting. The broken wing was jagged and flaming. The
plane turned tail up, plummeted past my gun port and was
no more.

Death here is distant, inaudible, impersonal; there are men in
the plane, but they have no names and no faces, and Bendiner
does not try to imagine their terror. As always in the air war, it's
the plane that dies.

The passage I have quoted is from a bomber narrative, but
you will find similarly vivid accounts of the deaths of planes in
fighter pilots' memoirs from both wars. These are the places
where even the dullest prose takes life—these and the fighters'
accounts of dogfights. Accounts of the actual deaths of men, on
the other hand, tend to be laconic and emptied of feeling:
"From this flight Bubble Waterston did not return" and "There
was no sign of him at all, and his body was never recovered."
That note of near indifference is a convention of flying narratives—conventional enough to be recorded in poems (Gavin
Ewart's "When a Beau Goes In") and satirized in films (Danny
Kaye's RAF pilot in *The Secret Life of Walter Mitty*). It is mainly
an English convention and no doubt comes from the tradition
of English reticence; but I think it also has to do with the
remoteness and insubstantiality of death in the air.

The Battle of Britain was the great romantic war of machines
in the air. The North African campaign was the great romantic
machine war on the ground. Like the Battle of Britain, it marked
a turning point in the fortunes of the Allies. "Before Alamein we

never had a victory," Churchill said. "After Alamein we never
had a defeat." Like the air war, the desert war has had many
narrators, but one in particular merits our attention. Keith
Douglas has a secure reputation as one of the finest poets of the
Second War, but he also wrote a prose book—wrote it hastily,
between battles, the way the Spitfire pilots wrote their instant
air-war narratives, to get the story down while there was time,
yet wrote it brilliantly. His *Alamein to Zem Zem* is an extraordinary accomplishment, given the circumstances of its writing; it is
a classic narrative of the war in the North African desert.

Douglas was not the usual war poet, at least not if our
models are First War poets like Wilfred Owen. He came into the
army desiring war and was restless until he found it. When it
looked as though he might be left in a rear-area job during the
desert campaign, he ran away to the front lines and talked his
way into a tank command. (You don't find many soldiers who
run in that direction.) He loved the desert fighting—the spacious
maneuvering, the surprises, the danger. When he was wounded
he seemed unaffected; he simply recovered and hurried back to
his regiment. "I like you, sir," his batman said. "You're shit or
bust, you are." That's death or glory in the language of the
troops; and so he was. War suited him, and the book he wrote
about it is more than simply a narrative: it's an enthusiast's cele-
bration of war.

The war Douglas wanted was a *personal* one; that's always
the romantic civilian's dream. "I am not writing about these
battles as a soldier," he says at the beginning of his book,

> nor trying to discuss them as military operations. I am
> thinking of them—selfishly, but as I always shall think of
> them—as my first experience of fighting: that is how I shall
> write of them. To say I thought of the battle of Alamein as
> an ordeal sounds pompous: but I did think of it as an
> important test, which I was interested in passing.

He didn't care about the causes and reasons for war, he says; such things are for the financiers and parliamentarians.

> But it is exciting and amazing to see thousands of men, very few of whom have much idea why they are fighting, all enduring hardships, living in an unnatural, dangerous, but not wholly terrible world, having to kill and to be killed, and yet at intervals moved by a feeling of comradeship with the men who kill them and whom they kill, because they are enduring and experiencing the same things. It is tremendously illogical—to read about it cannot convey the impression of having walked through the looking-glass which touches a man entering a battle.

It's striking how similar this idea of war is to Hillary's: for both men war was an adventure and a challenge that was made more exciting by the abstract drama of either killing or being killed. Douglas was making the romantic volunteer's case for war—not for this Good War alone, but simply for war. That case is not often made so explicitly in modern war narratives, but men feel it, and especially very young men, like Hillary and Douglas. War is a test—of courage, of manhood, of self—that they are anxious to pass; and it is a *romantic* one, beyond anything else that life is likely to offer them.

The desert-war romance began with the journey there, a long sea voyage (how many of the troops had been aboard a ship before?) down the length of Africa, with stops at romantic ports of call—Freetown, Cape Town, Durban—and then up the east coast and through the Red Sea to Suez and then Cairo. When they came ashore, romance was there too; here is Neil McCallum, infantry subaltern, traveling in a boxcar to a base camp near Geneifa:

> Outside the wagon the night was like a scene from a Ramon Navarro film in the 'twenties. Gold and silver sand in the full Egyptian moon, the luminous incredible stars,

white adobe houses piercingly bright against the darker
sand, and the curved droop of palm leaves. Each time the
train stopped, for reasons meaningless to us, the desert
receded into the darkness. The moon was splendid and the
chill of the night air pouring into the box-car was like a
flow of cold liquid.

Like many another soldier groping for an image adequate to
what he saw and felt, McCallum turned to Hollywood and
found one there. Not exactly a war-in-the-head, more a desert-
in-the-head.

As troops moved out from Cairo and Alexandria into the
desert battle zone, they became aware of the vast strangeness of
the desert, its emptiness and silence and loneliness. Some found
that strangeness beautiful—the vivid colors of the precipices, the
biblical scenes, and always in the distance the mountains on the
horizon—"jagged brown peaks going straight up and down like
a child's drawing." Others were overwhelmed by its nothingness: "The desert," one British soldier wrote, "omnipresent, so
saturates consciousness that it makes the mind as sterile as itself.
It's only now you realise how much you normally live through
the senses. Here there's nothing for them." But they all were
moved by the landscape they fought in, and sooner or later they
tried to make its power actual in their narratives. In the later
phases of the campaign, when the Afrika Korps was in accelera-
ting retreat, the massive, changing scenes are often as much a
part of the soldiers' consciousness as the fleeing enemy. John
Guest, an English aesthete turned artillery officer, describes a
view seen during the campaign in Tunisia in early 1943:

The other day, when I was motor-cycling on some errand,
the road wound up a mountain. Finally, as I came over the
top of the pass, I was confronted suddenly by a fantastic
panorama of valleys, hills, huge crags and mountains of
rock. I myself was in brilliant sunlight while all in front was

deeply shadowed by black clouds like oily smoke from which lightning zigzagged on to the mountain-tops. Between me and this yawning inferno was a rainbow so hard and artificial against the darkness that you could have hung clothes to dry on it; and beneath the rainbow, illuminated by a shaft of livid light, was a great ridge of pallid rock like jagged broken teeth. It was a landscape-painter's nightmare.

Even Private Crimp, who had found the desert so sterile to the senses, had to acknowledge the impressiveness of those Tunisian mountains when he fought there in the same campaign:

The eastern mountains (towards which our front is directed) look fine this morning. Over them all, like a giant wave, rears the surging crest of massive Zaghouan, highest point in all Tunisia. But the most prominent feature lies nearer at hand, looking only a mile or so off, though probably about five: a peculiar, double-peaked eminence, of considerable height, standing out distinctly against the mountain wall behind. Obviously of volcanic origin, it rises in strange isolation like a couple of pustules from the face of the plain—unnatural, forbidding, and repellent.

The place-names of the battle zone were as strange and exotic as the landscapes: Argoub el Megas, Sidi Barka, Bou Kournine, Souk el Arba, Medject el Bab. In every way, North Africa was a romantic place to fight a war.

It was also a good place for a war from a military point of view. Deserts offer ideal battlefields, as T. E. Lawrence had learned in another desert. In those wide, arid emptinesses armies can maneuver, charge, and withdraw, and the machines of war and the men who command them can be put to extreme tests. "There is satisfaction," Christopher Seton-Watson wrote during action on the Libyan frontier,

in the feeling that here is something to be defeated and
mastered, nature at her worst. I suppose Kipling would call
it a man's life. And for hundreds of miles around there is
one occupation—war. War in surroundings that cannot
suffer, where there can be no distractions. I feel that I'm
"getting down to it."

And later, looking back on the campaign after it was over, he
added: "The greatest joy of all was that feeling of freedom of
movement and space—the unique characteristic of desert warfare." That sounds like something a fighter pilot might have
said; and indeed the desert seems to have felt, to men who
fought there, as free and spacious as the sky.

That joy in freedom of movement is evident in all the stories
of the desert war. It was a war fought with machines—with
tanks, mobile guns, armored cars, and trucks for the infantry—
but it was not fought mechanically; it was not, that is, a matter of
grinding mass against mass. You get a sense, from the memoirs,
of men acting in small units, or independently, moving rapidly
over large distances, altering plans, making local decisions, and
always in large empty spaces where the first problem was to find
the enemy. Crimp the infantryman describes how, when
German tanks appear, his entire battalion leaps aboard trucks
and "scarpers" ten miles back; "apparently," he writes, "these
'scarpers' are accepted desert technique." And Seton-Watson,
the artilleryman, roams about the desert in an armored car,
looking for targets. Nobody hunkers down in one place for
long, there are no static trench lines; armies swirl and separate
and regroup like clouds.

For tankmen like Keith Douglas, the desert was a glorious
opportunity: it meant a return to cavalry tactics—the swift,
swooping attacks, the hunting and chasing, the moments of one-
against-one fighting. Tanks entered battle as squadrons and
were directed by radioed orders from the commanding officer,
but in the dust and noise and confusion of the desert fighting

(as Douglas tells it), there were often times when an individual tank commander had to act independently—advancing, firing, and retreating by his own decisions. The effect, in his narrative, is of battle handed back to the men who are fighting it, though confusedly—very like the war in the air, as fighter pilots tell it.

The romance of tank war, like that of the air, must have something to do with the way the killing is done—distantly, most of the time, and unwitnessed. Douglas, at the beginning of his book, writes abstractly and loftily about killing and being killed, as Hillary did; but he never mentions killing another man—his targets are machines. There are many dead men in his story—Germans, Italians, British—scattered over the battlefields, as they are in any war. But in this war, because it is spacious and mobile, they are mostly objects that the tanks roll by. Douglas looks down on them as he passes; they tell, he thinks, a cruel story. But it isn't his story; in his machine, he is raised above death and insulated from it, and he passes on. Mobility is a kind of forgetfulness; and the dead recede like the past, like the landscape.

There are passages in Douglas's book in which he stops in his war of movement to examine the dead, sometimes even to sketch them (the first edition of *Alamein to Zem Zem* contains his drawings of dead soldiers), as though these dead held some secret about what death is like in a war of machines. After the battle of Galal Station, he approached an abandoned Italian tank and peered into the turret:

Gradually the objects in the turret became visible: the crew of the tank—for, I believe, these tanks did not hold more than two—were, so to speak, distributed around the turret. At first it was difficult to work out how the limbs were arranged. They lay in a clumsy embrace, their white faces whiter, as those of dead men in the desert always were, for the light powdering of dust on them. One with a six-inch hole in his head, the whole skull smashed in behind the remains of an ear—the other covered with his own and his friend's blood, held up by the blue steel mechanism of a machine gun, his legs twisting among the dully gleaming gear levers. About them clung that impenetrable silence I have mentioned before, by which I think the dead compel our reverence.

It is a complex response to death. At first Douglas reads the scene in a soldierly, detached way, like a tankman, seeing the occupants of the turret as "objects" that are "distributed" within the tank space, avoiding their humanity. But then the tone shifts; perhaps it is his civilian eye that turns those objects into friends or lovers and his objectivity into reverence. The two bodies are intertwined with the mechanisms of their war machines, as though men and tank were one organism, a dead centaur. Douglas now knows how tankmen die. And knowing, he can feel a reverence for them. But there is no romance here; the dead, up close, forbid it.

There is romance, though, in another group of men who die, the senior officers of Douglas's regiment. It had been one of those county cavalry regiments, made up of weekend soldiers commanded by hunting-and-shooting country squires. The horses had been replaced by tanks, but the squires remained in command—arrogant, exclusive, eccentric men like Douglas's CO, "Piccadilly Jim," who wore suede boots with his uniform and smelled of pomatum, who talked about horses and hunting and ignored junior officers who didn't hunt. And like Guy, the second in command, whom Douglas describes:

> He was fantastically rich and handsome, and appeared, as indeed he was, a figure straight out of the nineteenth century. He was charming. His ideas were feudal in the best sense—he regarded everyone in the regiment as his tenants, sub-tenants, serfs, etc., and felt his responsibilities to them as a landlord. Everyone loved him and I believe pitied him

a little. His slim, beautifully clad figure remained among our dirty greasy uniforms as a symbol of the regiment's former glory.

Douglas resented men like Guy and Piccadilly Jim, but he also admired them, and when they died—as they all did before the North African campaign had come to a close—he mourned them. They were, he wrote in a poem, a "gentle obsolescent breed of heroes ... Unicorns, almost." What he mourned in them was the death of the old officer caste, the end of the Grenfell world. War seemed to come naturally to them; it was their métier, and they fought with an easy confidence and skill, and a kind of casualness, that no civilian soldier could hope to acquire. New men, temporary officers like Douglas, could feel only envy, reluctant admiration, and nostalgia for what they represented—a dream of soldiering in which war was a game of skill and all the players were skillful. I understand that dream. In my own part of the war, which was far from Douglas's, I felt the same way about the Old Marines, the sergeants and warrant officers who wore campaign hats and had been in China or Nicaragua and could sink a Japanese destroyer from the shore with a trench mortar (or so the Old Corps mythology went). We knew they were narrow-minded, rigid men, harsh in their discipline and strict in their application of the rules. But they were brave and unquestioning in their service, and a lot of them died doing it. They induced in us amateurs a nostalgia for a life of simple, entire commitment to war; they were part of the romance that we had come too late to share.

By the end of *Alamein to Zem Zem*, Douglas has become a seasoned, combat-wise tank commander; not Piccadilly Jim, but a soldier who is good at his job and loves what he does. The fight for the desert is over, Von Arnim, the German commander, is a prisoner, and Rommel has left Africa. It has been a great Allied victory. And yet the tone of Douglas's ending is not triumphant:

We repeated over and over again in our thoughts and conversation that the battle was over. The continual halting
and moving, the departure at first light, the shell-fire, the
interminable wireless conversations—and the strain, the
uncertainty of to-morrow, the fear of death: it was all over.
We had made it. We stood here on the safe side of it, like
swimmers. And Guy, lying under the flowers in Enfidaville
cemetery, Piccadilly Jim, buried miles behind us, Tom, and
all the others, back to the first casualties, during Rommel's
attempt to break through to Alexandria: they didn't make
it, but it's all over for them, too.

　　And to-morrow, we said, we'll get into every vehicle we
can find, and go out over the whole ground we beat them
on, and bring in more loot than we've ever seen.

That's what it was like, all of it—the tense movements, the
deaths, and the *loot*, which, coming at the end, deflects the tone
from mourning and makes it tough and ironic, like a good soldier of that war.

Because they fought in small machines, Hillary and Douglas
had elements in their wars that infantrymen and the men in the
big machines don't have: a wide space to move in, a mobile
mechanism to be skillful with, and a certain independence of
action. Perhaps in the end those elements would not have been
sufficient to preserve war's excitement; perhaps if these two
young men had lived long enough to look back on the war, they
might have turned cynical or bitter or angry about it. But they
didn't. Douglas was killed in Normandy on D-plus 3; Hillary,
having talked his way back onto flight orders, took off on a
training flight one cold January night in 1943 and crashed. Both
died doing what they wanted to do, engaged in and so far as
one can tell still excited by their military crafts. They might have
changed; but I don't think so. War had given them the action
and the romance that they hoped for; they had had Good Wars.
That may seem a bitter paradox in Hillary's case; but I think it is
nonetheless true. So perhaps a Good War is not a matter of

morality after all; perhaps it's only a matter of space, and freedom, and the right machine.

Writing about the renewal of romance in the Second War, I have had nothing to say about the most *un*romantic kind of soldiering—the infantry. The infantry has always been the ordinary, indistinguishable mass of armies, the place where they put you if you have no preference and no skills. The war stories that those ordinary men tell, the stories of walking war, differ in fundamental ways from the stories of the young men in machines, the long-haired boys. Infantrymen's narratives are narrower in the range of their vision, smaller in scale, more identified with groups than with individuals, more determined by the contingencies of battle, more concerned with survival than with action. For the majority of men who fought in the Second War, these are the stories that tell the common truths.

In some ways, all infantry stories are the same, whether the teller is Rifleman Harris in the Peninsular Wars or Rifleman Bowlby in the Italian campaign; they all say: keep your head down and your rifle clean and do what you're told when it's possible. But there are also differences. One difference between the two world wars is simply that the Second War was the *second* to be fought by civilian soldiers, which means that in 1939 there was a tradition of civilians at war. By then the first generation of civilian soldiers had written their books, and some of the men of the second generation had read them and even quoted them in their own books (Douglas, for example, quoted Sassoon). But even if they hadn't read the books, they knew the tradition: they could sing "Mademoiselle from Armentières" and "Tipperary" (Americans as well as British knew them; those songs were part of our childhood), and they had heard stories from men who had been there, a father or an uncle or the man next door. They knew that men who were soldiers in modern wars came home again and reverted to being ordinary civilians. Soldiering was a temporary thing, a period you passed through, like high school. Any guy on the block could do it, should do it, would do it.

There are two notable consequences of this circumstance, this second-generation civilian-soldier army. I've mentioned them both: one is the conscious condition of civilianness, the sense of the soldiering self as a kind of impostor, out of place, unprepared, and ignorant of what is happening or is going to happen—not a *real* soldier. The other follows from it: the awareness that such a man in uniform may be, probably will be, a comic figure at least some of the time. These attitudes changed armies; they also changed the stories the soldiers of those armies told, gave them a civilian note of skepticism, and made their war ironic in the telling.

An example of what I mean is this passage from *And No Birds Sang*, the fine memoir by the Canadian writer-naturalist Farley Mowat. Mowat, an infantry lieutenant in the Hastings and Prince Edward Regiment, is leading his men in their first combat operation, a beach landing in Sicily. They have come ashore and moved inland until stopped by a barbed-wire obstacle. There they fall prone and begin to fire their weapons, until a voice ahead of them cries: *"Hold your fire, you clods!"*

> Such was our astonishment that we immediately obeyed, never pausing to consider whether or not this might be an enemy ruse. Action was called for, and it was up to me to do the calling.
>
> "Fix bayonets!" I shrilled.
>
> And so we went into our first and last bayonet charge in a war in which the bayonet was an almost total anachronism.
>
> We scrambled over the wire, ripping our shorts and shirts and flesh, and went galloping clumsily up the slope. As we reached the crest we discovered why we had not all been slaughtered during this suicidal attack. A group of commandos was just completing an assault from the rear of the hill: only, instead of waving bayonets, they were sensibly hosing streams of lead into the buildings.

"Core!" a commando sergeant said to me after we had finished sorting ourselves out. "You chaps *did* look loverly! Just like the Light Brigade. Never seen nothin' like it 'cept in that flick with Errol Flynn!"

What is this anecdote doing at the beginning of Mowat's book? Well, listen to the voice. It's the voice of an absolute civilian, a young man ignorant of how wars are really fought and totally unprepared to lead men into battle. But it's also an amused, comic voice: in *this* war, it says, being hopeless can be funny. Here at the start Mowat is confirming the essential civilianness of the war he's in. This time that will be the norm: it will be OK to be incompetent.

(There is another civilian element here worth noting—the presence of Errol Flynn, the war-in-the-head out of the movies. From now on, the heroes of war movies will figure as ironic examples of how war *isn't* fought, of the difference between the fantasies of moviegoing civilians and the real thing.)

In the course of the hard fighting that followed—across Sicily and up the Italian peninsula—Mowat changed: he became a soldier. But not entirely; the civilian remained an audible presence, a voice we hear mocking his own attempts at soldiering and hating the brass hats and behind-the-lines bureaucrats. The note of self-directed irony, which says, in effect, "I'm not really a soldier and never will be, even when I've learned to do the job," is a characteristic narrative voice of the Second War. You hear it in Douglas as well as in Mowat. I hear it in my own war memoir. We all learned it from the same models, the classic narratives of the First War. Or perhaps it would be more precise to say that we learned it from the decade in which those narratives first appeared—from the Great Hangover of the Twenties. What we found there was not so much bitterness or disillusionment as a wariness, a determination to be armed against heroics by irony.

There are a number of other things about Mowat's book that make it, to my mind, a classic of military civilianness. One is his

continuous astonishment and outrage at the way war is conducted, how it is planned by behind-the-lines brass hats and
carried out in confusion that is sometimes farcical and sometimes mortal. Another is his way of describing military activities
with the eye and the vocabulary of a kid from Ontario who has
never heard or seen such things before. Here is an example:

> I had scarcely rejoined the platoon when the day was rent
> by a rasping, metallic screeching that rose to an ear-
> splitting pitch and volume, culminating in a series of stu-
> pendous explosions that shook the solid rock beneath my
> cringing flesh. A blast of furnace-hot air buffeted me, and
> six coiling plumes of smoke and dust sprang, towering,
> above the castle ruins.

What has happened? He doesn't know, and neither do we. It's
like a riddle: what is it that rasps and screeches and blasts hot
air? The answer (in the next paragraph) is: an artillery rocket,
the kind the Germans called Nebelwerfer and the English
Moaning Minnies. But how could a civilian, or a civilian soldier,
know that?

Mowat's book was not published until 1979, more than
thirty years after the events it describes. By then Mowat had
written more than twenty books. Does that matter? Does all that
literary experience simply make him a better writer, or does it
do what Calvino feared memory would do: does it turn his war
into "a piece of narrative written in the style of the time"? A
little of both, I think: war becomes anecdotes, wonderfully told
but *shaped*, well made; memory and style open a distance
between the story and its telling. This is not a criticism of the
book; it is simply an observation of the action of time and experience upon memory.

Mowat had his antecedents in the First War, among the literary young officers like Sassoon and Graves who came to see
their war ironically but took their commissions seriously and in
time became responsible officers. There are no antecedents that

I know of for Rifleman Bowlby; his *Recollections* couldn't have been written about any previous war. His is a new voice in the soldiers' tale: the voice of a civilian who fights his war but is not essentially changed by it or seduced to its values.

Like Mowat, Bowlby fought in the Italian campaign, from somewhere south of Rome to somewhere north of Florence (as in most personal narratives, the geography is rather vague). Like Mowat, he was an infantryman, and like Mowat, he was in heavy, close-range fighting in that mountainous terrain. But there the similarity ends.

For one thing, Bowlby was not an officer but a common rifleman, though he was something of an odd man out, since he had been to an English public school (Kipling would have called him a "gentleman ranker"). Such a position has advantages for the teller of a war story; he can see his fellow soldiers with an outsider's eye, like an anthropologist among savages. Bowlby saw the coarse lives of common soldiers, and recorded them with an exact, unjudgmental fidelity: the horseplay, the crude jokes and songs, the quarrels, the complaints, the discomfort of their daily existence. Some of this is farcically funny: a man goes for a swim and loses his teeth in the river; a Spandau begins to fire and Bowlby's underpants come down; he gets stuck in his own slit trench. It's comic war, "pure Laurel and Hardy" as Bowlby says; and more often than not, *he* is the comedian. You won't find such self-directed humor in earlier narratives.

But Bowlby's war is more than simply farce; it also contains violent and fearful action. There is fierce fighting, none of it in major battles, not the sort of thing that got into the newspapers, just a few men attacking a village or a hill, full of confusion and panic and fear. Good men die, and weak men desert; German corpses are found along the roads, and men loot them. And all this is inextricably mixed with the comedy. The instability of tone that I've mentioned before as characteristic of modern war memoirs is constant in Bowlby.

One tone is absent, though: the top of the range, the note of high emotions and heroics, which other civilian-soldier narrators reach for on occasion to render courage and skill and death in battle, is not in Bowlby's register; his approach to war doesn't allow for heroism. You'll get a sense of what that approach is, essentially, from the epigraph he chose for his book, a remark attributed to the Duke of Wellington: "All soldiers run away. It does not matter as long as their supports stand firm." *The Reflections of Rifleman Bowlby* is about running away, ducking and dodging, keeping one's head down, and *not* being heroic.

Here is a brief example of that approach. Bowlby is asleep in a slit trench near Lignano:

> I was woken by a roar of explosions. Paralysed with fear I listened to a mortar-barrage sweep over the Company. Five Platoon's Brens opened up. Forcing myself to look over the parapet I saw Mr Simmonds [the platoon commander] jump out of his trench.
>
> "Six Platoon!" he yelled. "Come to the help of your friends!"

Thus far this is classic war stuff; it could be from the pages of *The Boy's Own Paper*, or from Henty. But from here on it is different:

> None of us moved. For a moment Mr Simmonds stood upright in a pelt of shrapnel, then he jumped back into his trench. Humphreys, who had dug himself a "lean-to" trench, caught my eye. We grinned.

This confrontation is not between a brave soldier and two cowards; it's between a man trying to play a soldier's role and two civilians exercising a civilian prudence. It would be wrong to call that prudence *cowardice*, as wrong as to call it *courage;* those concepts are simply not included in Bowlby's understanding of war. Indeed, there are no concepts at all in his war, none of the Big Words that name the military values. There are only the particulars of these men, in these mountains, in all this confusion of fighting; while one man is dying, another is getting caught in a hedge, or losing his false teeth—farce and death crowd in upon each other. This doesn't mean that Bowlby's war was fought without tragic cost; two-thirds of his battalion were casualties. What it does mean is that it was fought, by some men, in a different spirit. Bowlby motionless in his trench is not a model of the way soldiers have traditionally behaved; or at least it isn't the way they have told their stories. Here is an ironic, self-mocking individual consciousness that remains untouched by military values and unmoved by exhortations to be brave. There must have been many Bowlbys in the citizen armies of the Second World War, though not many who were as frank.

Bowlby's story is a sharp reminder that between the two world wars, ideas of courage and cowardice had changed. In the Second War courage remained admirable, men did brave things and were given medals; but too-flamboyant courage was mocked as what movies stars did, Errol Flynn stuff, and death-or-glory was a synonym for folly. "Keep your nut down," one of Bowlby's mates advises him. "Death or glory boys don't last." And another memoirist from the same campaign proves the wisdom of that advice. Raleigh Trevelyan, a subaltern in the Rifle Brigade at Anzio, recalls his friend Monty, rumored to have been recommended for the Victoria Cross:

> I don't know the full story of what he did even now. Apparently he found Mike's platoon pinned down by spandaus and anti-tank guns.... Although his own men were reduced by casualties to section strength, he rallied them into following him in a great death-or-glory charge across the open. All the while he was cracking his usual absurd jokes and chanting the tune of the regimental march. Every one of them was killed.

That's a splendid story in the old tradition—the rush to the aid of a platoon in trouble, the jokes, the regimental march. But look at the last sentence. Death-or-glory boys don't last, even if they do get VCs.

Attitudes toward cowardice had changed even more, a fact that the British Army recognized when it removed cowardice from its list of capital offenses in 1930. Other crimes against war, like mutiny, treachery, and desertion, remained punishable by death, but when nearly two hundred British soldiers mutinied at Salerno in 1943, only three (all of them sergeants) were condemned to death, and those sentences were commuted to prison terms. Military executions for military crimes were felt to be inappropriate in a people's army. "When a citizen Army is fighting the battles of this country," a British MP observed in the Commons in 1945, "the death penalty should be abolished and penal servitude drastically reduced in order to conform to the wishes of the people."

After Italy, the last chapter of the European war—the invasion of Normandy and the final march to Germany—seems a very different story, almost a different war. It's most different, in the tellings of it, in the sense one gets of its enormous scale. From the beginning, when troops and matériel gathered at the ports and airfields of southern England, the numbers were vast: an invasion fleet of 7,000 vessels, 15,000 aircraft, an assault force of 150,000 men, 18,000 parachutists, 50,000 vehicles. The men who have told their invasion stories didn't usually know those numbers, but they were aware of the mass: how the Channel was covered with "an enormous armada of vessels" and the beaches were jammed with men and equipment, and how "the airspace above the battlefield was almost as congested as the ground below." The effect of this mass on the personal narratives is to cast a huge shadow on the importance of the human presence, to make the operation seem a battle of many machines, and war itself a huge machine with replaceable parts, both mechanical and human. What happened to individual men depended on what the machines did: if a landing craft stopped short of the beach, men drowned; if a transport carrying paratroopers flew too low, men struck the earth before their chutes could open, making a sound "like large ripe pumpkins being thrown down to burst against the ground"; if a tank was hit by gunfire, it "brewed up"—that is, burned—incinerating its crew.

A large-scale operation, then; but because of its wide extent, and the ways men entered it, also many small-scale ones. Men who struggled ashore on D-day were among thousands, yet many felt themselves "abandoned, alone, and uncared-for in the world" as they hunted for their units and their officers and wondered what to do next. Men who were there remembered the noise, and the debris, and the confusion, not the fighting. Charles Cawthon was an American infantry officer in that landing, and his account of the day has a ring of authority—deep in details, honest, as responsible as a man could be in that great disorder. He tells of ominous signs—how the battleships stopped shelling and the air cleared of planes, how the tide swept laterally along the beach and scattered units, and how "the first assault wave, already on the beach, did not resemble a battle line as much as it did heaps of refuse, deposited there to burn and smoulder unattended." Cawthon commanded a boat team, but he landed alone and spent the next hours running up and down the beach, looking for his men, for senior officers, for some leadership and direction. His is a confused story of confusion—how could it be anything else? "Mine is an account," he says

> of one soldier's groping through the fog of battle that lay so heavily over that day, and that still conceals parts of it. To try to make this search appear systematic and well-reasoned would be entirely false. It was haphazard and followed no logical pattern; I was aware only of what was occurring immediately around me, and I moved in a constricted compartment of sight, sound, and emotion.

Inland, the paratroopers were even more scattered and constricted. Dropped into darkness, often in the wrong place, they

found themselves alone or with a few other troopers, in a dark
maze of Norman hedgerows, not knowing where they were or
in what direction they should move. Here is one such soldier,
just landed at midnight:

> Small private wars erupted to the right and left, near and
> far, most of them lasting from fifteen minutes to half an
> hour, with anyone's guess being good as to who the victors
> were. The heavy hedgerow country muffled the sounds,
> while the night air magnified them. It was almost impos-
> sible to tell how far away the fights were and sometimes
> even in what direction. The only thing I could be sure of
> was that a lot of men were dying in this nightmarish
> labyrinth. During this time I had no success in finding
> anyone, friend or foe. To be crawling up and down
> hedgerows, alone, deep in enemy country with a whole
> ocean between yourself and the nearest allies sure makes a
> man feel about as lonely as a man can get.

In this strange battle of lost, uncertain, isolated men, the
usual acts and emotions of war occurred: men felt (and confessed) fear, killed, saw their first dead friends and enemies,
acted bravely, died. In all that it was like any battle. What was
different, as the tellers tell it, was the *scale* of the confusion and
of the destruction. We've seen the anti-landscapes of other wars
and battles; this one is marked, in men's memories, by the
extent of the battle wreckage, and the amount of it that was
wrecked machines. Cawthon was sent, on the second day of the
assault, to where the exit from the beach met the coastal road:

> There is a dreadful sameness to such scenes: fragments of
> torn metal, masonry, vegetation, and bodies. The smell is of
> burned explosive, oil, cloth, wood, metal, flesh—a combina-
> tion of odors that never clears the memory. All of these ele-
> ments crowded the scene at Vierville, for the shells had hit
> into a jam of vehicles tailgating up from the beach, tearing

and throwing them about. The wounded had been removed, but the dead were still there.

Dead machines, dead men: interchangeable parts. Another man, a tank gunner moving inland from Caen, saw a desolate, pitted lunar landscape that stirred the war-in-his-head; it was

> country fought over and destroyed like the Somme or Passchendaele battlefields of the Great War. Pocked with shellholes. . . . Scarred with slit trenches. Littered with shattered vehicles and instruments of war. Studded with shredded trees and crumbled houses. Sullied above all by the stench of unburied dead, animal and human. The stench creeps in through the periscope fittings like a live, breathing fog.

As the invasion went on, Normandy became that anti-landscape, littered with the used-up materials of a machine war—tanks, trucks, crashed gliders, guns—and with graves and unburied bodies, the whole scene a testimony that this last chapter of the war in Europe would be won by sheer multitudinousness, both of men and of the machines they fought with (one machine for each three men, according to the D-day statistics I quoted above). That fact was most clear to the men who fought in the confined spaces around the beachheads, where everything the Allies had was thrown against the enemy, and then thrown away.

Once Normandy had been made secure, the story of the war's last chapter changed again. From this point on, it would be a war of swift, large movements, interrupted by counter-attacks and delaying actions and by some bitter pauses, as at Arnhem and Bastogne, when the war machine stopped for a time. You will get a sense of what that war of movement was like from the journal of a Canadian infantryman, Donald Pearce. Pearce came ashore in Normandy in September 1944 and moved north. The map in his book marks his northeastward advance: Caen, September 5; Desvres, September 11; Ambleteuse (near Calais), October 4; Ghent, November 5; Knocke-sur-Mer, November 13; Wyler (in the Reichswald), November 22; Niel, December 18; Goch, February 10; Udem, March 3; Zutphen (in the Netherlands), April 3. Ten positions in seven months, and always forward, toward the heart of Germany.

As the advance proceeded, against weakening German resistance, it became, men said, "a cushy war." In France and Belgium and the Netherlands the conquering troops were welcomed by the liberated people with wine and kisses and cheering, and they responded by sharing their rations and giving their chocolate to children, and even in one story arranging a child's birthday party. By the time they entered Germany, "a relaxed air extended to the front," Cawthon wrote:

> Losses for the past month had been low, and, with heavy traffic returning from hospital, the ranks were full. This, combined with certainty of victory, the promise of spring, and the satisfaction of campaigning in the enemy's country and having access to his possessions, gave a pleasant aspect to the war. The few jeeps and weapons carriers allotted an infantry battalion became so laden with "trophies" that their weapons cargo was smothered.

Your enemy's possessions are yours: that's a soldier's creed. There was good looting in Germany.

Narratives of this relentless advance ought to be full of excitement and self-satisfaction and the smell of victory. But on the whole they aren't. Why not? Perhaps because it was a different Allied army that fought in those last months, a new army of inexperienced men, many of them conscripts, some of them, at least, without enthusiasm for the war they'd been dragged to. Narrators mention stragglers, and Paris was said to be full of deserters, and troops in the line seem, from tellers' anecdotes, to have been less soldierly, less keen to kill Germans, than their predecessors had been. Donald Pearce tells of an incident on the Rhine on Christmas Day:

> Today, just before noon, Fraser, a slightly odd-ball rifle-man in the platoon, who is somewhat given to fits of rashness, slipped out of our company area unnoticed; when he was finally pointed out to me, he was half a mile away, silhouetted against the white fields, loitering near the riveredge, unarmed, head down, hands in pockets, making a deliberate target of himself for German snipers just across the river. He came back an hour or so later; said he had exchanged waves and other greetings with several Germans on the other bank, and that they tossed their hats into the air and threw snowballs at him, like schoolchildren, and displayed no interest in shooting at him.

It's like the Christmas Day truce of 1914, when nobody fired on the Western Front. But what kind of war is *that*? One can't construct a theory on a single story, but this one suggests what other narratives confirm, that the will to make war had weakened among the troops as the war in Europe approached its end.

The army of the enemy was different too. American and British soldiers looked at the dead and the prisoners of war and saw too-young faces, sixteen-year-olds, fourteen-year-olds, even younger: they were fighting *children*! They were also still fighting seasoned veterans, SS and Panzer troops, but there weren't enough of those old fighters left, or enough supplies for them, to win battles; the German army had become a retreating, surrendering, last-stand-fighting force. American officers told stories of German execution squads patrolling behind their own lines and hanging soldiers caught away from their units. That may or may not have been true—I don't know—but the stories capture the Allied sense of the spirit of the other side. By then the war had been won and lost; yet it went on, and perhaps that is why the narratives of the end are shadowed. Maybe the excitement and pleasure of war are in the undetermined contest.

As with other war theaters' stories, those of the Northwest Europe campaign don't all end with the last shot. Men were wounded and were sent back to England, or they became exhausted by war and were relieved (there were plenty of replacements now). Usually their stories end when their personal wars end, short of victory, with tired men relieved to be out of the fighting and alive. But even the narratives of men who stayed in the war to the end aren't very celebratory. Douglas Sutherland, generally a lighthearted teller in the manner of Verney and Bowlby, is gloomy as he rolls into Germany on his last page: "It was," he says, "an immensely depressing experience." Cawthon is not much more cheerful:

> We were still in the assembly area on 5 May, when complete German surrender was announced and Victory in Europe proclaimed. The 2nd Battalion's reaction was not boisterous: Truck horns were sounded, a few rifle shots were fired in the air, and there was tapping of German wine stocks. In general, though, the foot soldier's reaction was subdued and, it seems to me, in keeping with the mood in which he fought the war: conviction, determination, unstinted effort, no little courage and sacrifice—and little exultation.

That, I think, is as near as you will get to the voice of the Good War, there at the end of the European fighting. Cawthon still believed in the virtues of his men and his cause. But he wasn't exultant.

I'm aware that I've been writing about Second World War memoirs as though that war was fought entirely in Europe and North Africa. For many Europeans it was, and one sometimes has to

remind them that the war was in fact *two* wars, fought on opposite sides of the earth, wars that began at different times, more
than two years apart, and ended at different times.

The war in the Pacific and Southeast Asia was a vast one,
fought both on the largest scale, in the great fleet-hunting carrier battles, and on the smallest, a few thousand men fighting
for a coral island or a jungle clearing scarcely large enough to
hold them. But when I think about the battles fought out there,
I conclude that what was most different about them, compared
to the battles and campaigns in Europe and North Africa, was
their utter remoteness from the continents, the history, the civi-
lizations that men from Western nations knew. In North Africa
you went back to rest in Cairo or Alexandria, where an ancient
Mediterranean culture began; if you flew in the RAF or the
Eighth Air Force you returned to England from your missions,
to cities and villages with a history that was part of your own; in
Italy you marched through the classical past, and if you were
foresighted, like Raleigh Trevelyan, you took a Baedeker with
you; the armies of the Normandy invasion moved north past the
great battle sites of French and English history, Crécy and Agin-
court and the Somme.

The Pacific war wasn't like that: Southeast Asia and the
islands were remote, exotic places where everything was different, where the people had brown or yellow skins and spoke
strange languages, and where the landscapes were hostile to
Westerners. Amid all that strangeness there were colonial cities,
where Westerners had lived comfortable colonial lives, but they
don't figure in the stories much; once Singapore and Manila fell
war moved away from those patches of civility, to the jungles
and the islands. Out there the war life was all there was: no history was visible, no monuments of the past, no cities remembered from books. There was nothing there to remind a soldier
of his other life: no towns, no bars, nowhere to go, nowhere
even to desert to. Reading narratives of the jungle campaigns
one occasionally comes upon a village or a plantation or a native

hut, but the general sense they give is not of the imposed order of human occupation, but of a green and threatening mystery.

The island battles seem, in memory, even emptier. On those scattered outcrops of rock and coral there had been communities, though they were different from anything Western soldiers knew; but they were fragile, and war had obliterated them. Okinawa, where I fought, had had an ancient culture, but it had simply been erased from the earth by the bombing and shelling of the American attacking forces. In Naha, the principal city, only a single wall remained upright; Shuri Castle, the island's great medieval fortress, was a pile of rubble; and the native people—such as had survived the bombs and shells of the invasion—had been herded into camps, where American troops didn't see them. The island I saw wasn't a human habitation with a society and a past; it was only a place to fight a battle, where everything that was intact and recognizable had been brought ashore by the invading Americans.

So the narratives of the Pacific war, though they have their civilian-soldier voices, have less of another kind of civilianness, the sense that the war was being fought in a human place, where a local life had been lived that was domestic and ordinary and like life back home, until it was entered and damaged and disrupted by war, by *us*. "A destroyed city is a terrible sight," Donald Pearce wrote, recalling his entry into the Belgian city of Xanten. "How can anyone record it?—the million smashed things, the absolutely innumerable tiny tragedies, the crushed life-works, the jagged homes, army tanks parked in living-rooms—who could tell of these things I don't know; they are too numerous to mention, too awful in their meanings." The Pacific war didn't move men to such identification with the civilian victims of war and their smashed lives.

The difference is evident in the narratives of that war. Consider, as an example, one of the best of its kind, E. B. Sledge's *With the Old Breed at Peleliu and Okinawa*. Sledge fought as a marine infantryman in two of the bitterest of the island battles.

In the first, at Peleliu, sixteen thousand marines fought ten thousand Japanese for an island six miles long and two miles wide. Sledge's account of the battle is deep in details, yet he mentions nothing that is not either natural terrain or a military installation; there are no villages, no buildings, no civilians, and no loot—only an airfield, pillboxes, caves, rocks, underbrush, swamps. Everything is battlefield, and every action is battle. In his account of his thirty days there, nothing happens except fighting, killing, and dying: it is personal war of an intensity beyond any other narrative I know.

Okinawa, where Sledge's second battle was fought, was a much bigger island than Peleliu, but it is not much different in Sledge's story. When he first went ashore, there were signs of a traditional rural society: small fields and gardens, an empty farmhouse, a few Okinawans, a horse. But as he fought, those signs were erased from the landscape, and it became as strange and empty as the moon, or Peleliu. Here is Sledge's view of the battlefield from Half Moon Hill below Shuri Castle, late in the operation:

As far as I could see, an area that previously had been a low grassy valley with a picturesque stream meandering through it was a muddy, repulsive, open sore on the land. The place was choked with the putrefaction of death, decay, and destruction. In a shallow defilade to our right, between my gun pit and the railroad, lay about twenty dead marines, each on a stretcher and covered to his ankles with a poncho—a commonplace, albeit tragic, scene to every veteran. Those bodies had been placed there to await transport to the rear for burial. At least those were covered from the torrents of rain that had made them miserable in life and from the swarms of flies that sought to hasten their decay. But as I looked about, I saw that other Marine dead couldn't be tended to properly. The whole area was pocked with shell craters and churned up by explosions. Every crater was half full of water, and many of them held a

Marine corpse. The bodies lay pathetically just as they had been killed, half submerged in muck and water, rusting weapons still in hand. Swarms of flies hovered about them.

This was once a landscape; now it's an anti-landscape, a space that can be defined only in terms of war's destructions—the bodies and the shell craters. There are no living creatures, no human habitations, no cultivated fields, not a tree or a road or a fence. Only the railroad suggests that peaceable human beings might once have lived here. In its devastation it resembles the anti-landscape of the Somme; but with a difference. A mile or two behind the lines on the Somme, there were towns and fields untouched by the war, where a man might go to find ordinary life much like what he had known at home; there was no such place, no such life, on Okinawa.

One other element in the Pacific war is important for the story: that is the feelings that the men who fought the Japanese, on the ground and hand-to-hand, had for their enemies. Sledge describes those feelings, and the consequences:

The attitudes held toward the Japanese by non-combatants or even sailors or airmen often did not reflect the deep personal resentment felt by Marine infantrymen. Official histories and memoirs of Marine infantrymen written after the war rarely reflect that hatred. But at the time of battle, Marines felt it deeply, bitterly, and as certainly as danger itself. To deny this hatred or make light of it would be as much a lie as to deny or make light of the esprit de corps or the intense patriotism felt by the Marines with whom I served in the Pacific.

My experiences on Peleliu and Okinawa made me believe that the Japanese held mutual feelings for us. They were a fanatical enemy; that is to say, they believed in their cause with an intensity little understood by many post-war Americans—and possibly many Japanese, as well.

This collective attitude, Marine and Japanese, resulted

in savage, ferocious fighting with no holds barred. This was not the dispassionate killing seen on other fronts or in other wars. This was a brutish, primitive hatred, as characteristic of the horror of war in the Pacific as the palm trees and the islands. To comprehend what the troops endured then and there, one must take into full account this aspect of the nature of the Marines' war.

This fierce hatred is not to be explained away as simply the feeling of the soldiers of one race for the soldiers of another. No doubt that was part of it; but there were other, more immediate reasons. The Marines saw their enemies as different from themselves in two fundamental, fearful ways. One difference was that the Japanese fought suicidally, without any evident sense of self-preservation, and this meant that they would attack in banzai charges, or would infiltrate Marine lines at night armed only with a bayonet, to kill and be killed. No American soldier would do that, nor any Briton or Frenchman or German, or could even imagine doing it; such behavior came out of a state of mind that seemed so alien as not to be human.

The other difference was their cruelty and brutality. History provides plenty of evidence of that: in the rape of Nanking, the treatment of Korean women, the prisoner-of-war camps. Sledge saw it in another form, close up, on Peleliu:

As we moved past the defilade, my buddy groaned, "Jesus!" I took a quick glance into the depression and recoiled in revulsion and pity at what I saw. The bodies were badly decomposed and nearly blackened by exposure. This was to be expected of the dead in the tropics, but these Marines had been mutilated hideously by the enemy. One man had been decapitated. His head lay on his chest; his hands had been severed from his wrists and also lay on his chest near his chin. In disbelief I stared at the face as I realized that the Japanese had cut off the dead Marine's penis and stuffed it into his mouth. The corpse next to him had been treated similarly. The third had been butchered, chopped up like a carcass torn by some predatory animal.

If this ghastly flourish of Battlefield Gothic were from some document of the First World War, I would dismiss it as propaganda, the work of a civilian in London or Paris, stirring up the people against the Hun. But I believe this, because it is an eyewitness account, and because I trust Sledge's honest directness. It explains what was most special about his war—its hatred.

You will find that hatred in memoirs of many Asian and Pacific battles, wherever British or American troops met the Japanese: in Malaya, Burma, in the Philippines, and in the prisoner-of-war camps (of which I will have more to say in a later chapter). It is a hatred that has endured, untempered by time, in many men's minds. A striking example is the British novelist George MacDonald Fraser, author of the much-admired Flashman novels. Fraser wrote *Quartered Safe Out Here*, his recollection of the war in Burma, fifty years after the events he records. Here are some of his comments on the enemy he faced there:

> Putting a grenade into a bunker [full of Japanese soldiers] had the satisfaction of doing grievous bodily harm to an enemy for whom I felt real hatred, and still do....

> No one underestimated Jap: he might be a subhuman creature who tortured and starved prisoners of war to death, raped women captives, and used civilians for bayonet practice, but there was no braver soldier in the whole history of war, and if he fought to a finish ...

> As to the Japanese of fifty years ago, there is no question that he was viewed in an entirely different light from our European enemies. Would the atomic bomb have been dropped on Berlin, Rome, or Vienna? No doubt newspaper reports and broadcasts had encouraged us, civilians and

military, to regard him as an evil, misshapen, buck-toothed barbarian who looked and behaved like something sub–Stone Age; the experiences of Allied prisoners of war demonstrated that the reports had not lied and reinforced the view that the only good Jap was a dead one. And we were right, then.

A gifted, intelligent, sophisticated writer remembers back over half a century, and the enemy he remembers is still evil and sub-human, still "Jap." The hatred he expresses is not just a feeling; it's a fact of the Asian war, it's history.

There was another war in the Pacific, which was interwoven with the island war and yet was distinct and had its own story— the naval war, which began at Pearl Harbor and effectively ended in May 1945, with the sinking of the *Yamato*, Japan's largest and last battleship. That war—so huge, so scattered, and so costly in lives and ships—what was it like? One might try to answer that essential question by comparing the sea war to the wars in other theaters that we've been considering. It was, first of all, like the desert war—a war, that is, of maneuvering in a great empty space, a war of enemy-hunting and attacking, only much larger, infinitely expanded. It was like the European air war too, in a way, in that it was fought in both large and small machines. In the largest vessels, the battleships and the carriers, no individual could possible have felt in control of his own fate, whereas in the smallest—the PT boats, for example—the com-mander at least might be persuaded that his actions were freer and self-determined. Submarines seem to have felt both like fighters and like bombers, depending on the circumstances. Like fighters, they were hunters; but like bombers, they were also the hunted, and at such times, as they lay silent and motion-less upon the ocean floor while depth charges exploded around them, their crews must have felt the same helpless fatalism that bomber crews felt over Ploesti or Berlin.

The sea war was like the island war, in the sense that it was a

war fought in isolation. A fighting ship is a closed society, like
an attacking force on a small island—separate and entire. Within
itself it is complete; outside it there is only the indifferent emptiness of the sea, nowhere to go, *no elsewhere*. To a landsman (like
me), that shipboard life seems one that would induce claustro-
phobia and agoraphobia at the same time, a world at once too
small and too vast.

Among the capital ships, the ones that figured most importantly and dramatically in the Pacific war were the carriers; the
two crucial naval battles—Midway and the Coral Sea—were both
carrier battles. Those battles have two quite distinct stories:
what happened on board the ships—the defensive story—
and what happened in the air—the offensive part. In the pilots'
stories there is freedom of action: fighter pilots choose their
opponents, dive-bombers choose their targets. But for the crews
of the carriers the story is different; their ships were targets of
attacks against which individuals could do very little except
endure. Every man must do his duty, Lord Nelson said; but
whatever he does, if he is aboard a ship in battle, he cannot save
his own life, and over his efforts there must hang a heavy
fatalism.

Consider, first, the pilots' war. It was much like the European
war of the fighter planes. Carrier-based planes were small, compared to the four-engined monsters, the B-17s and B-24s and
B-29s, that the bombing squadrons flew. They were single-
engined and maneuverable, and held at most a crew of three,
and though they attacked in squadrons, the pilots had considerable freedom of action to choose their targets, and attacked
individually. Every naval pilot's memoir that I have seen is first
person singular when it comes to the point of combat, in the
same way that Battle of Britain memoirs are (and the memoirs
of tank officers, too). In the air above the enemy's fleet, the
spirit was every man for himself.

There was one difference, though, between the European air
war and the war that was fought in the air above the Pacific: that

is the feeling that comes from flying in an empty sky over an empty, endless ocean. Out there, the enemy had first to be found—a cluster of ships somewhere in all that space; and after the attack the planes had to find their way home, to another ship cluster somewhere over the horizon, and reach their own carrier while they still had fuel enough to land—if the carrier was still afloat, after the enemy's attack. It was a flying war of intense insecurity and uncertainty, as fearful as the European bombers' war, but different—emptier, more remote from any familiar, comfortable thing, and with its own special kind of fear: where is safety, in all this space? Why fly one way rather than another? What will happen to me if I don't find the ship? There ought to be a psychological name for this sense of a self astray in vastness: the speck-in-space syndrome—will that do? It was a powerful and upsetting part of the air war at sea.

And the man below, the ordinary sailor on the carrier in battle—what about him? For that story, there is no better source than Alvin Kernan's *Crossing the Line*—an extraordinary book, written fifty years after the events it describes but as sharply detailed as any contemporary account could be. Kernan was an ordnance man on the *Hornet* when it was sunk in the battle of Santa Cruz, near Guadalcanal; later he served on the *Enterprise* and was a gunner in torpedo planes. Kernan's job on the *Hornet* was to arm the carrier's planes; once they were launched, he had nothing to do until they returned except wait for the planes of the Japanese task force, which the *Hornet*'s planes were attacking, to attack the *Hornet* in return. Here is his account of what happened when they arrived:

> In the ordnance shack, just below the flight deck, we could see nothing, only listen, feel the vibrating steel deck, and slide back and forth with the steep turns of the ship that came in quick succession. When the new 20-millimeter guns spaced along the catwalks began their continuous rapid firing, we knew the attack had commenced and that

the dive-bombers were coming down and the torpedo planes—for the Japanese still used them to deliver with deadly accuracy the big blows—were making their runs at water level. . . .

Then, just up the passageway, past the dive-bomber ready rooms, near the admiral's quarters, there was a huge explosion. A bright red flame came like an express train down the passageway, knocking everything and everybody flat. A Japanese plane, hit, had suicidally crashed the signal bridge and then ricocheted into and through the flight deck just forward of the area where we were sitting. Its bombs rolled around and did not go off, but its gas tanks had exploded. We got up and ran to the other, after, end of the passageway and by a ladder there up onto the flight deck. . . .

But the flight deck was afire, and so the men returned to the hangar deck below, in time to see a Japanese torpedo plane crash through the ship.

It had already done tremendous damage when it crashed into the gun sponsons on the bow of the ship. . . . One of the compartments he hit on his way through the ship was a blanket storage, and his plane had set the blankets afire and scattered them burning and smoldering the length of the hangar deck. The navy had fine white blankets with blue bands—these were officers' blankets—and the smell of burning wool mixed with fuel oil remains my dominant sense impression of the day.

It's an extraordinary scene. Here are men under attack and threatened with death, yet they can do nothing but run from deck to deck and witness the destruction of their ship. Where is *courage* here? What would it mean, there on the burning hangar deck, to be *brave*? Even Marc Bloch's minimal definition, of standing without trembling, seems irrelevant: what difference would it make if these men stood? It isn't that they are cowards;

they aren't: in Kernan's story he is courageous whenever circumstances allow him to be. It's simply that such terms don't
apply to this situation. What we see here is an extreme case of a
modern circumstance of war: absolute helplessness in the face
of a violence too huge to oppose, the condition in which
fighting men become victims.

And the dead in this inferno?

Among the burning and smoldering blankets dotted about
the deck were bodies, some terribly burned, others dismembered, some appearing unharmed. The burns were the
worst to see, huge blisters oozing fluid, the tight charred
smelly flesh, the member sometimes projecting as if
straining for some final grotesque sexual act.

In the war at sea, as in so much of modern war, the enemies
you kill die invisibly and at a distance; ships sink beyond the
horizon and men drown, planes are shot from the sky and sink
into the sea. But your own dead are near at hand, to be seen,
and smelled, and dumped over the side, with the rest of the
wreckage.

For the Japanese, the naval war in the Pacific ended in defeat
and, on the way to defeat, suicide. First there were the kamikaze
pilots, who volunteered to crash their planes into enemy ships.
These suicide attacks began in late 1944, when it seemed clear
that Japan had lost its war. They couldn't make any difference
in the outcome, and they didn't; their goal, as it appears to a
Westerner, was not victory but death—death in war, death with
honor. As the Japanese defeat became more certain the following spring, with the invasion of Okinawa, the kamikazes
increased in numbers. Now they were conscripts, inexperienced
pilots with little flying time, flying older, often obsolete planes;
most of them were shot down before they reached their targets,
though some got through and sank or damaged ships.

What was it like to stand on the deck of a ship and see an

enemy plane approaching and know that the pilot intended to fly straight at you until his plane struck your ship, and plane and ship, pilot and you, all exploding into nothing? Many men who were there have told us how it was. This example is from James J. Fahey's *Pacific War Diary.* Fahey's ship, the cruiser *Montpelier,* is under air attack in Leyte Gulf, late in November 1944; Fahey is at his post on a gun mount:

> ... exploding planes overhead were showering us with their parts. It looked like it was raining plane parts. They were falling all over the ship.... The men on my mount were also showered with parts of Jap planes. One suicide dive bomber was heading right for us while we were firing at other attacking planes and if the 40mm. mount behind us on the port side did not blow the Jap wing off it would have killed all of us. When the wing was blown off it, the plane turned some and bounced off into the water and the bombs blew part of the plane onto our ship. Another suicide plane crashed into one of the 5 inch mounts, pushing the side of the mount in and injuring some of the men inside.... A Jap dive bomber crashed into one of the 40mm. mounts but lucky for them it dropped its bombs on another ship before crashing. Parts of the plane flew everywhere when it crashed into the mount. Part of the motor hit Tomlinson, he had chunks of it all over him, his stomach, back, legs, etc.... The explosions were terrific as the suicide planes exploded in the water not too far away from our ship. The water was covered with black smoke that rose high into the air. The water looked like it was on fire.

A naval battle in which the sky rains airplane fragments and the sea is on fire is a new kind of war strangeness. But stranger, I think, is what happened then.

> Parts of destroyed suicide planes were scattered all over the ship. During a little lull in the action the men would

look around for Jap souvenirs and what souvenirs they were. I got part of the plane. The deck near my mount was covered with blood, guts, brains, tongues, scalps, hearts, arms, etc. from the Jap pilots. One of the Marines cut the ring off the finger of one of the dead pilots. They had to put the hose on to wash the blood off the deck. The deck ran red with blood. The Japs were spattered all over the place. One of the fellows had a Jap scalp, it looked just like you skinned an animal. The hair was black, cut very short, and the color of the skin was yellow, real Japanese. I do not think he was very old. I picked up a tin pie plate with a tongue on it. The pilot's tooth mark was into it very deep. It was very big and long, it looked like part of his tonsils and throat were attached to it. It also looked like the tongue you buy in the meat store. This was the first time I ever saw a person's brains, what a mess. One of the men on our mount got a Jap rib and cleaned it up, he said his sister wants part of a Jap body. One fellow from Texas had a knee bone and he was going to preserve it in alcohol from the sick bay. The Jap bodies were blown into all sorts of pieces.

A different shower—of human body parts—covers the ship's deck. What is most interesting is the tone of Fahey's response. War has just done something unimaginable, and Fahey is astonished by the sight—but he is not appalled, not moved by the presence of human dead. The dead Japanese pilots remain fragments, all sorts of pieces, souvenirs.

These episodes, the attack and the scene on deck afterward, are strange, but once told about them, we find them comprehensible; in the same situations, we might react the way Fahey did, be excited by the exploding planes and curious at the ways in which a body can disintegrate. Fahey is an imaginable witness. But what about those other men, the kamikaze pilots themselves? Their thoughts and emotions seem beyond imagining, off the scale of what we might do. And how can we ever

know, anyway? For surely, given their vocation, they couldn't
leave their war narratives; how can you write a memoir of your
own suicide? But there is one book, at least, written by a young
Japanese who was conscripted as a suicide pilot but never quite
reached the point where plane and target met. When I read
Ryuji Nagatsuka's *I Was a Kamikaze*, I found that we were much
alike, two university students interested in Western literature,
both pilots—I on Okinawa, he a thousand miles north—both
twenty years old when the war ended, each anxious to do his
job and to survive. If we had met, I thought, I'd probably have
liked him. But I wouldn't have understood his willingness to
die, as it were, against his will. And I wouldn't have known how
to decide whether his commitment to death was an act of
courage or something more mysterious and less creditable.

I've mentioned another kind of suicide: the sinking of the
Yamato. Its commander took his ship out of port in May 1945
and headed south for Okinawa, without fighter cover and
without hope. American navy planes found the ship in midocean
and attacked in wave after wave with bombs and torpedoes; and
there the *Yamato* died, slowly, like a bull in a corrida. There is
no American account of the ship's sinking that I know of, but
there is one by a young Japanese officer who was aboard when
she went down. Mitsuru Yoshida's *Requiem for the Battleship
Yamato* tells the story of the death of a great ship; but it does
something more. It explains, not entirely but a little, the state of
mind of a people for whom defeat was not enough.

The oddest thing about the Second World War is how fragmen-
tarily and insecurely it persists in our imaginations fifty years
later, how, for all its huge drama, it is not our favorite war and
has not produced a canon of classic war books, as the First War
did. You can test the truth of that proposition very simply: make
a quick list of the great books of the First War; then list the
great ones of the Second. The first list will come quickly and
will be more or less the same for any English or American

reader: *All Quiet on the Western Front, Good-bye to All That, Memoirs of an Infantry Officer, A Farewell to Arms,* Owen's poems. The second list will come slowly, if it comes at all, and will have no uniformity from reader to reader. The canon of the Second War does not exist.

Why is that? Perhaps because it was simply too big, with too many different battles, on too many battlefields, too many stories that will not merge and meld, as those of the Western Front did, into a single tale. Or maybe because it was the *Second* World War, a vast event but a repeated one, a footnote to be carved on the First War's memorial stones, something else to be remembered on Armistice Day.

Or maybe it was that this war was not a disillusioning one, but remained to the end a Good War. That doesn't mean that the men who fought in it didn't feel anger and frustration at the *ways* in which it was fought and at the follies and stupidities of their leaders. There were failures of intelligence and errors of judgment, inadequate supplies and incompetent commanders; men died under friendly fire, or in defense of indefensible positions, or attacking impregnable ones. Read Terence O'Brien's *Chasing After Danger,* an RAF pilot's recollections of the defense of Singapore, written nearly fifty years after the city fell but still full of fierce anger at "the idiots who commanded us"; read Elmer Bendiner on the Schweinfurt raid.

Still, the ground bass of the soldiers' tale of the Second War remains an affirmation. Men who fought in it, in even the fiercest fighting, didn't regret their service, either at the time or later. O'Brien didn't, Bendiner didn't. One of Fergusson's Chindits, deep in the Burmese jungle, said: "Well, this may be hell, but I wouldn't have missed even this part of the trip"; and George MacDonald Fraser, remembering his part of the Burma campaign, wrote: "Glad I was there; I wouldn't have missed it for anything." And Eugene Sledge, veteran of two terrible Pacific island battles, could end his narrative with these sober words:

Until the millennium arrives and countries cease trying to enslave others, it will be necessary to accept one's responsibilities and to be willing to make sacrifices for one's country—as my comrades did. As the troops used to say, "If the country is good enough to live in, it's good enough to fight for." With privilege goes responsibility.

Those are recruiting office feelings, an ordinary young man's reasons for enlisting; they were still intact in him at the end, after all the killing.

There have been attempts in recent years to impose the tone of the First War's tale on the Second War and argue that they were essentially the same. Here, as an example, is the physicist Freeman Dyson, in his *Weapons and Hope* (1984):

The two world wars seemed totally different to the people who fought in them and lived through them from day to day, but they begin to look more and more alike as they recede into history. The first war began with the trumpet blowing of Rupert Brooke and ended with the nightmares of Wilfred Owen. The second war began with the mourning of Day Lewis [Dyson has been quoting Cecil Day Lewis's poem about the Spanish Civil War, "The Nabara"] and ended with the anger of Jimmy Porter [the bitter young man in John Osborne's *Look Back in Anger*]. In both wars, the beginning was young men going out to fight for freedom in a mood of noble self-sacrifice, and the end was a technological bloodbath which seemed in retrospect meaningless.... In both wars, history proved that those who fight for freedom with the technologies of death end by living in fear of their own technology.

Because Dyson was writing a cautionary book about nuclear weapons, and because he was writing at the end of the Cold War era, it suited his ends to make all modern wars alike. But he was wrong, in many ways, in his hasty identification of the two world wars: wrong about the mood in which young men went to war; wrong about their moods at the end; foolishly wrong to base his arguments on the literary works of four writers, only one of whom had any experience of fighting. One is in a delicate position, quarreling with such a learned man who is taking such high moral ground. But we must seek better sources than Dyson's for the real tales of the two world wars—we must look to the men who were there. They tell us that the wars were different in fundamental ways, and they show us what the differences were.

One difference is in the ways they ended. The First War ended in a traditional way, in a steady battering advance by the Allied armies, which forced the Germans at last to unconditional surrender (though as I said, the soldiers' stories don't usually terminate so neatly). The Second War wasn't like that; imaginatively, its progress toward inevitable victory was interrupted and altered by two events that brought at the end a shock-wave of suffering: in the late winter and early spring of 1945, Allied troops liberated the Nazi death camps; and on August 6th a B-29 of the United States Air Force dropped the first atomic bomb on Hiroshima.

The immediate effect of the atom bomb on the story of the Pacific war was obvious and apparent; suddenly and unexpectedly, the war was simply called off. There would be no invasion of Japan, no great conclusive battle, no victory won by hard fighting. Many soldiers serving around the world believed they were committed to take part in that last assault; troops in Europe and in the United States, as well as those scattered across the Pacific islands, *all* believed they'd be in it and that the casualties would be terrible. (If every ex-soldier who will still tell you that his outfit was scheduled for the invasion force had actually hit the Japanese beaches, there wouldn't have been space for them all to stand.) There was relief among those men, that it was all over and they were still alive; but there was also a kind of disappointment, a letdown. The proper fighting end of the story had been cut off; there would be no final curtain to their drama.

The liberation of the camps, insofar as it enters the European war narratives, had a less obvious effect. The story didn't change—Germany still had to be entered and defeated. Only the tone changed, and the sense of what the enemy had all along been like.

The effects of these two events were profound: with them, the nature of what was possible in war changed. Imaginations that had managed to comprehend two world wars would have to extend their capacities to encompass new meanings of power and of evil; there would have to be new war stories, the stories of the victims.

CHAPTER FIVE

What Happened in Nam

The story of the Vietnam War is a cautionary tale for our time, the war story that can teach us most. World wars are in the past now, or so it seems; but intervention for political reasons in other nations' revolutions and civil wars—these are still possible. And recent history tells us they are likely to end in humiliation and withdrawal. But for the people of the United States, the Vietnam War is more than a lesson in political unwisdom. It lingers in American minds like the memory of an illness, a kind of fever that weakened the country until its people were divided and its cause was lost. That fever is in the narratives Americans have written about the war, and it makes their soldiers' tale different from the tales of other modern wars—not simply because the United States lost, though that had not happened before, but because in the loss there was humiliation and bitterness and the burden of complicity in a nation's moral failure.

It didn't begin like that. Young Americans enlisted in the beginning for the same reasons they had gone to fight in other wars: because their leaders told them it was right to go; out of patriotism; out of curiosity ("I enlisted because I wanted to see what a war was like"); to fight an evil force in the world ("we believed we were ordained to play cop to the Communists' robber"); to gain respect ("I wanted to be a man of honor"). That positive initial mood is easy to understand. These were the sons of men who had fought in 1941–45, and the war-in-the-head that they took with them to Vietnam was the Good War. They expected to do in Vietnam what their fathers had done in Normandy and Italy and Guadalcanal—enter a struggle on the right side, fight hard and win, and be praised for it. That didn't happen. The intervention in Vietnam stretched out to be America's longest and most unpopular war and as it continued, the faith in the good cause leaked away, and a failure of will poured in. Before it ended, the war had become an anti-war myth of national dishonor. A Bad War after a Good War: it was like a fall from grace.

You will get a sense of what that myth became from these words of Ron Kovic, a man who was there and wrote about it in a well-known memoir, *Born on the Fourth of July*. The words are not from the book, though, but from a spontaneous outburst at a conference on Vietnam war literature in 1986:

> When I saw the wall for the first time, I said, "My God, fifty-eight thousand American boys killed because of the United States Government's foreign policy." Fifty-eight thousand killed because they lied to us, because they used us, because they fed us with all this crap about John Wayne and being a hero and the romance of war and everything we watched on television. They set up my generation, they set us up for that war. They made us believe that war was going to be something glorious and something beautiful, just like they set up the veterans of World War I. The bands were playing. Everybody told us to go.

The core of the Vietnam myth that most of us know is in that angry outburst: that the war was fought not for moral but for political reasons, and wrong ones; that it exploited the innocent; that it was nourished by government lies and by the deceptions of mass culture (with the implication that government and culture were in collusion); that it split the nation into Them and Us; and that young men who were killed in it died for nothing.

There are two other elements in that conference speech that are important to the myth: "the wall"—that is, the Vietnam Veterans Memorial in Washington, with its 58,000 names, bearing none of the Big Words of war, making no gestures, but simply naming the dead—a visual symbol of the war's meaninglessness; and Kovic himself, a paraplegic, one of the war's permanently damaged men, raging from his wheelchair against the war, a man whose anger is in his injury—which They did to him.

Other veterans have protested that Kovic was not the innocent victim he imagined himself to have been; that he had served one tour of duty in Vietnam and come home, and had volunteered for a second tour, in the course of which he was wounded. He knew, they say, what the war was like. It doesn't really matter. The point is that in his story—both the written account and the spontaneous oral one—he saw himself and his fellow volunteer soldiers as victims of the war and not as its agents. That notion is an important part of the Vietnam myth—or at least of one version of it; it is fundamental to the psychiatrists' story (to which we will return) and to many representations of the war in films and novels.

It was just like World War I, Kovic said, and indeed you can hear in his words echoes of the anger that was felt by soldiers of that earlier war. Not that he borrowed his bitterness—a man paralyzed for life doesn't need to borrow—but he wasn't the first angry veteran; there already existed a literature of anger against war in the books of the First World War. The analogy he made has become a commonplace: Vietnam was to the United States what the First World War was to Britain—a war of national disillusionment that changed the way a generation thought about its country, its leaders, and war itself.

Like most commonplaces, this one is partly true and partly false. Certainly there are strong similarities between the two situations, and especially in the feeling some fighting men of both wars had that they had been betrayed by their elders, the Old Men in power who sent young men to war. But there are

also differences. There was no civilian reaction to the war in
World War One England comparable to the antiwar demonstra-
tions during the Vietnam years. When British veterans came
home in 1918 there were victory parades with flags and bands,
and a cenotaph was built in Whitehall to commemorate the Glorious Dead; nobody spat on the returning soldiers, nobody
called them baby-killers. Vietnam veterans straggled home sepa-
rately, as their year-long tours of duty ended, and were ignored
or mocked. One veteran, who had lost an arm in the war,
returned to his university campus, to this greeting:

> In the fall of 1968, as I stopped at a traffic light on my walk
> to class across the campus of the University of Denver, a
> man stepped up to me and said, "Hi."
>   Without waiting for my reply to his greeting, he pointed
> to the hook sticking out of my left sleeve. "Get that in
> Vietnam?"
>   I said, "Yeah, up near Tam Ky in I Corps."
>   "Served you right."

Narratives of the war play variations on that sad anecdote: men
come home, no one is glad, and the war goes on.

So the men who fought in Vietnam had a different sense of
betrayal from the men of the First War: they had been doubly
betrayed—by the politicians and generals, and by the war protesters of their own generation. This double betrayal informs
the Vietnam soldiers' tale and gives it its peculiarly dissonant, disappointed tone. Here is an example, from Robert Mason's *Chickenhawk*, the narrative of a helicopter pilot in Vietnam
in 1965–66. Mason is in his tent with a fellow pilot named
Connors:

> It didn't help that the anti-Vietnam-war demonstrators
> were becoming prominent in the news. With the company
> in a black mood, the protesters' remarks were so much salt
> in our wounds. No one likes being a fool. Especially if he
> finds himself risking his life to be one.

"I think I'd rather kill one of those fuckheads than a goddamn gook!" yelled Connors. He threw a magazine on the ground inside our tent. "Cocksuckers think they know everything! Did you read that?" He spoke to no one in particular. It was late, and I was up, writing a letter on my cot. "That asshole says that Ho Chi Minh was sold out by the Americans! He says that gook was once our ally and that we let a British colonel turn South Vietnam back to the French!" He stopped. I looked over. He sat on his cot in his shorts with a beer in his hand, staring angrily at the canvas wall behind me. His face calmed when he saw me. "You ever heard that before, Mason?"

"That was the first time," I said.

"Do you think it's true?" he pleaded. To him, I was an educated man, having been to college for two years.

"No," I said.

The most striking thing about that passage is surely its language; you won't find Connors's vocabulary in the memoirs of any previous war. The conventions of publishing would have prevented it, of course, but that is not the only reason for its absence. Men wrote, I think, with a sense of the dignity of war, and of soldiers, that forbade the transcription of their coarsest common speech. But for some memories of Vietnam, that language seemed a necessary part of the story: it was the idiom of the war. And notice that Connors's verbal anger is directed not at the North Vietnamese or the Vietcong but at American opponents of the war he is fighting. He has *two* enemies, and the one he hates most is the one back home, in his own country.

Another thing about this passage: Connors is angry about the *history* of the war he is in, which nobody has explained to him. All wars have their antecedent causes, no war begins with the first shot; but Vietnam was peculiar in that a war had been going on there for twenty years before United States combat troops arrived. It was a long and disgraceful story, of which the Americans were to act out the closing chapters. But what had

happened before they arrived? Could it be that they shouldn't
be there? Was their country at fault? Were they on the wrong
side? Had it perhaps *never* been a Good War? Connors is a type
of the American soldier in the Vietnam narratives: ignorant of
the history he is stuck in, confused and angered by his own generation back home, distrusting his leaders, trying to believe that
patriotism and duty are still virtues and to preserve his faith in
the good American cause, in a war that had gone wrong.

Loss of faith wasn't the only thing that was wrong about the
United States' war in Vietnam: the *army* was, wrong for a democratic nation. The Vietnam War was the first American war from
which the middle classes were substantially exempt. I asked a
lawyer friend of mine who had fought in Vietnam how many
men from his own middle class he had known there, and he
replied:

> As far as I can tell, nobody from my social class had to go.
> Nobody. People got out with endless educational defer-
> ments, by entering the proper profession (teaching was
> one), by joining the National Guard ... by pretending to
> be homosexual, dropping sugar in their urine sample and
> showing up as a diabetic, by fathering a child, by going to
> Canada or England or, in one case of a public school kid I
> grew up with, Sweden, but then he'd actually allowed him-
> self to be inducted so he had to desert to get out of going.

This is only one man's testimony; but anyone who taught in an
American college during those years, as I did, remembers the
reigning spirit of evasion. Among the students it was not considered dishonorable to avoid the draft; the dishonorable (and
stupid) thing was to go.

A nation chooses its war story when it chooses the men who
will fight its war. For the Vietnam War, the United States chose
not to send the middle-class young men who had written the
war narratives of the two world wars, but sent instead young
men from the lower end of the social ladder—the rural and

urban poor, the unemployed and unemployable, with heavy concentrations from the areas where jobs were scarce: the cities and the South. Many were from minorities, though their number has been exaggerated; of the total American forces serving in Vietnam, ten percent were black and another ten percent were Hispanic.

General Westmoreland, who commanded U.S. forces in Vietnam, added two other categories to describe that army: "category four" and criminals. "Category four," he explained in an interview, "is a dummy. You can probably make a soldier out of ten percent of him." By criminals he meant "the type of person who had been dismissed by a judge from a criminal charge if he would join the Army and go to Vietnam. And that did happen. So that introduced a weak-minded, criminal, untrained element into the Army." This is the commanding general of American forces in Vietnam speaking of his troops: we are back with Wellington and the scum of the earth. Worse, really; Westmoreland thought the deferment of college students had lowered the quality of officers too, and "that brought about the commissioning of people like Lieutenant Calley" (of the My Lai episode).

This is certainly what the myth says: that the Vietnam War was fought by an army of ill-trained, pot-smoking, drug-taking slum dwellers led by amateur, incompetent junior officers. That's the version told in postwar films of the war and in some journalistic accounts. But it isn't the story the narratives tell. Their story is that most of the men who fought were volunteers, or men who chose not to evade the draft, and that they went to the war for simple, patriotic motives, as their fathers had gone to World War II. They were ordinary young Americans—the narratives tell us that: poor, maybe, but neither criminals nor "category four." If the army degenerated, it wasn't because its soldiers were degenerates from the start; it was because the *war* degenerated.

Two other things about this army. It was young: Westmoreland said the average age of his troops was less than nineteen, as compared to an average of twenty-four in Korea and twenty-six in the Second World War. An army of eighteen-year-olds, away from home for the first time, with only a few months of training to turn them from boys into soldiers, unused to taking responsibility or making moral decisions, dropped into an alien and fearful place—what kind of army would that be? It would be an army of uncertain, frightened boys.

It was also an army of short-timers. "Short-timer" is an army term (borrowed, apparently, from prison slang) for a soldier who has only a few weeks left to serve. In Vietnam, in comparison with other American wars, everyone was a short-timer— you spent 365 days "in-country," as they put it, and were then rotated back to "the world." Washington expected a short war and didn't want a stockpile of either matériel or men when it was over. A recruit was inducted, trained, flown to Vietnam, and assigned to a combat unit, where he found himself a stranger among strangers. No one belonged to a unit for as long as a year; there couldn't possibly be any strong sense of the unit as an entity, or any collective trust. (What would the stranger next to you do in a firefight? Could you trust a boot lieutenant with perhaps less time in-country than you had to lead you into battle and out again?) So the troops counted the days from the moment they arrived, like prisoners in some foreign jail.

For these short-timers the war was a measured interval between home and home. In that situation, they were bound to hang on to their civilianness, learning the defensive rules of war—how not to get killed—but not really trying to become soldiers, not all the way through, like the regulars. They brought their civilian tastes and habits with them—their radios, their tapes, their paperbacks and their comic books—and what they didn't have the army provided. It's striking how zealously the army nurtured the back-home needs of the troops: forty-two ice cream plants were built in-country, hot meals and ice were flown in to combat landing zones, beers and Cokes were always available, and so were the latest movies. It was as though the generals had persuaded themselves that the American spirit and loyalty of the troops in the field could be sustained forever, regardless of how the war went, if only they had enough American products to consume. Those consumer goods litter the memoirs like empty beer cans along an American highway, and help to give them their characteristic dissonant note of the totally familiar in the totally strange.

Most of all, there was the music that was their generation's voice. Every soldier seemed to have his radio and his tapes, and the Armed Forces Radio was on the air to make sure that he could hear his favorite rock and roll. It was a rock-and-roll war. You can get a sense of the importance of that music to the men who were there simply by looking at the copyright credits in their published narratives: Simon and Garfunkel, Crosby, Stills and Nash, the Beatles, Bob Dylan, the Rolling Stones, Frank Zappa, Jimi Hendrix—they're all there, because their songs are part of the story. One narrator, John Ketwig, took his title from a Dylan song and dedicated his book to John Lennon. Together those songs provided the war with its own distinctive music; but they provided more than that. They offered the men who were there a rhetoric and a set of attitudes—brash, anti-establishment, often explicitly anti-war. Armies are traditionally and necessarily authoritarian and disciplined; but the music this army moved to was neither of those, was indeed the opposite.

You won't find such a rhetoric of opposition woven into the narratives of the two world wars. If there are songs at all, they are sentimental ones like "Keep the Home Fires Burning" and "We'll Meet Again," or soldiers' satires from the oral tradition, like "Hanging on the Old Barbed Wire" and "Bless 'Em All." But for this war, those back-home songs of alienation and protest were the right words: they were the war generation's own litera-ture. Listening to them, as one Vietnam veteran told me, "it was like we never left home." But home was now a troubled and divided place, as many of the songs said; and the cause of the trouble was the war.

All those comforts of home—and others too—were made extravagantly available when troops moved out of combat for R & R (rest and rehabilitation). In the combat zone, life was as difficult and as uncomfortable as in any war of this century— or so it sounds in the memoirs: worse than the Western Front (which had no malaria and no leeches), as bad as Guadal- canal (which had both). But in the towns in the safe areas, and along the China Sea beaches, and in Asian cities outside Viet- nam (if you were an officer), life was lived in a glut of American products and American comforts—beer and ice cream and hot showers. And bars. And bar girls. And venereal disease.

Of course, there have always been camp followers and brothels, and soldiers have always got drunk and got laid; we know from history about the licentious soldiery. But that side of war had not figured much in modern narratives of war until Vietnam. There is a kind of puritanism that prevails in accounts of the two world wars: partly, I suppose, because of the middle- class backgrounds of the volunteers who wrote the books, and partly because of a sense that war, and only war, was the sub- ject. There were brothels, both official and unofficial, in France during the First War, and venereal disease was a serious problem for the Allied armies; but such subjects are scarcely mentioned in the memoirs, and there are almost no reported sexual encounters.

Memoirs of the Second War also tend to ignore the sex lives of soldiers. That was sometimes more a matter of geography than morality—if you fought on the Pacific islands, for example, women weren't going to be much of a problem—but it seems also to have been a matter of moral atmosphere, in the telling if not in the doing. It was, after all, the Good War; whores would have been out of place in its story.

In Vietnam things were different: sex was everywhere—another consumer product, more readily available to nineteen-year-old soldiers than it could ever have been back home. In that small, impoverished country, many young women were willing to sell their bodies. And away from the towns, in the combat zone, there were women who could be forced into sexual acts, because soldiers had power and women had none. The ubiquity of sex is one reality that distinguishes this war from the others. There is another: that those sexual acts—so cheap, so casual, and often so violent—should be reported in the war narratives, that the sexual story should be felt to be a necessary part of the whole truth of Vietnam.

The short-timers' war in Vietnam went on for eight years, fought always by replaceable, temporary soldiers, like a football game played entirely by substitutes, who had to learn the rules of the game as they went along. The game was nothing like the war-in-their-heads that they brought with them, nothing like their fathers' war; or their grandfathers', for that matter. Every war is strange, as I've said, to the civilian-soldiers who fight it; but the strangeness is always different. In Vietnam it was the land, the people, the culture, that were strange. And the enemy too. The North Vietnamese Army didn't have the big machines that make modern armies powerful and visible—the tanks, the heavy bombers, the big artillery. In this war, masses of men and weapons would not confront each other along an established front, as in the First World War, or move swiftly in mechanized attack, as in the great campaigns of the Second. Instead the NVA fought swift, surprising local actions and then disappeared, leaving the American troops to hunt for them. And the Vietcong guerrillas moved invisibly in the dark, lying in ambush and setting land mines and booby traps, so that every bush and every path was threatening.

The narratives of the men who were there tell us what it was like to fight that kind of war:

We walk through the mines, trying to catch the Viet Cong
Forty-eighth Battalion like an unexperienced hunter after a
hummingbird. But he finds us far more often than we do
him. He is hidden among the mass of civilians or in tunnels
or in jungles. So we walk to find him, stalking the mythical,
phantomlike Forty-eighth Battalion from here to there to
here to there. And each piece of ground left behind is his
from the moment we are gone on our next hunt.

In effect, we commuted to and from the war. We went into
the bush for a day or two or three, returned for a brief rest,
and went out again. There was no pattern to these patrols
and operations. Without a front, flanks, or rear, we fought a
formless war against a formless enemy, who evaporated
like the morning mists, only to materialize in some unexpected place. It was a haphazard, episodic sort of combat.

Of course, the Americans never owned anything except the
ground they stood on. We were supposed to be winning a
war, but we didn't dare move outside our perimeters at
night.

How is a formless war, a war without a front, to be won? The
answer of the American generals was: by attrition—kill more of
the enemy's troops than they kill of yours: kill so many that they
lose the capacity and the will to fight. That had also been Marshal Haig's strategy on the Western Front in the First War; but
there was a difference. Haig's men knew who their enemies
were—they were the men in the field-gray uniforms over there
on the other side of no-man's land. Westmoreland's troops had
no such certainty; their enemies could be anybody.

If killing was the goal, then the number of enemy dead, the
daily body count, would measure the army's success. Those
numbers were very large, and if attrition had worked, the
Americans would have won the war. The North Vietnamese
Army and the Vietcong together lost nearly half a million men,
while American losses were only 58,000—plus a quarter of a mil-

lion of their South Vietnamese allies, who tend to be forgotten in the calculation. It didn't work, but the body counting went on, to be reported at home on the evening news as evidence of military success.

In that grim accounting, American soldiers couldn't readily distinguish Vietcong guerrillas from civilians, and often made no effort to do so. Civilians were killed distantly by bombs and napalm and artillery shells, and at closer range in infantry attacks on their villages; and the troops as they advanced saw the people they had killed, including the women and the children and the old. That had not happened as a usual thing in other wars: Landscape with Dead Civilians was a new image of war, which became part of the story. Here is an example, from Tobias Wolff's *In Pharaoh's Army*. The Tet offensive has just ended, and the Vietcong who for a time occupied the Delta town of My Tho have been blasted out by American artillery and bombing planes. Once the town is secure, Wolff visits it:

> The place was a wreck, still smoldering two weeks later, still reeking sweetly of corpses. The corpses were everywhere, lying in the streets, floating in the reservoir, buried and half buried in collapsed buildings, grinning, blackened, fat with gas, limbs missing or oddly bent, some headless, some burned almost to the bone, the smell so thick and foul we had to wear surgical masks scented with cologne, aftershave, deodorant, whatever we had, simply to move through town.

The aftershave and the deodorant are a good touch: products that American males use to avoid smelling bad, used here to protect them from the smell of death.

In the stories that Vietnam narrators tell, the killing, which was the point of the strategy, appears to be random, accidental, arbitrary, often brutal. The army printed up rules of engagement and distributed them among the troops; but in the field there were no rules. The enemy was invisible, or indistinguishable among civilians, and all Vietnamese looked alike to the young short-timers; how could a soldier kill in a discriminating, careful, soldierly way? And how could he avoid killing wrongfully? Robert Mason tells of a training question that was asked of all prospective grunts: What would you do if you were the driver of a truck loaded with soldiers, traveling very fast down a muddy road, flanked on both sides by steep drop-offs, and a child suddenly walked into your path? Would you try to avoid the child, and drive off the road to certain death? Or would you run over it? Everybody knew the right answer: kill the kid. Mason tells the story to illuminate his account of flying his helicopter over a village where an innocent-looking crowd of Vietnamese is bunched around a man with a machine gun. What do you do? You kill the kid. Mason's gunner machine-gunned the whole crowd.

Rod Kane has another story: An infantryman, the kind they called a "tunnel rat," is crawling through an underground Vietcong tunnel and comes to a large room at the end. He can hear voices. "I lay there," the tunnel rat says, "wondering ... The war room? Officers' quarters? Weapons room? Man, I'm gonna get me a medal!" He throws a grenade into the room. "So," Kane asks, "did you get your medal?" The tunnel rat shakes his head. "I blew up a teacher and a classroom full of kids." Those dead children are everywhere in Vietnam narratives: they become a convention, like Homeric metaphors. Many children were killed in the war; but the point is not simply a mimetic one. Every narrator selects his anecdotes and so sets the tone and makes the point of his narrative. The dead children are what Vietnam *meant* to the men who tell its story, just as the corpses of last year's dead were the meaning of the Western Front.

There are other stories of killings that were simply executions—or murders: twenty-one captives in a row, shot dead by an angry sergeant; peasants working in a field shot for target practice; an old woman killed for spitting in an officer's face.

Violent deaths: of course—war *is* violent; but also brutal deaths, and brutal in the telling. And the brutality continues even after death: bodies are dragged through the narratives—maimed, dismembered, violated, hideous, stinking bodies. And body parts.

One might explain the omnipresence of the dead as a necessary consequence of the American policy of attrition; if the score is what matters, then you must have bodies to count, even if they arrive in pieces, like the Vietcong soldiers in Frederick Downs's *The Killing Zone*, who have blown themselves up with their own land mine:

> There were three penises, two complete faces, which looked like masks they were so complete, five soles of feet, three hands, and a few other parts. The largest body part was a section of a rib cage with parts of four rib bones connected to a small section of the shoulder.

But the need to count bodies doesn't explain what Downs's men did with them. One stood a dismembered hand upright in the soft earth and placed a cigarette between two of its fingers. "It looked great," Downs says.

> It looked like someone lying underground had paused in the motion of moving his cigarette from his mouth to his side. Everyone took pictures of this bizarre construction. We never thought it was ghoulish.

Why not? It *is* ghoulish. But acts like this one were evidently common among American troops, so common that the ugliness ceased to be apparent. Soldiers dishonored the enemy dead, cut off their ears and strung them on strings for souvenirs, spit on them, urinated on them, preserved their skulls as ornaments. These degradations are told in detail in the narratives; they make the story barbaric and the Battlefield Gothic horrible. But they also make it commonplace.

Though before we generalize too quickly about the

particular ugliness of the Vietnam War, we should remember that mutilation of the dead has been part of military behavior from the beginning of wars. If you kill your enemy, his body belongs to you, it's part of the loot: that seems to have been taken for granted since the Philistines cut off Saul's head and fastened his body to the wall of Beth-shan. Certainly it was the view of some Americans during the Second World War—in the Pacific theater, that is; I never heard of a GI cutting a souvenir off a German or an Italian corpse, but I flew with a Marine captain who kept a Japanese ear in his pocket. And in 1944 *Life* magazine, that arbiter of popular opinion, could print a photograph of a pretty American girl with a "Jap skull" on her desk, a souvenir from a boy-friend in the Pacific.

Nevertheless, stories like these are a marked feature of Vietnamese narratives. What was it that made this war so brutal and so savage? Perhaps, as Caputo says, it was the circumstances of the war: that it was both a civil war and a revolution; that it was fought in jungle; that it had been preceded by twenty years of terrorism and fratricide, and the Americans had simply inherited this climate of cruelty. Or perhaps it was in the way the American army had been slung together; perhaps it was the short-timer mentality that made it cruel. A sergeant tells Caputo: "Lieutenant, I've got a wife and two kids at home and I'm going to see 'em again and don't care who I've got to kill or how many of 'em to do it." Or perhaps it was the army's youth: another sergeant says, "Before you leave here, sir, you're going to learn that one of the most brutal things in the world is your average nineteen-year-old American boy." Probably the truth includes all of these explanations: a war of inherited brutality, fought by young, untrained boys trying to survive for so many days in a country to which they felt no commitment. Those soldiers, in that confused and fearful war, would do things that a more disciplined, long-term army wouldn't have done.

Or is it possible that they enjoyed it? "Why did we want to kill dinks?" Downs asks himself.

After all, we had been mostly law-abiding citizens back in the world and we were taught that to take another man's life was wrong. Somehow the perspective got twisted in a war. If the government told us it was alright and, in fact, a must to kill the members of another government's people, then we had the law on our side. It turned out that most of us liked to kill other men. Some of the guys would shoot at a dink much as they would at a target. Some of the men didn't like to kill a dink up close. The closer the killing, the more personal it became.

Others in the platoon liked to kill close in. A few even liked to torture the dinks if they had a prisoner or cut the dead bodies with knives in a frenzy of aggression.

A few didn't like to kill at all and wouldn't fire their weapons except to protect their buddies.

Mostly, we all saw it as a job and rationalized it in our own way. Over it all ran the streak of anger or fear that for brief moments ruled us all.

It's a retrospective passage, like Rifleman Harris's memory of the roasted Frenchman; an older man, after his war, looking back on himself as a short-time soldier and asking, with a kind of astonishment, "Why did we want to kill?" Not why did we kill—no soldier needs to ask that question—but why did we *want* to? He offers several answers: because men are twisted in war; because we were told it was right; because we were frightened and angry. And the worst answer of all: because we like to kill other men. If that is true, then the sergeant was right about young Americans: they *are* brutal. One might venture one other answer: that the strategy of attrition, which made dead Vietnamese more valuable than living ones, made killing a virtue. But the passage isn't really an answer to its question; it's a meditation on the strangeness of this war, in which young men not only could kill but could develop tastes in the way they did it.

The one event of the war that stands as the worst-case symbol of all the brutality and inhumanity and anger and fear is the massacre that occurred in March of 1968 when Charlie Company, 1st Battalion, Eleventh Infantry Brigade, Americal Division, led by Lieutenant William Calley, entered the undefended village of My Lai and slaughtered every living thing they could find there—hundreds of Vietnamese civilians, including old men, women, and children, the village livestock, even the chickens. The men who did it were ordinary men, typical of the American troops then in Vietnam, insofar as statistics can measure what is typical: young (around twenty, most of them), some enlisted and some drafted, some black and some white. They were all new to the army and new to Vietnam (they had been in-country less than three months); and because the company had taken casualties from ambushes and mines, they were frightened and angry. So they killed the people, violated the women, and razed the village.

The words "My Lai" and "Calley" stuck in the imaginations of the men who served in Vietnam and in time entered their narratives as names for what was most wrong about the Vietnam War: the indiscriminate killing of civilians. They died in huge numbers—by one estimate three million out of a population of fifty million, nearly sixty civilians for every dead American soldier. In the Good War, the annihilation of villages and their inhabitants had been something the Nazis did at Lidice and Oradour; in this war, My Lai was what *we* did. To some civilian soldiers it seemed impossible. "Maybe I was naive," David Donovan wrote, "but I found it unbelievable that an American infantry platoon at My Lai had slaughtered women and children just for the hell of it." He *was* naive; it happened, and not only at My Lai. Young men found themselves killing unarmed and innocent people—in fear, in panic, or with a numbed indifference, or because "killing dinks" was what they were there for.

Here is an example. It's from an oral history of the war—a new kind of war narrative that came out of Vietnam to tell the soldiers' tale in voices that in earlier wars were silent:

It was a little straw-hut village. Had a little church at the end with this big Buddha. We didn't see anybody in the village. But I heard movement in the rear of this hut. I just opened up the machine gun. You ain't wanna open the door, and then you get blown away. Or maybe they booby-trapped.

Anyway, this little girl screamed. I went inside the door. I'd done already shot her, and she was on top of the old man. She was trying to shield the old man. He looked like he could have been about eighty years old. She was about seven. Both of them was dead. I killed an old man and a little girl in the hut by accident.

The men who were there saw more than dead people. As they slogged through the country on "search and destroy" missions, or flew over it in helicopters on the way to battles, they saw what their intervention was doing to the country they were defending. Personal narratives register the ruination: the crops destroyed, the villages razed, the fields made dead and sterile. Of course, every soldier who moves across fought-over ground sees the devastation that war inflicts; I have quoted accounts of battlefield anti-landscapes from both world wars. But Vietnam was different; there the destruction was not simply a consequence of war, it was a *policy*. If you destroy villages and their crops, you deny the enemy food and support, so the theory went.

Because there was no front and the Vietcong would be anywhere, devastation could be anywhere too. And Vietnamese villages were fragile—it was as easy to destroy one as not to (the Zippo lighter was a piece of American technology as destructive as the B-52). But the destruction, as the narratives tell it, was also *local*, one village in a valley, and then another valley, another village, treated like this:

All the empty huts and storehouses could never be destroyed with bombs and shells, so we had another task. The Blues [the author's platoon] would search deserted

villages, many of which had beige stucco Catholic churches
crowned by the one true cross, and burn every standing
structure. Huts and haystacks were set aflame; rice caches
were soaked with aviation fuel and burned. On some days
we would burn so much rice and so many huts that in the
evening our day's route would be marked by dozens of
columns of rising white smoke, extending back across
some silent valley or another.

The remaining livestock could not be left to feed the
Communists, so the platoon shot pigs and chickens and
machine-gunned water buffalo. Sometimes the grenadiers
would use water buffalo as target practice for their 40mm.
grenades. The damage one of those grenades could do to a
big animal was appalling.

Those columns of smoke from burning villages are a part of the
war landscape, as narrators remember it.

Some men saw more than that: they saw that a culture—
ancient, stable, and peaceful—was being destroyed. They looked
at the villages they were sent to annihilate and saw Paradise
Lost. Robert Mason remembered a village in the Kim Son
valley. Enemy troops were reported there, and he flew one of
the helicopters that carried the attacking infantry in. After the
village had been secured, he looked around. There were the
usual signs of a successful mission: a pile of VC corpses, captured weapons, the smell of burning houses and burned flesh.
But there were also vestiges of the life that had been lived there
before the Americans came: along the river's edge native boats,
woven like baskets, and across the river a giant waterwheel,
built entirely of bamboo.

I examined one of the basket boats. The weave was so tight
and precise that it stopped water. There was no calking
between the flat strands, yet the boat did not leak. Both
basket and wheel were built from material found growing
around the village. I wondered how our technology was

going to help the Vietnamese. Maybe after we had killed off the people—like these villagers, who knew how to live so elegantly in this country—the survivors would *have* to have our technology. That waterwheel was as efficient as any device our engineers could produce. The knowledge that built it was being systematically destroyed.

What Mason saw was a pyramid of destruction: dead men, a dead village, a dead culture. It was a vision of the consequences of the American way of war.

There were also the American dead—fewer of them, but present in every story. They appear much as the dead do in other war narratives, though many of them died in a particular way that is an insistent part of the Vietnam tale, not shot but blown apart. Because the North Vietnamese Army and the Vietcong didn't have the big machines, they made war with the small technology they had, and especially with the hidden weapons—land mines and booby traps. Any time, anywhere, the man ahead of you on the trail or beside you in the rice paddy might suddenly lift into the air, to fall to earth broken and dead.

Or not *quite* dead, for it was a war of many wounds that were terrible but not mortal. An American serviceman in World War II had one chance in twenty-five of being wounded; in Vietnam the odds were one in eight. And if the wound came from a mine or a booby trap, it was likely to be a terrible one; any of the many doctors' narratives will tell you just how terrible:

> I did another patient. He stayed in shock, while losing his whole right leg and his left leg, at the knee, one testicle, a thumb and a finger.... I wonder that he survived the surgery.

> Today, one of my patients went through the whole case on oxygen alone! He was so hurt that he could not tolerate an anaesthetic. We took off both his legs and several fingers.

* * *

Today ... we had horrible casualties! My first was a double
amputee, who died, but was resuscitated successfully.

Advances in military medicine had been such that combat-
zone wounded who would have died in any previous war could
be evacuated by helicopter, operated on, pumped full of new
blood, and kept alive: paralyzed, perhaps, or without legs, but
alive. "In Nam," one doctor wrote in his diary, "if they take you
off the choppers alive, or just a little dead, it may hurt a lot, but
you'll live." It wasn't the first war to produce amputees, of
course—one remembers Elisha Stockwell's wagonload of legs—
but it was the first in which the mutilated wrote books that bore
witness to their mutilation. Kovic's *Born on the Fourth of July* I
have already mentioned. Frederick Downs's *The Killing Zone* is
another (he lost an arm to a "Bouncing Betty" land mine, a kind
that flies into the air and explodes waist high). But the most disturbing account is in Lewis Puller, Jr.'s *Fortunate Son*, the narrative of how the only son of the Marine Corps' most decorated
general went to Vietnam and was terribly wounded there—and
lived.

Puller's account is a war story, but only briefly an *action*
story. He trained, was sent to Vietnam as a second lieutenant,
joined a Marine infantry company, and went into combat. Soon
he found himself in a firefight with North Vietnamese troops,
and separated from his own men. His weapon jammed, and he
saw that all he could do was run for cover. The action ended
like this:

> I knew only that the firepower advantage of the NVA
> squad I had just encountered would be neutralized if I
> could reach the men milling at the crest of the hill. With
> only a few meters left to cover in my flight, a thunderous
> boom suddenly rent the air, and I was propelled upward
> with the acrid smell of cordite in my nostrils.
>   When I landed a few feet up the trail from the booby-
> trapped howitzer round that I had detonated, I felt as if I

had been airborne forever. Colors and sound became
muted, and although there was now a beehive of activity
around me, all movement seemed to me to be in slow
motion. I thought initially that the loss of my glasses in the
explosion accounted for my blurred vision, and I had no
idea that the pink mist that engulfed me had been caused
by the vaporization of most of my right and left legs. As
shock began to numb my body, I could see through a haze
of pain that my right thumb and little finger were missing,
as was most of my left hand, and I could smell the charred
flesh, which extended from my right wrist upward to the
elbow. I knew that I had finished serving my time in the
hell of Vietnam.

This is Battlefield Gothic, a style we know about; only this time
it is first-person: the Gothic horror is the teller's own body.
Puller's is the true voice of the terribly violated man, at the point
where he ceases to be an agent of war and becomes its victim.
What is most striking about it is that its principal emotion is
astonishment; the outrage and the pain would come later.

Narratives of damaged men like Puller and Kovic confront
us with a paradox: the medical science that saves soldiers' lives
extends their suffering—beyond action, beyond treatment, even,
to the ends of their lives. For some of those men, it was the suffering, not the fighting, that was the war story; the figure at the
center of their narratives is not a soldier but a victim. And even
beyond the end of the recorded narrative, we know that the
story of suffering went on. Puller suffered until the day in 1994,
more than twenty years after he was wounded, when he committed suicide.

Victims make a difference in the Vietnam story. And so do
journalists. Before the memoirs began to appear after the war, it
was the journalists who were the witnesses; bland and official
sometimes, repeating the army's optimism; but sometimes as
shocked and bitter as any grunt. As long as the war went on, it
was their stories that told the world what it was like, and it was

through them that the reaction against the Vietnam War was articulated to the American people. Their testimonies appeared in widely read books like David Halberstam's *The Making of a Quagmire* (1965, the year the United States entered the war as a combatant nation) and Seymour Hersh's *My Lai 4* (1970) and Frances FitzGerald's *Fire in the Lake* (1972), and in the work of journalists like Gloria Emerson, Michael Herr, and Jonathan Schell. By the time the American involvement ended and the troops went home, in 1973, a vivid, emotional anti-war tale of the Vietnam War existed. But it wasn't the soldiers' story—that hadn't been written yet.

This phenomenon, the wartime expressions by journalists of a fierce reaction against the war, didn't happen in either of the world wars: not in the first because press censorship was absolute, not in the second because no significant anti-war reaction took place. But Vietnam was different; journalists there were free to observe, to photograph, and to film pretty much as they wished. And the state of media technology meant that what they wrote today could be printed in tomorrow's paper, and what they put on film could be projected onto hometown television screens on tomorrow's evening news.

It was probably the visual images that made the first powerful impact. Readers who are old enough will remember some of the pictures. A South Vietnamese police chief shoots a suspected terrorist in the head; it's a close-up photograph, and you can see the man's head distort as the bullet strikes it. Children run down a road, away from the smoke of what is apparently their napalmed village; a little girl in the center is naked and crying. In both of these photographs the viewers are intimately involved: we are close witnesses to an execution; it is toward *us* that the crying child runs. Images like these entered early into what became the myth of the Vietnam War, the horror story that Americans carried in their heads. They made it a different kind of story, in which the folks at home became witnesses to war's terror as it happened.

A consequence of pictures like these, and of newspaper and magazine reporting that was often highly critical of the war, was the creation of an uneasy sense of complicity in the killing among home-front civilians, beyond what they had felt in other wars. And among the fighting troops too; for a unique feature of this war was the way in which news coverage circulated—first to the States as journalists' stories, and then back again to the combat zone as their printed reports. In the soldiers' war narratives, they read *Time* and *Newsweek* and *Life* and are troubled by what they read (that's what Connors is doing in the foul-mouthed passage I quoted above from *Chickenhawk*). As they endured their war, they read accounts of what they were doing that told contrary stories—pro-war if the source was the official body counters, anti-war if it came from the protesters, but not *their* story either way. Those conflicts among versions of reality that we call *irony* were in place very early in the war; you might say, indeed, that the war in Vietnam was ironic from the beginning, that its essential meaning was the *absence* of a single coherent meaning in its events.

You'll find that principle of ironic incoherence expressed in the very form of the best-known of journalists' books on the war—Michael Herr's *Dispatches*. Herr was in Vietnam in 1967—the year leading up to the Tet offensive; his pieces were published in *Esquire* in 1968–70 and in revised versions as a book in 1977. *Dispatches* is not, in fact, dispatches: not, that is, a journalist's daily reports from the combat zone. Rather, it is a series of vignettes, arranged like a surrealist movie to create one long, disorienting image of the war. There are extended episodes in the book—most notably the story of the battle for Khe Sanh—but no continuous narratives, no clear chronology, no beginning or ending beyond Herr's own entry into and withdrawal from a war that also had no clear beginning or ending and no continuity.

Instead of a story line, Herr held his war together with three powerful metaphors. One is that experiencing the war was like taking drugs, like being stoned. The book is full of dope smokers, on both sides; a Marine tells Herr that the Vietcong are "doped to the eyeballs (sure they smoke dope, it gets them crazy)." Most Vietnam narratives by actual soldiers don't have much to say about drugs, and it must be from books like Herr's that the drugged-out version of the war took form, to be taken up later by filmmakers.

Herr's second metaphor is in that Marine's remark I just quoted: experiencing the war was like being crazy. Everybody is crazy: the combat troops, the enemy, the people who write the official press releases (Herr calls their stories "psychotic vaudeville"). The craziness of war isn't a new idea—Herr acknowledged his debt to Joseph Heller's *Catch-22*—but it is an effective one. We must remember, though, that like the drugs, it was a figure of speech for the war, as seen by a skeptical reporter, and not a statistical reality.

The third metaphor is, like the other two, a figure of derangement and unreality: the war is like a movie. Herr's book is full of movies—the romantic/heroic Hollywood movies that are American boys' imagined wars, their fantasies, their expectations, their dreams of glory (what Kovic called "all this crap about John Wayne and being a hero and the romance of war").

> I keep thinking about all the kids who got wiped out by seventeen years of war movies before coming to Vietnam to get wiped out for good. You don't know what a media freak is until you've seen the way a few of those grunts would run around during a fight when they knew that there was a television crew nearby; they were actually making war movies in their heads, doing little guts-and-glory Leatherneck tap dances under fire, getting their pimples shot off for the networks. They were insane, but the war hadn't done that to them. Most combat troops stopped thinking of the war as an adventure after their first few firefights, but there were always the ones who couldn't

let that go, these few who were up there doing numbers for the cameras. A lot of correspondents weren't much better. We'd all seen too many movies, stayed too long in Television City.

Herr is saying more here than simply that these young men went to war with a war-in-their-heads; he is saying that in their minds, Hollywood-reality *was* reality, that life in a media-glutted culture made it impossible for them to see what they did, except as movies. If that is true, then there was another element in the uniqueness of the Vietnam story: it was filtered through films.

Dispatches was a popular success because Herr is a gifted professional writer. ("Professional" is an important word in that sentence: his book is complex, allusive, and constructed beyond what any one-book soldier could manage.) But it was popular also because in it Herr created an image of the war that an American public wanted: a war world of absolute difference from any other place on earth, emptied of meaning, values, coherence, reasons—all those concepts that had leaked away. He populated that world with an American army that was divided into two parts: bland army bureaucrats, who kept well away from the fighting and told the official lies; and grunts, a fighting force of weird, twisted men with old faces and twitching hands, spaced-out rock-and-rollers, drug takers high on war, men who'd "flipped over," victims of the war they were still fighting. In Herr's Vietnam, the war lovers are psychopaths. By the time *Dispatches* appeared, to say that it was "the best book to have been written about the Vietnam war," as a *New York Times* reviewer did, or that it was "the best book I have ever read on man and war in our time," as John Le Carré did, was to make a political statement—and a politically correct one. By then we all had a Vietnam war-in-our-heads, and it was more or less Herr's.

In *Dispatches*, Herr did one thing with particular brilliance: he used the troops' own vocabulary and made it into a new literary language. Some of that language was army slang—the

words and phrases by which soldiers separate themselves and
their world from the outside world of civilians, a way of ex-
pressing their conviction that if you weren't there you can't
understand. Some of it was the common obscenities of the
American street. But some of it was new to army talk, because
the army in Vietnam included a substantial new presence, inner-
city blacks. They added their own jivey, street-smart vocabulary
to the general stew of soldiers' speech, and those memoir
writers with the best ears heard it and filled their books with
faithful dialogue. Listen to this speech, from William Merritt's
Where the Rivers Ran Backward. A soldier is telling how his platoon built their encampment on ground above an enemy tunnel
system:

> We'd camped right on top of that mofo. Had our perime-
> ter out all round the hill. Guards. Claymores. Trip wires.
> Set out all our shit. And them dudes was under us. And
> inside us. They probably had doors in the dirt like those
> hairy spiders on TV. Could have cut us all up. Them mofos
> bad, bro. They don't play.

Merritt's book is full of such well-heard speeches, and so are
many others. But Herr went a long step farther: he made that
speech his own. Any page of his book offers illustrations. Here
are two taken more or less at random:

> Sitting in Saigon was like sitting inside the folded petals of
> a poisonous flower, the poison history, fucked in its root no
> matter how far back you wanted to run your trace.

> At the bottom was the shitface grunt, at the top a Com-
> mand trinity: a blue-eyed, hero-faced general, a geri-
> atrics-emergency ambassador and a hale, heartless CIA
> performer.

Into the middle of the serious thoughts about how it was in
Saigon and in the command structure of the war, Herr drops

"fucked" and "shitface," as though they were the only right and proper adjectives for the occasion. This isn't a matter of linguistic realism; Herr is not quoting the common soldier, as Robert Mason quoted his fellow pilot Connors; he's speaking in his own authorial voice. He saw that language like this was appropriate for the story of the Vietnam War, that its coarseness, ugliness, shockingness—whatever term you choose—was a just analogy for the ugliness of the war itself.

That isn't the only rhetoric of the war's story; other men managed to write their memoirs without obscenity—or nearly so. David Donovan's *Once a Warrior King* is an example; so is James McDonough's *Platoon Leader*. Their different rhetoric has mostly to do, no doubt, with the fact that they were officers, writing in the role they played in the field—as leaders, examples, men in authority. It's a military difference that is also, as a rule, a class difference: officers were mostly middle class and with some university education; enlisted men mostly weren't. Maybe sometimes it had to do with the wars they fought: Donovan worked with a four-man Special Warfare team in an isolated village in the Delta—a serious job, but distanced from the dust and blood and fear of the rice-paddy-and-jungle war that the infantry fought.

Herr was distanced too; he was in Vietnam as a reporter, not as an infantryman, and that fact separates him from the other narrators in this book. He was there and not there; as he frankly explained: "I was there to watch." He came as close as an observer could to living the soldiers' war; but still there is a difference between watching and warding, between the voyeur and the combatant. Herr could go where he wished, witness what he wanted to see, and catch a helicopter out; he wasn't stuck in the war, and that makes his story different from the stories of the men who were really, entirely *there*. Nevertheless, he watched with observant eyes, and he listened with well-tuned ears; he heard the war in all its voices—the commanders, the journalists, the Vietnamese, and the shitface grunts—and from

those voices he invented a rhetoric that for us is what the war
sounds like.

Dispatches is not so much a narrative of the Vietnam War as a
nightmare version of it—a stoned, crazy war movie. None of the
soldiers' narratives I know equals Herr's in inventiveness of
action, language, and character, but they share the nightmare, its
causes and its narrative consequences. The causes are clear—
they are the ways in which the Vietnam War was different from
other modern wars: that it was a long war fought by short-
timers; that many of the troops came from the lowest rungs of
the American social ladder; that they fought a war without a
front, a war of attrition; that they fought against the pressures of
emerging anti-war opinion.

The consequences for the storytelling are just as clear. A
war without a front is necessarily a war without a direction, a
story without a plot. There is no narrative continuity in Vietnam
stories because there couldn't be: a man's combat could begin
anywhere in the eight-year war and end a year later; during that
year he would go into the jungle to "search and destroy," come
out, go in again—like a commuter, as Caputo said. Or spend
some months defending a bridge somewhere, move to the
jungle, go back to the bridge (that is Frederick Downs's story)—
all of these moves apparently arbitrary and related to no grand
strategic intention. Nor were they shaped by military events—the
fighting of a crucial battle, or a great campaign, or a final victory.
There is no *momentum* in them; and without momentum they
aren't really narratives, not in the customary sense of the term.
Rather, they are gatherings of disconnected incidents—stories of
small fierce actions, ambushes, exploding mines, burning villages, interspersed, sometimes, with anecdotes of nights out of
the combat zone, in the towns, with women and drink. These
pieces of a fragmented war are separate from each other, linked
only by a common ugliness and violence, strung together like
souvenir ears on a string, just things that happened in one man's

one-year hunk of a long and formless war. The formlessness is the form.

Perhaps for that reason, because the fighting itself had no meaning, many Vietnam war narratives neither begin nor end with the teller's time in combat, or even with the beginning and ending of American involvement in the war. Often they begin in the innocent postwar years of the 1940s and 1950s, with the sons of the Good War growing up: Ron Kovic in a Long Island suburb, playing baseball and dreaming of becoming a Marine; Robert Mason, a farm kid in Florida, yearning to fly; Rod Kane in Philadelphia, who wants to smoke Camel cigarettes and be a paratrooper; Lew Puller in Virginia, who wants only to be a Marine like his heroic father. They begin in American innocence because that's what was lost, in the mythic telling of the Vietnam War.

They end at various points—when a man's tour ends, or when he looks out of a civilian airplane and sees his hometown below, or when the wound that has taken him out of the war heals. Many of them share a common ending, which is the end, not of the war itself, but of *their* war: at the Vietnam Veterans Memorial in Washington, on Veterans Day, November 13, 1982, the day the memorial was unveiled in Washington and the veterans marched in their own parade. Kovic was there (I quoted his reaction at the beginning of this chapter); David Donovan was there, looking for the names of his own dead; Rod Kane was there, looking for the place where his name would be; Bill Merritt was there, looking to be sure his name *wasn't* there; John Ketwig was there; and Lew Puller in his wheelchair. Being there with those names—57,939 of them—was clearly a kind of conclusion.

The mood on that occasion was complicated. The monument was in a public place, but it wasn't exactly official: the veterans themselves had paid for it; and neither was the parade: it, too, was theirs. The veterans who marched that day seem to have felt

most of all relief, a sense of a burden lifted from them, and of
completion of a war that had never properly ended. Rod Kane
wrote:

> It's like an enormous weight being lifted from our shoul-
> ders with every step. This is like taking care of one hope,
> one dream we all shared when talking of coming home. It
> doesn't make the war worth it, but it puts the period at the
> end of the sentence of surviving it.

For some, the mood was celebratory, or almost so. Here is
Donovan's account:

> And I finally got my parade. For one day it was like being
> in the army again. It was Veterans Day, November 13. The
> word got around in crisp military terms; parade assembly
> time was 0845 hours. Old soldiers tried to remember how
> to fall in, dress right, and keep in step. Everyone was
> feeling so good that the fine points of parade technique
> didn't really matter. We were getting our parade! That was
> enough in itself.
>
> The uniform of the day was old combat boots worn
> white with age, faded jungle fatigue shirts over old blue
> jeans, and service headgear of every description. On
> November 13, 1982, after more than ten years of waiting,
> the American Army of Vietnam moved out for its splen-
> didly ragtag parade down Constitution Avenue.
>
> As we made the sweeping left turn from the Mall onto
> Constitution Avenue, I could see clearly down the broad
> street. The sidewalks were crammed with cheering people.
> Since I was on the outside of the front rank, people
> reached out to shake my hand and pound my back. I
> wasn't special, I was just accessible. Men, women, and chil-
> dren were cheering and waving flags. The most common
> cheer was "Welcome home! Welcome home!" Our forma-
> tion was more like a rambling cattle herd than soldiers on
> parade. It was so bad it was good and added to the joy of

the occasion. Nobody was worried about anything, everybody was having a good time.

The swelling was in my chest again, the tears kept filling my eyes, but this time not from sadness—it was from pleasure and immense relief. A parade! For me. A great weight was lifted from my shoulders. Cheering crowds, smiling women, waving children—simple things really, but things soldiers have always yearned for and always will.

By this account it was a kind of parody of a victory parade: a ragtag army, without bands or a reviewing stand of officials, out of step and out of uniform, marching on its own, and so parading its sense of rejection by the society it had served and suffered for. But also a reconciliation: "Welcome home! Welcome home!"—ten years late. An ironic parade for an ironic war.

And there was the monument itself, the least declamatory of war memorials. It, too, is a war text of a sort, but not one that turns memory into style or freezes the Big Words of war in stone. What the wall says is, in the grunts' phrase, *It don't mean nothin'*—except that men die in war. And perhaps one other thing: that wars don't end when the fighting stops, that there must be a parade, a monument, some formal acknowledgment of the human cost and of the public's awareness of it.

The soldiers' tale of the Vietnam War is the whole long sweep of emotion and disillusionment from the American dream of innocence and the Good War to the body count on the wall. The story of the eight years of actual war is a stretch in the middle of the tale that could be graphed as a humpbacked curve, beginning with the landing of the first Marine battalions in March 1965, rising to the top of the hump in 1968, when more than half a million American troops were in-country, and then declining as the long disengagement began, until the last combat troops departed early in 1973 and the war was returned to the people it belonged to.

Most of the outstanding soldiers' narratives of the war come

out of combat service in the earlier years of the war, on the
upward curve of the graph: Caputo, Kane, Kovic, and Mason
were all there in 1965–66; Downs and Tobias Wolff arrived in
1967; Merritt followed in 1968. Why should the early fighting
make the best stories? Perhaps because the real subject of the
tale is the loss of faith, the process by which the simple conviction that Americans fight only Good Wars was lost. Perhaps
after that there was no story left to tell, only formless anecdotes
of death and violation.

Clearly there was a turning point in the mood of the war; it
occurred about 1968. That was the year of the Tet offensive,
which taught American commanders just how powerful and
mobile their enemies were; and of the My Lai massacre, which
should have taught them how undisciplined and demoralized
their own troops were (but evidently didn't). Here, three years
into the war, the American spirit turned.

But perhaps the causes of that turn were not in the war itself,
but in events back in the United States. In 1968 Martin Luther
King and Robert Kennedy were assassinated, Lyndon Johnson
decided not to run for a second term, and the Democratic Party
Convention self-destructed in Chicago. One could surely argue
that from that point on, the central story became the one that
was acted out back home. Or say that the two war stories, the
one in-country and the one back in the world, became entangled, each hampering the other, until the war was lost.

At the time of the 1968 Democratic Convention, William
Merritt was in an Oakland army barracks waiting to be shipped
out to Vietnam, and he watched the convention on the dayroom
television set. Here is part of his impressionistic account of that
tangled experience:

> The camera flicked to a pep rally. Crowds chanting.
>   "HO, HO, HO CHI MINH ..."
>   "... currently unable to interview Mayor Daley, who is
> jeering at Senator ..."

"HO, HO, HO CHI MINH ...
THE NLF IS GONNA WIN ..."
Political chants. Ugly. Meant to outrage. And to hurt.

"This is just in, Walter. Hugh Hefner is reported to have been clubbed by police outside the Hilton. No word yet as to the extent of his injuries."

"HEY, HEY, LBJ—HOW MANY KIDS DID YOU KILL TODAY? ..."
"HEY, HEY, LBJ—HOW MANY KIDS DID YOU KILL TODAY? ..."
... Early the next day we were marched onto buses and driven to Travis for our flight to Vietnam. It was such a quiet ride. The Democrats were still rioting over Chicago when we left. And for two more days after that.

A war is being fought in Chicago, authority against anarchy, old against young. And a young man is going to the *other* war, which he is going to fight for the sake of the turmoil behind him.

Merritt came late among the memoirists. His war began at the turn, in 1968, when the war had gone sour both in Vietnam and at home, and the difference is there in his attitude and in his tone—a bit melancholy, ironically amused at the mess that the war had become, but not angry, because he went to war not expecting much. It's a memoir of the Fall. Most of the memoir writers who did their fighting earlier didn't publish their books until after the war. A few, like Tim O'Brien, published parts in magazines in the late war years, as Herr did (and Lieutenant Calley too), and their pieces helped to shape American attitudes in the downhill years of the war; but generally the memorable war narratives began to appear only after the troops had gone home. Some were published in the 1970s, more in the '80s, a few in the '90s (Tobias Wolff's *In Pharaoh's Army*, for example, in 1994), though diminishingly, as if the initial impulse to recover the sense of what it was like had run its course.

This curve of memoir writing is not surprising: a similar pattern can be found after the two world wars, though the First War writers delayed for a decade and the Second War writers waited longer (some are still being published). But what is different about the Vietnam narratives is that by the time they were written, a myth of the war had already been constructed. I don't mean the official version that comes out of every war—that story was dead, because the United States had lost. I mean the revisionist witness, the voices that said, "*This* is the way it *really* was, this is what that war meant." Those voices came early in the Vietnam War—from journalists, from the television screens in American living rooms, from protesters in American streets. The soldiers' tale of the war, when it took shape in the postwar years, would draw on that already existing myth, affirming or denying it, but acknowledging that it existed, that before the war ended it had been judged.

Actually, by the time the war ended there were two myths firmly in place, which told two different stories: the Myth of the Bad War, which said it was an immoral adventure that should never have been begun, in which American boys were killed and a nation was devastated; and the Myth of the War That Was Lost, which said the army could and would have won, if it had been allowed to fight as it wished. The two myths were opposites, politically; what they had in common were bitterness and a sense of national shame. Either way, it had been a wasteful and destructive folly that reflected on every American and disgraced the men who fought in it. The consequence was a national hangover, like the one the British suffered after the First War but worse and longer, because the hungover nation had lost its war.

The principal Vietnam narratives were written during the years of that long hangover and in the shadows of those two contrary myths of the war, and their stories reflect those circumstances. You can see the effects in individual episodes, how they tend to be not simply about fighting but about *killing*, often the wrong people, so that the episodes become little parables of the war.

You can see the effects also in the ways the narratives use

the traditional language of military values, the Big Words like "courage" and "duty" and "heroism." Those words survive, but without a clear moral base; they are simply words for extraordinary kinds of behavior.

This is a common condition in modernist writing: it's what sustains the bullfighters and hunters in Hemingway's stories and the seamen in Conrad's novels; it's what Hemingway called grace under pressure and Conrad called fidelity. You find it in many Vietnam narratives. For example, in Caputo's *A Rumor of War*. Caputo's tone is generally cynical and ironic, the tone of an after-the-Fall narrative, yet he can describe the death of a fellow officer as a "hero's death" and mean it quite unironically. Though the war was over and lost, it was still possible for a teller to bootleg a Big Word like "hero" into his narrative; it just wasn't possible to tell a heroic story heroically all the way through. The consequent fluctuation of tone, in and out of irony, is not uncommon in Vietnam memoirs.

Take the passage in which Caputo describes the "hero's death" of Captain Reasoner:

> We split a beer and talked about the patrol he was taking out in the afternoon. His company was going into the paddy lands below Charlie Ridge, flat, dangerous country with a lot of tree lines and hedgerows. Reasoner finished his beer and left. A few hours later, a helicopter brought him back in; a machine gun had stitched him across the belly, and the young corporal who had pulled Reasoner's body out of the line of fire said, "He should be covered up. Will someone get a blanket? My skipper's dead."

How flat and workmanlike that sounds, just a story of a Marine going out to do his job and coming back dead. But then there is that touch of tenderness for the dead captain: "He should be covered up.... My skipper's dead." The emotional links between soldiers, and between officers and their men, are difficult to render, because though the attachments between men in war can be strong—stronger than peacetime friendships—they are mostly inarticulate. Caputo does it delicately here.

Then he tells what had happened:

> Out on the patrol, his company had run into a couple of enemy machine-gun nests. He had charged one of the guns single-handedly, knocking it out of action. Then, having fired his carbine at the second gun, he had run to pick up one of his wounded and was killed.

There's fidelity—the officer who is faithful to his men. But where are the brave adjectives, the rhetorical ruffles and flourishes of a heroic story? Caputo suggests where they were:

> They gave Frank Reasoner the Congressional Medal of Honor, named a camp *and* a ship after him, and sent the medal and a letter of condolence to his widow.

"They"—the top brass, the people in Washington, the Old Men who run wars—have stolen the language of heroism; Caputo can only tell the story, and tell it ironically. Irony is the inescapable tone of modern war.

Courage, and even heroism, were possible in Vietnam; even the bitterest of the war-hating narrators have their stories of brave men. But the courage that is reported in the narratives is not usually demonstrated in acts against the enemy; stories of killing VCs are often terrible, sometimes murderous, and are told without positive moral weighting. It's the protective acts—recovering one's own wounded, or the dead, or covering a withdrawal—that carry moral and emotional value.

Courage and heroism were possible in Vietnam narratives; the *ideal* of courage, the Heroic Man of the war tradition, wasn't. Or rather, he was, but only as a ridiculous celluloid figure. As such, he was present in Vietnam in men's minds, and he is in the narratives they wrote; his name is John Wayne. Kovic, you will remember, said angrily that "they fed us with all this crap about John Wayne and being a hero," and there is much evidence of the currency of Wayne's name in the combat zone as a term identifying all those daring individual acts that succeed in the movies but are only dumb stunts that will get you killed in a real war. When Frederick Downs sees one of his men firing an M-60 machine gun from his hip, he shouts, "You can't hit anything firing that thing like John Wayne"; and Caputo's commanding officer says, "I don't want anyone going in there thinking he's going to play John Wayne." And in oral histories of the war, which come as close as written words can to the way ordinary grunts spoke, the usage is the same: "He saw where the machine-gun net was, and he tried to do the John Wayne thing"; "I didn't see no tanks in Saigon.... I was expecting for the tank to come up there and do the John Wayne type of things." For the Vietnam generation, "John Wayne" was the Hollywood war-in-their-heads, exposed and mocked by the real, bitter thing. It's a sign of how completely the old values had faded that Wayne, the hero of the Westerns and war movies that the Vietnam War generation had grown up on, and the embodiment of what seemed a particularly American kind of independent courage, had become a soldier's joke, an anti-hero, everybody's example of how *not* to fight a war.

John Wayne's wars were adventurous and romantic; but there was no adventure in Vietnam, and no romance. How could there be, in a war in which the goals were to kill Vietnamese in the largest possible numbers and to hold fortified positions against assault? Mass killing and defensiveness don't make heroic war stories. Occasionally a memoir tells a story of hand-to-hand fighting, one man killing another with a knife or a bayonet, but it isn't heroic combat; it's too sudden and desperate for that. As for war in the air, which had provided romantic adventure stories in the two world wars, it didn't seem to produce any in Vietnam. American fighter planes were based there, and sometimes they engaged enemy Migs, and there were dogfights of a long-distance kind, and planes were shot down. By the end of the war, five American airmen had shot down five or more enemy planes, and so were officially aces. But not in the romantic sense of the word; it was too late in the history of aerial warfare for that: the planes were too fast, the electronic weapons were too automatic, the distances between planes were too great, to make their combats war stories. Reading about them is like reading about video games. There were no McCuddens or Pappy Boyingtons in Vietnam. Nor were there memorable bombers' stories, though the B-52s did their best to bomb North Vietnam "back to the stone age." Neither fighters nor bombers have become part of the soldiers' tale. Helicopters have, and there are excellent helicopter pilots' memoirs; but not romantic ones. Indeed, the only romantic figures in the Vietnam story are the journalists (in their own narratives, that is). It was a happy accident that Michael Herr's comrade in journalism in Vietnam was the son of Errol Flynn, one of the great celluloid heroes, and that he disappeared romantically into Cambodia, "MIA to say the least," Herr concluded.

But for the men who fought it wasn't a romantic war; it was brutal, fearful, and cruel, and so are the stories they told of it. Those memoirs were mostly written in the decade or so after the war had been abandoned, and they are touched by the sour emotions of that time. Some of the tellers had gone home to become antiwar activists, and they chose their stories, whether intentionally or not, for their polemical impact. The dead children, the burned villages, the poisoned earth, the acts of wild, unnecessary destruction, all tell that war story against war, and often tell it vividly, memorably. A description in John Ketwig's ... *and a hard rain fell* of a napalm-burned Vietnamese child is so gruesome that I can scarcely bring myself to quote it. Ketwig sees the child, "a pathetically skinny boy of about seven or eight," in an army evacuation hospital, patiently waiting to be treated.

The little fellow had an unruly patch of jet black hair, and dark eyes that seemed to recede above his cheekbones to burrow into deep, dark sockets and hide from the horrors of his world. There was no reflection, no childish sparkle in those eyes. The reason was obvious. His legs were a horror of blackened, crispy shards of burnt flesh. Above the meager shorts, his torso, also black, seemed bubbled like an overbaked pizza. His right shoulder disappeared into the horrible mass of his chest, a diagonal lump of melted black putty that fell to his navel, then rose on another diagonal to exit near the left shoulder by way of four stubby pink protrusions. His right arm had been melted to his chest in a searing ball of flaming napalm. The boy's right fingers jutted out of his chest like pink worms, clawing uncontrollably. The dry black bubbles rose up his neck and chin, angling off to obscure only half his mouth. I watched him nod to shoo a pesky fly.

As I read that passage I found myself asking: Did Ketwig really see that melted little boy? Could a child with such injuries possibly survive? I don't know the answers, and in a way it doesn't matter: that sight is a necessary part of his story, a symbol of the guilt that he and many other decent young men felt about their war.

Guilt, in many Vietnam narratives, is a *structure* (as it is in crime novels). For the guilty, escaping from the war back into "the world" won't be a sufficient ending to their story; there will have to be something like judgment. For Caputo, that judgment is a classic courtroom scene, in which he is tried for the premeditated murder of two Vietnamese civilians. He is acquitted, but he feels guilty. For Kovic, judgment is life as a paraplegic. "I think," he says, "that maybe the wound is my punishment for killing the corporal [of his own platoon] and the children [Vietnamese]." For Mason, judgment is a conviction for drug running, back in the States. All of them are guilty, of a crime that is more than their own: guilty of their nation's war.

That common feeling of guilt doesn't seem to have afflicted men in other wars, or at least it hasn't gotten into their stories. Other men have killed civilians—the Eighth Air Force over Berlin, for example, and the Germans over London, the men who invaded Okinawa, the firebombers of Tokyo, submarine crews that attacked civilian ships in both world wars, and before them the British at Badajoz, the French at Leipzig and Moscow, the Israelites at Ai and Bethel, any army attacking any city—but have come away apparently guilt free. Men don't seem to feel guilt for what they do in war, so long as they have the support of their fellow soldiers, the authority of commands, and the approval of the civil society behind them. Distance is a factor; I have no statistics (how could there be any?), but my sense, from the memoirs, is that in Vietnam there was more close-range, visible killing than in other modern wars. Certainly there were more *images* of killing, filmed and reported and released to newspapers and television news broadcasts at home, and then returned through the same media to the troops in the field. Other armies have not been shown what they've done, not in that graphic way.

Losing is part of the guilt story too. Losers' narratives, from any war, show us clearly that to be one of the defeated is a kind of guilt. If I had fought harder, says the loser, my nation and my cause would not have failed, my friends would not be dead. That isn't true of every defeated soldier, of course; some blame their generals, or the people at home, or the odds, or mutter about betrayal. But for some, loss is guilt.

In our society, guilt is a psychological as well as a moral problem, and it isn't surprising that many narratives of the Vietnam War don't end when the fighting ends but continue in psychiatric hospitals and group therapy sessions with other veterans, fighting what a tunnel rat I know calls "the war after the war." So many stories end there in that after-war that psychiatrists have given a name to the problem: post-traumatic stress disorder. PTSD is to Vietnam what shell shock was to the First World War—a new kind of war damage, a new suffering that military medicine wasn't prepared for.

Collectively, those sufferers add an epilogue to the story of the Vietnam War: an after-myth, you might call it, or the Psychiatrists' Tale. Some of their stories are in their books (some of which were written as therapy); others are quoted or summarized in the writings of psychiatrists who have treated them. These stories constitute a new kind of personal narrative of war, and a disturbing one for a nation committed to the idea of a citizen army. For the assumption implicit in the idea of an army composed of temporary civilian soldiers is that when the war to which they were called is over, they will revert to being the civilians they were before. Clearly that has been historically the case for many men of many volunteer and conscripted armies; they may have been changed by war, but not so much changed that they were incapable of re-entering their old lives. The Vietnam story seemed to challenge that assumption. Here was a war fought on such terms, in such conditions, that many of the men who were there could not re-enter the society they had fought for but were left on the outside, disqualified from ordinary living.

This is Rod Kane, in a group therapy session in a Veterans Administration hospital:

"Mr. Kane, do you have trouble with your concentration?"

"Trouble with concentration?" I stare at her defensively. I forgot her name already. "Not necessarily, I concentrate on the war, or drinking ... but I'm not here because of my concentration problems, or my memory. I will say that if I've had trouble with anything since Nam, it's been sleeping.... One reason I drink so much, so I could pass out and not have to worry about nightmares. Or course, after a while, all the booze in the world couldn't keep them down. ... I mean, there are booby-trap nightmares that speak for themselves. Instant replay nightmares where, asleep or awake, I play the same scene over and over again. There are nightmares that combine Viet Nam action with stateside stuff. Christ! Do I have to get into all this right away?"

And a passage from a psychiatrist's record of a veteran's words:

I haven't really slept for twenty years. I lie down, but I don't sleep. I'm always watching the door, the window, then back to the door. I get up at least five times to walk my perimeter, sometimes it's ten or fifteen times. There's always something within reach, maybe a baseball bat or a knife, at every door. I used to sleep with a gun under my pillow, another under my mattress, and another in the drawer next to the bed. You [the psychiatrist] made me get rid of them when I came into the program here. They're over at my mother's, so I know I can get them any time, but I don't. Sometimes I think about them—I want to have a gun in my hands so bad at night it makes my arms ache.

So it's like that until the sun begins to come up, then I can sleep for an hour or two.

And two cases summarized by a psychiatrist:

Bob, a Texan, describes, how he stiffened suddenly in crowds, looked around fearfully, and thought, "These New Yorkers all look alike. How do I know who's friend and who's foe?" Then he shook himself, and realized: "Hey, they're all your friends. This is Times Square, U.S.A." Two years after a nonpsychiatric discharge, following four years of Marine combat duty in Indochina, Bob is still seized by these unpredictable episodes of disorientation and panic.

Tom remembers: "I was a helicopter door-gunner.... All I want now is to forget the look on their faces as we shot them down ... to forget what death spasms look like, to forget what it feels like when your hooch [Vietnamese hut] is blown apart. *They* may suffer the defeat, but *I'll* never forget my pleasure in killing my first 16-year-old 'Commie for Christ.' *I* carried out the orders. *I* carried the guns." At the local VA Tom was given phenothiazines and told to return in six months. His nightmares were unaffected except by his own treatment: every night, after work, he hurtled along the local freeways on his motorbike for hours; when he tumbled into bed, exhausted, he knew he would sleep without nightmares.

Certain elements in these narratives appear so often as to become almost conventions: the paranoia, the acts of sudden irrational violence, sleeplessness, alcoholism, the inability to hold a job or preserve a marriage or feel love. Collectively, they describe what happens to men when war takes them so far beyond the limits of ordinary human behavior that they can't find their way back. To call that collective story an after-myth of the war is not to suggest that their sufferings were not real but simply to note that it has become a widely accepted account of what the Vietnam War did to the men who fought in it. That story places Vietnam veterans with the subjects of the next chapter, with the *victims;* they are, it says, victims of their own war, and they have been compared, by one psychiatrist, to survivors of Nazi concentration camps.

That story has been absorbed into the Vietnam story for the same reason that all war myths are accepted—because it gives events a comprehensible shape that is consistent with the myth of the war itself—the Bad War that was lost. Because the war was wrong, because children were killed and a country was devastated, men who fought there were devastated too. No one can doubt that some men suffered after the war and behaved as the stories tell us they did. No one can doubt, either, that many other men *didn't* suffer, or not in that disabling way, that after their tour of duty they went home, got jobs, raised families. And more than that, they weren't sorry they'd gone. A 1980 Veterans Administration study, quoted in Stanley Karnow's *Vietnam: A*

History, reported that 71 percent of the Vietnam veterans polled
were glad they went to Vietnam, 74 percent claimed to have
enjoyed their war, and 66 percent would be willing to serve
again. Were those men all war-loving psychopaths? Of course
they weren't; they were ordinary men, like those in other wars
who afterward confessed that they wouldn't have missed it.
Some of those ordinary men wrote their war stories, and I've
quoted a couple (Merritt is one, Donovan is another); but on
the whole those stories have not entered the canon of Vietnam
memoirs. The war that we know, the Vietnam myth, is not their
war. If it were, the myth would have no moral; if men could
fight in that Bad War and come out of it undamaged and nos-
talgic, what would the war *mean*? But they are nonetheless as
valid, as truth-telling, as valuable, as the worst accounts of
slaughtered innocents and damaged lives. The soldiers' tale of
Vietnam is *all* of the stories. We must not choose among them.

Compared to the other wars I've talked about in this book,
the Vietnam War was a small-scale affair. It began as a local conflict, fought first against French domination and then internally
as a civil war, until it attracted the intervention of more powerful
nations. Yet it was a war of international significance, as important in its time as the Spanish Civil War was thirty years earlier.
Like the Spanish war, it came to be seen as a moral issue for the
world. In streets far from the conflict, in London and Paris as
well as in American cities, people marched to protest against a
war that was not their own and yet was (again, the similarity to
the Spanish Civil War is striking). The effect on the American
people was, as I said, like the effect of the First World War on
the British: it left them with a national postwar hangover. That
hangover is not cured yet.

CHAPTER SIX

Agents and Sufferers

I n a translation of Aristotle's *Poetics* that I sometimes use is a sentence describing tragic characters as those "that may have been involved, as either agents or sufferers, in some deed of horror." There are agents and sufferers in war too: the soldiers who perform the cruel deeds of war, and those others, soldiers and civilians, to whom the deeds are done. War stories have traditionally been told by the *agents*—the men of power who fight and kill; the *sufferers*—the helpless, the unarmed, the captive, the weak—all those human beings caught up in war and killed or maimed or imprisoned or starved simply because they were powerless and were there—these have had no voice.

In our century this has changed; for the first time, narratives of suffering have been written by the sufferers. These narratives have radically altered the geometry of the modern soldiers' tale, adding to the usual story of army against army a different war story—of armies against humanity. We might call those possible stories, taken together, the Literature of Atrocity, or perhaps the Sufferers' Tale.

Cruelty beyond the confines of the battlefield runs through the whole long story of war. Troy is sacked in Homer; cities are looted and burned, and defeated armies are slaughtered in the Old Testament and in Thucydides. Wellington's armies in the Peninsula ravaged the cities they captured; when the Japanese took Nanking in 1937, they entered upon an orgy of

223

murder, rape, looting, and arson that continued for weeks and cost 300,000 lives; the massacres at Babi Yar and My Lai were the actions of soldiers under orders and against civilians. One might think of armies as the most disciplined of human institutions; but in some circumstances—and especially when troops aroused by combat meet a helpless enemy—discipline dissolves, command descends to sadism, humanity is forgotten, and everything is allowed. "Doesn't anyone realize," Rod Kane wrote, "that in Nam, in war, anyone can do anything at any given time?" That's an exaggeration: not *anyone*, not *anytime;* but sometimes in war, because war runs on power, and when power confronts powerlessness, atrocities are possible.

Violence against the helpless seems a constant or, at the least, a frequently recurrent element in war; but peoples of civilized nations have wished, and even come to believe, that wars could be conducted in ways that would reflect their civilization. And so international meetings were called, and conventions were agreed on and signed—the Geneva Conventions, the Hague Convention—describing not the way war was actually fought but an ideal of modern war, how war would be if it were civilized.

These conventions were written over three-quarters of a century, from the time of the American Civil War to just after the Second World War. It was during the latter half of this rule-making period that *atrocities* entered the story of war: not the deeds themselves—they had always been there—but the idea that in a war between civilized nations, certain actions must fall outside the limits of decent war-making, and these could be classified under one collective label as crimes against humanity. The First World War wasn't a month old before atrocity stories—ostensibly firsthand accounts by eyewitnesses of German outrages—began to appear in English newspapers and pamphlets. These accounts of the German advance into Belgium told how civilians were shot, hanged, tortured, burned, buried alive, how women were bayoneted, children were beaten, babies' brains were dashed out against the ground, how entire villages were razed and their inhabitants murdered.

These gruesome stories were not the work of journalistic hacks (or not all of them were); my source for the cruel acts I've just described is *The German Terror in Belgium: An Historical Record* by the young Arnold Toynbee. Many similar books were published in the early years of the war, including the report of an official British government committee chaired by the distinguished historian Viscount Bryce. All of them report and confirm similar acts of violence.

There had never been such a Literature of Atrocity before; why did it appear at this time? The answer seems simple enough: England and her allies needed a brutal enemy. At a time when international conferences were writing rules for civilized war, democratic nations had to be mobilized for a war that would be total and *un*civilized. Hatred of the Germans would have to be generated among both the troops and the civilian population, and for that a propaganda of atrocities would be a flammable fuel. A general rule applies: To make a people forget their humanity in war, make their enemy inhuman. And perhaps another: To mobilize civilians to support a war, tell them stories of other civilians suffering.

But though the instant historians of the war told atrocity stories, those stories weren't war narratives—weren't, that is, authentic first-person testimonies of experiences. They were simply gatherings of anecdotes, rumors, hearsay, sheer invention—propaganda in the world's first propaganda war. There are no genuine victim narratives of the First War, so far as I can discover. Nor do atrocities appear as true events in the narratives of the men who were there; no soldier recalled actually seeing an Australian crucified, or a baby spitted on a bayonet, or a priest hanged by his church bell rope. Some German narratives record executions of *francs-tireurs* and hostages, and the burning of resisting villages, but that's all.

When English soldiers heard the propagandists' reports of

German atrocities, they didn't believe them. Robert Graves devoted a passage in *Good-bye to All That* to dismissing such stories:

> Atrocities. Propaganda reports of atrocities were, we agreed, ridiculous. Atrocities against civilians were surely few.... By atrocities we meant, specifically, rape, mutilation and torture, not summary shootings of suspected spies, harbourers of spies, *francs-tireurs,* or disobedient local officials. If the atrocity list was to include the accidental-on-purpose bombing or machine-gunning of civilians from the air, the Allies were now committing as many atrocities as the Germans.... For true atrocities, that is, personal rather than military violations of the code of war, there were few opportunities.

Graves thought he knew what "true atrocities" were, but he confessed that he wasn't sure where to draw the line between atrocities and ordinary killing. "For instance," he wrote,

> the British soldier at first regarded as atrocious the use of bowie-knives by German patrols. After a time he learned to use them himself.... The Germans regarded as atrocious the British Mark VII rifle bullet, which was more apt to turn on striking than a German bullet.

Other observers had the same definitional problem: at various times during the war, journalists described as atrocious submarine warfare, aerial bombing, gas, slapping a prisoner, burning Louvain, and bombing the Mount of Olives in the Holy Land.

Some of these offending acts were clearly not gratuitous cruelties inflicted by individuals upon the weak but simply the consequences of advances in military technology. Technology drives war, as it drives everything else in modern society; technological advances continually create new and better ways of killing, which seem atrocities until men grow accustomed to them and use them themselves. In this sense, the First War was modern war in its infancy; science offered new weapons—bombs, gas, flamethrowers, tanks—and armies used them, though to some people they seemed beyond the limits of decent war. The casualties from these innovations were relatively low; most men were killed with weapons invented in the nineteenth century—with long-range artillery and machine guns. As for civilian casualties from the new scientific weapons, they were relatively light; in the entire course of the war, for example, German zeppelin and bombing-plane attacks on England killed only fourteen hundred people. Many Englishmen regarded those first air raids as atrocities.

What all this suggests is not that war became more atrocious in the First World War but that the instruments of cruelty changed, and that the world at large became more aware of what war might do, not only to soldiers but to civilians. Because this was the first propaganda war, what the citizens of combatant countries thought they knew about it was melodramatic and had much to do with cruelty. And because it was the first modern technological war, they knew that cruelty could come in many ways, that it might fall from the sky or rise from the sea to burn or drown innocent people, who would never see their executioners. And because the armies in the field were made up of civilian soldiers, the line between their sufferings and the sufferings of civilians was not distinct; men-at-arms took personally what happened to persons outside the army, who might have been themselves or their families, and civilians at home felt the sufferings of soldiers, who were their fathers, their husbands, their sons.

By the time the First War had ended, the possible scope of the soldiers' tale had altered and expanded. Atrocity stories, though mostly spurious, had thrust into the consciousness of both soldiers and civilians the recognition that war could inflict great pain beyond battlefield wounds, and upon persons who

were not fighting; and the new technology had made it possible
for ordinary people to imagine a future war in which the distinction between combatants and noncombatants would not exist
and everyone could be a victim. War's cast of characters had
expanded enormously; and that expansion added a new question for war narratives to answer: "What sufferings were
inflicted on the helpless?" Answers to that question would make
the soldiers' tale of the next world war very different from the
tale of the one before.

Stephen Spender once remarked that bombed cities were to
the Second World War what the Western Front was to the
First—the essential image of the war. One can see what he
meant: the fact that in the Second War historic cities of Europe
and Asia were attacked and destroyed from the air made that
war unique, and the memorable records in films and photographs of those ruined cities—the shells of buildings, the
unidentifiable streets, the landscapes of ashes—are images of
that uniqueness.

The wars against cities added another difference to the story
of the Second War: once cities were targets, it became a war
against civilians. Strategic planners called it "a war to destroy
morale," but since you can't separate morale from the people
who have it, it was a war against civilians, who died in the war in
far greater numbers than fighting men did. Were those attacks
atrocities? In the judgment of the winners, they weren't; at the
Nuremberg Trials, the bombing of cities, though it violated the
Hague Conventions, was not regarded as a crime against
humanity, and no one was tried for it. The burning cities were
simply the inevitable consequences of the weapons available: if
four-engined bombers exist and incendiary bombs exist, then
Dresden will burn (and fifty thousand people will die) and
Tokyo will burn (one hundred thousand dead). But not Paris,
not Rome: there *were* restraints; destruction was not simply scattered like seed in a field. Military justifications could be offered
for the raids, and were: certain cities could be called military tar-

gets—unlike Lidice and Oradour, where destruction was entirely punitive, cruelty for terror's sake.

One might expect that the tale of such a war, in which some forty million civilians died, would include many civilian narratives—perhaps even a number proportional to the number of the dead. That isn't the case; narratives by civilian survivors of the great air raids are rare compared to the many narratives by the men who flew above them and dropped the bombs. Why is that? I could venture some possible explanations. Perhaps it is simply that nobody had told the civilian tale before, that there were no models and no tradition. Wars were *soldiers'* stories, and always had been. Or perhaps helplessness and passive suffering and random death did not seem important subjects, compared to infantry attacks and armored columns and planes flying through flak. Or maybe an enemy six miles in the air above you is not sufficiently substantial to oppose, and without opposition there is no story.

However you explain it, there are not many civilian narratives. But there are some, and they tell us how it feels to be down there on the ground, expecting an attack and then undergoing one, and what a city or a town looks like after the bombs have fallen and the raiders have flown home. The best of those narratives are by women, which shouldn't surprise anyone; statistically, there were more women than men in those cities. But it's more than statistics, surely; attacks on cities and their civilian populations are attacks on life, security, families, communities, stability—elements that women would protect if they could. Men bomb, women protect: is that it? The formulation is perhaps too simple; still, the war story of the cities does tend to confirm it.

What was it like, then, to be in the cities when the bombers came? Here are three accounts, by women from three countries and three different social classes. First, from the *Berlin Diaries* of Marie "Missie" Vassiltchikov, a White Russian aristocrat caught in the German capital when the war began. On the morning

after an air raid she leaves home for her office in the Foreign
Ministry:

> At first our Woyrschstrasse did not look too bad; but one
> block away, at the corner of Lützowstrasse, all the houses
> were burnt out. As I continued down Lützowstrasse the
> devastation grew worse; many buildings were still burning
> and I had to keep to the middle of the street, which was
> difficult on account of the numerous wrecked trams.... At
> the end of Lützowstrasse, about four blocks away from the
> office, the houses on both sides of the street had collapsed
> and I had to climb over mounds of smoking rubble,
> leaking water pipes and other wreckage to get to the other
> side.... I caught sight of the mail box into which I had
> dropped that long letter to Tatiana the night before; it still
> stood but was completely crumpled. Then I saw my food
> shop Krause, or rather what remained of it.... But poor
> Krause would be of no help either now.

Then to Leningrad, where Elena Skrjabina, a middle-class
woman with two young sons, is living during the German siege.
After a bombardment she goes out to look at the stricken streets
of her neighborhood:

> A few scenes have etched themselves into my memory,
> probably until I die: a house demolished almost to its foun-
> dations, but one wall remained, still papered in the favorite
> cornflower design. There is even a picture hanging on it, as
> straight as ever. Above a heap of bricks, cement, and
> beams, a whole corner of an upper apartment of another
> house was preserved. In the corner, an icon; on the floor,
> toys, scattered everywhere as if the children had just fin-
> ished playing. Further down was a room half buried under
> debris, but against the wall, a bed with fluffy pillows, and a
> lamp ... household items, surviving by chance, open to the
> eyes of passersby—silent witnesses to the fact that someone

or something alien tore mercilessly into the private life of people and barbarously defaced it.

And the third: Nella Last, an English working-class housewife living in Barrow-in-Furness. Hers is a smaller-scale story, with smaller-scale ruination in it: not a city, but her house, after an air raid:

I've a sick shadow over me as I look at my loved little house that will never be the same again. The windows are nearly all out, the metal frames strained, the ceilings down, the walls cracked and the garage roof showing four inches of daylight where it joins the wall. Doors are splintered off—and there is the *dirt* from the blast that swept down the chimney. The house rocked, and then the kitchenette door careered down the hall and plaster showered on to the shelter. I'll never forget my odd sensations, one a calm acceptance of "the end," the other a feeling of regret that I'd not opened a tin of fruit salad for tea—and now it was too late!

Different cities, different scales of devastation, but the same story: a woman in a place that had been familiar and the foundation of her life—a home, a street, a city—made strange and insecure. Nothing much is said about the origins of the ruin; planes fly over, guns fire, but the men who control them and the cause they serve have no identity and are not opposed. War comes like some terrible natural disaster, to be witnessed and endured.

And yet all three of these women were agents in their lives: they did oppose, in their own ways, and they were as courageous as any battlefield soldier. "Missy" Vassiltchikov, amid the ruins of her fashionable Berlin life, was active in the 20 July plot on Hitler's life and waited anxiously as her friends were arrested and executed. Elena Skrjabina acted in the only way she could: she fled Leningrad with her family on an odyssey that took her

the length of Russia, to the Caucasus, and then west with the
Germans to the Rhineland. Hers is a less romantic story than the
plot, but it's epic in its way—a quality you can best feel by
tracing it on the map in her book. As for Nella Last, her small-
scale story is neither epic nor romantic, but it is quietly courageous—a nervous housewife who was afraid of machines and
loud noises, holding her family together, comforting her neigh-
bors, simply enduring, until peace and quiet returned, and her
house was restored, and the war seemed "a nightmare that had
passed and left no trace."

In the minds of the strategic bombing theorists, those
women on the ground were the enemy: it was their morale, as
much as the soldiers', that was the target of those high planes.
And since they were weaponless, one might think that they were
simply war's victims. But they aren't victims in their own narratives; they are too vital and active for that. They don't regard the
war as an evil inflicted on their helplessness, they don't say that
what is happening to them is atrocious, they don't speak of
hatred or of anger. For them, war is simply a catastrophe to be
dealt with. They oppose, they protect, and they survive. But they
don't fight; war, when it reaches them, has gone beyond combat
to include the lives and deaths of civilians as a part of its tale.

Prisoner-of-war narratives are like the women's narratives, in
that they tell the story of the *other* side of war, where human
beings suffer but do not fight. Soldiers have been taken prisoner for as long as wars have been fought; but stories of imprisonment are not common among the war narratives of the old
wars. To be captured has always been a humiliating thing for
professional soldiers, something that shouldn't happen to a man
who was good at his job. Modern war has changed the weight
of individual responsibility somewhat—a pilot can't really be
blamed for being shot out of the air, nor a private for being
overwhelmed in a battle against the odds—but an odor of disgrace still hangs over many prisoners' stories. "The members of

the services to Malaya have not been blamed for the collapse of Singapore," wrote one of the men who was there in early 1942 when the city fell. "But in captivity they felt unhappy and ashamed, and rightly so. The defence of Malaya was shameful." Other prisoners, from other wars, have felt that shame too. It's not simply losing a battle; it's a more fundamental loss, the loss of one's identity as a soldier. All imprisonment diminishes, but a prisoner of war is especially deprived; disarmed, denied freedom of action, stripped of his signs of rank and his duties, he is dispossessed of what defines him—his soldiership.

The condition of dispossession is described in many memoirs. Here is one from a prisoner in Changi jail, where the Japanese put the British troops who surrendered at Singapore:

A defeated army is a strange thing.... The entire purpose of our mighty collective existence—the defence of the Naval Base and British power in the Far East—had been snuffed out.

What replaced our previous motive force was uncertainty, creeping in and growing stronger day by day, a negative force feeding on anxiety and fear. Before, we'd had the spring of aggression to keep us moving; now there was a kind of nervous elastic pulling us backwards. We still wanted to fight: but our bitter young energy had to be bottled up. We began to experience the overriding, dominant feature of POW life: constant anxiety, and utter powerlessness and frustration.

And another, from a young British officer captured by the Germans at Dunkirk:

Such imprisonment is a double tragedy. First, there is the loss of freedom. Then, since there is no apparent crime to expiate, unless it be personal folly, a sense of injustice scars the spirit. This bitterness of soul has clouded the life of many a strong man.

The prisoner of war is to himself an object of pity. He

feels he is forgotten by those who flung him, so he thinks, into an unequal contest. He broods over the causes of his capture, and to himself and his friends he soon becomes a bore, endlessly relating the story of his last stand. In these interminable reminiscences he unites with his fellow-prisoners in a chorus of protest at his sudden removal from active service.

Anxiety and powerlessness and bitterness: those are under-standable feelings for a prisoner. A soldier, who is what he does, is made powerless to act; though he is guiltless, yet he is justly imprisoned (for the Geneva Conventions affirm every nation's right to take and hold enemy troops); though he has been nei-ther tried nor sentenced, yet he is condemned to suffer confine-ment until either the war ends or he dies. One can see how such a man might feel that some accident of war—bad luck, or bad leadership—had caught him up and tossed him into nothingness, an unsoldier, forgotten, war's nobody, Othello with his occupa-tion gone.

But as I said, not all wars have made POW's stories a signifi-cant part of their soldiers' tale. In the First World War, for example, 190,000 British soldiers were captured, yet the story of their imprisonment is scarcely audible in the war narratives of that war. Either the men who were prisoners didn't write about their experiences at all, or they thrust them parenthetically into a short space in a long narrative, or they turned them into some other literary form. The novelist Charles Morgan was a POW but never wrote his story; J. R. Ackerley turned his POW experi-ence into a play; John Easton, whose "Broadchalk" chronicle is the best account of the fighting at Loos that I know, broke off his narrative at the moment when he was captured by German troops, as though the story that was worth telling ended there.

Why such reluctance to tell prisoners' stories in personal nar-ratives of that war? In some cases, it must have been the odor of disgrace. In others, the imprisonment simply didn't last long enough to make a story: prisoners were often exchanged, and some escaped. And perhaps there was another explanation: compared to the war in the trenches, imprisonment simply wasn't terrible enough to dwell on.

On this point, as on others, the war in Vietnam was similar to the First World War. There were American POWs, and some wrote personal narratives of their captivity, but their story is not a vital part of the tale of the war (I can't offhand think of a single soldier's narrative of Vietnam that mentions a man being captured by the enemy). The story in which POWs and MIAs (missing in action) did figure prominently and emotionally was the one acted out at home, where the issue of American boys unaccounted for was made part of the public's indictment of the government's conduct of the war.

The Second War is different: POW stories are an important part of its tale. Anyone who is at all interested in the war has read an escaper's story and knows about the Japanese prison camps. Why the difference? You could offer a statistical answer and say there were more prisoners in the Second War than in the First, and they stayed in prison longer, so of course there would be more and longer stories. But that won't do as an explanation; it wasn't the numbers in the prisons that make the prison narratives so integral to the tale; it was what was done to them there and, sometimes, what they did in return. For in that war, some prisons were places where the worst things that could be done to a soldier *were* done. Out of those places one powerful kind of prisoner's story came—the sufferer's story. But not the only kind: there is another, almost the opposite of the first— the escaper's story, in which the prisoner makes himself an agent in his own confined life. POW narratives of the war can be arranged along a continuum between these two poles: at one end the powerless sufferers, most of them veterans of Asian campaigns and prisoners of the Japanese; and at the other end the agents, veterans of European battles, captives of the Germans or the Italians.

Some soldiers would probably see this continuum as a graph of manliness, or even of simple humanity: at the bottom end men reduced to the lowest creaturely existence, lacking virtually everything that distinguishes men as human and makes their lives endurable; and at the top end men choosing and acting, and so affirming themselves as men. But it is more just to see it not as a graph but as a map of two hemispheres, one in which captors acted to extinguish humanity in their prisoners, and one where those in power (who, paradoxically, were Nazis) allowed prisoners—soldier prisoners, that is, and especially *officer* prisoners)—the minimum conditions of existence as human beings, and even a certain dignity as soldiers.

Consider first the military prisons of Europe. They produced POW stories—some firsthand personal narratives, some factual secondhand accounts—that were best-sellers in their time and are still well known: *The Colditz Story, The Great Escape, The Wooden Horse, The Tunnel.* One can see why such books were popular; they told the public the story it wanted to hear. They are all adventure stories that inject the old personal military virtues—courage, daring, ingenuity, endurance—into the anonymous mass narrative, with all its suffering and death, that modern war is. Coming as they did just after the end of the war, they made the war that had been won seem adventurous, almost fun.

The less-well-known, firsthand POW narratives of European captivity have much the same adventurous qualities. Anyone who reads widely among them will be struck by two things. One is that though the adventures they describe are exciting, they don't really seem dangerous. Men dig tunnels, and are caught, and try again, and escape, and are caught again, until at last they succeed. But escaping seems a venial crime to their jailers: in most of the narratives nobody is shot or even beaten; the escaper's usual sentence is a couple of weeks in a prison cell, the "cooler," and recidivists are treated no more harshly than first offenders. Both the actions of the stories and the tone in which most of them are told make escaping seem a game played between the prisoners and their captors, or an agreed-on rule of war: it is *your* duty to try to escape and *our* duty to prevent you. But there are no hard feelings; we're all soldiers, and this is the way war is.

But it *isn't* the way war is, not war as we have seen it in other men's memories: in these European adventure stories there are almost no killings and no corpses, and none of the other accompanying conditions of war—the roar and the stench of battle, the paralyzing fear, the grief. Their distinctive qualities are the opposites of all that: silence, freedom accomplished, and the exhilaration that comes from personal choice and action. The stories of the escapers aren't like other war narratives; they're romances.

The other striking thing about these narratives is the picture they give of prison life. One expects horrors: sadistic Gestapo interrogators, beatings, firing squads; they're not there, or not often. The practices of the camps are severe but military: soldiers controlling soldiers, all very Germanic. An escaper caught by the Gestapo hears himself addressed as "Herr Leutnant" and knows that he won't be shot; a newly captured airman, apprehensive because he is Jewish, is relieved to hear a German say: "He is a soldier like us, and therefore we must treat him as one of us." Some cruel acts are reported, but from the edge of the picture, as things that were done somewhere else to some other man. At the center there is only Prussian militarism.

Compared to possible battle conditions, life in the camps was surprisingly comfortable. (Once more one is faced with the improbable proposition that it wasn't so bad, really.) Consider this prisoner's testimony:

> We were fed more abundantly, probably, than any other community in Europe at that time. We had clothes, blankets, books, games, encouragement to study and the necessary material with which to work.... Before we left that

camp ... we had a library and well-furnished recreation
rooms. Also, at the top of the building, was a small silence
room where one might write in comfort. Here were
flowers, pictures, even a carpet. From the windows no wire
could be seen, nothing but distant woods and the far,
sunlit peaks of the Austrian Tyrol.

It all sounds like some Bavarian resort hotel. One must take
account, of course, of the fact that it was written during the war
and that the man who wrote it was still a prisoner, and had good
reasons for giving his hosts a favorable review; but other POWs
confirm most of the details: prison food, supplemented by
regular Red Cross parcels, was adequate, at least until late in the
war; books and writing materials were supplied; mail was delivered; plum puddings, sent for Christmas, arrived on time.

A comfortable-sounding life, and an oddly familiar one, for
the men who were there. I've been saying all through this book
that war is a strange and unimaginable experience, but these
memoirs of prison life are an exception: there is no *strangeness* in
them. The men who were sent to the camps seem quickly to
have made themselves at home there. Each camp became at
once an organized community, with a government, a class structure, strict codes of behavior, and a busy social life. Activities
were organized: one camp built a bobsled run and a skating
rink in winter, and when the ice melted in the spring sailed toy
boats on the puddles, and when the puddles dried laid out a
football field. There were plays and Christmas pantomimes, and
camp magazines were published. It was as though they arrived
knowing what to do, as though they had been there before. And
they had: what they constructed—the British, at least—in their
German jails and castles, and in Italian ones too, was English
school life all over again.

Like schoolboys, they imagined escaping from their confine-
ment. Cyril Rofe recalled how the RAF prisoners at Lamsdorf
thought about escape:

With the approach of spring, escape fever got a real hold on the compound. Hundreds of enthusiasts were doing their daily circuits and in every barrack there were men copying maps, planning routes and laying in all necessary stores. . . .

Many looked upon escape as a sport. It broke the monotony. They did not expect to succeed; they merely wanted something to do. The planning passed the time, the escape was a great adventure.

At the back of all this there is a military ethic: a soldier withheld from war should try to rejoin it and so recover his lost soldier-ship. But the motives Rofe describes are not so simple. Men plan escapes out of boredom, or for fun: "For me," one escaper wrote, "escaping was still a schoolboy adventure reminiscent of the books of G. A. Henty." They may not escape, or even try to, but if they draw maps and gather supplies, they will be making escape possible and so will not be entirely prisoners and victims. And those supplies—odds and ends of tools and clothing and forged documents, "keys, wires, knives, and useful bits of metal"—those, too, would be supports for the self; a man with a knife is not nobody. The maps must have been especially sup-portive: they confirmed the world beyond the walls and made its roads possible routes; you could get there from here.

I've mentioned the popular escape-adventure stories, the ones that were chosen by book clubs and made into movies. But to my mind the best account of escape from a German prison is not in any of them, but in a less-known escaper's narrative, Airey Neave's *They Have Their Exits*. It is best because Neave was an intelligent, reflective man, but also because history provided him with a fortunate frame for his story, which gives it unusual depth and resolution.

Neave was an English barrister when the war began, and a member of a Territorial regiment. He was called up and sent to France in 1940 with the first British troops, fought in the great retreating action toward Dunkirk, and was wounded and captured at Calais. For twenty months he was a prisoner of the Germans; he made two escape attempts that failed and then, on the third attempt, succeeded. For the rest of the war he worked to help the French Resistance and to assist Allied escapers. That experience, and his legal training, made him an appropriate member of the British staff at the Nuremberg Trials, where it was his job to serve writs on the imprisoned German war criminals. And so his story begins, unusually for a war narrative, at the end, as he enters the cell of General Keitel and hands him the charges against him.

Neave saw in this full circle "the poetic justice, with which Fate had brought me face to face with my former captors." But it is more than that: this is one war memoir that ends with a strong, symmetrical resolution, with evil identified and punished, and the good soldier explicit in his triumph. Most men who fight are not permitted such just rewards. Perhaps because Neave was there, or perhaps simply because he was a thoughtful, judicious man, the book that he wrote about his war is both a lively adventure narrative and a reflection on imprisonment and freedom, crime and crimelessness.

There is one further thing to say about *They Have Their Exits*, because it is a characteristic that narratives of European escapes share: it is a travel book. Neave escaped through Leipzig to Ulm and over the Swiss frontier, and then south through Vichy France to Perpignan and the Spanish border. For an Englishman of his class and education this was familiar territory; he spoke the languages, he knew the customs, and everything he saw he *knew*—the trains, the civilians and the clothes they wore, the food, the villages and towns. It's the *strangeness* point again, but reversed: there is no strangeness here, only a middle-class English officer on a European tour. And where is the war? It was never *here*, in these quiet places. If this is a war narrative, then *war* means something more than we thought; it includes

costumes, and disguises, and anxious train journeys, and sympa-
thetic civilians. And in Neave's case it included, at the end, justice. (Or not quite at the end: Neave survived his war, only to
die unjustly in another. In the postwar years he became a
Member of Parliament and was killed by an IRA car bomb in
1979.)

The familiar journey Neave took was the one to choose for
your escape, if you had a choice. As Cyril Rofe explained,

> Most escapers were satisfied to aim for Switzerland, France
> and Spain, or Sweden via the German Baltic ports. These
> were countries we all knew something about. It meant
> crossing Germany, possibly western Czechoslovakia, but
> we were all familiar with Germans by now and most pris-
> oners knew a few words of the language. It was like
> crossing a semi-civilized country where the dangers and
> pitfalls were known and could therefore be countered.

Those routes were possible if you were imprisoned in Germany;
but what did you do if the camp was in Poland? You headed
east, toward Russia. Rofe, the Jewish airman, escaped three
times from Polish camps, into the strangeness of Poland. Twice
he was caught—once by Polish civilians who handed him over to
the Germans because he was a Jew. The third time he reached
the advancing Russian Army. He had been on the run for five
weeks, and had crossed most of Poland on foot.

Rofe's journey was radically different from the Western
European tour; the terrain was unknown, the language incom-
prehensible, the people frightened and suspicious, even the
place names a mystery (he had a German map, but the road
signs were in Polish). Wandering, trusting strangers, begging for
his food, Rofe moved uncertainly toward the Eastern Front,
where the war was being fought (another fundamental difference from the western routes); only when he had passed
through the war to the other side would he be safe. But his

story doesn't stop there; it wanders on, to Moscow, to Mur-
mansk, and finally by ship to Britain, where it ends in December
1944, with the war still going on.

    This seems a right and appropriate ending for a POW's story;
escapers' narratives are completed when the escaper feels *free*—
which for most of them is when they reach home. Rofe's return
has no significance for anyone but him; he has been gone three
and a half years and has traveled four thousand miles to reach
his moment of freedom—not with loved ones in some dear
familiar place, not with his comrades in the RAF, but on a train
between Carlisle and London, in a fog, in a country still at war.

    And in his uniform, that's important; Rofe ends his story
restored to his first condition—he is an airman. That is the European POW's happy ending; "joining the fight again," as Neave
wrote, "is the main purpose of escaping." And how does Rofe
feel about all that he has undergone during those lost years?
Like so many other remembering soldiers, he thinks, at the end
of his book, "I would not have missed it for anything in the
world." Men like danger, hardship, and fear: we must accept
that; it's an *adventure*.

    The essential point about European POWs' narratives is that
they are told as adventures, in which men oppose their captors,
break from their captivity, and preserve for themselves and their
fellow prisoners the reality of action and freedom that makes
them men. Prisoners of the Japanese told other stories, which
are almost diametrically opposite to those told by European
prisoners. The ones we are most likely to know are sufferers'
stories in which starvation, disease, and the cruelty of the guards
turn prisoners into less than men, and in which the sustaining
hope is not freedom but simply survival. (One prisoner in four
would die in the Japanese camps; in the German camps the
death rate was one in twenty-five.) From those cruel camps in
Malaya, the Philippines, Korea, and the home islands, there
would be no escape. What prisoner would have the strength to

try, after such hardships? And where would he go? There are virtually no Asian escape adventures comparable to the European ones.

In the Asian narratives escape is a rumor, passed among prisoners who will never themselves escape but will only endure, or die. Word comes to Malayan prison camps that a man has slipped out of Singapore in a small boat; that escapers from Changi jail have been caught, and tortured and killed; that ten prisoners walked away from a Burma railway construction camp, of whom five died in the jungle and the survivors were captured. POWs in Manila hear that two men have escaped from Bilibid prison; that three officers who tried it at the Cabanatuan camp have been caught, beaten, and shot; that an army private has been caught after a week of freedom.

None of these is an eyewitness report; they are all rumors. Here is a typical rumor remembered:

> In February two escape parties, one consisting of Captain Pomeroy and Lieutenant Howard, the other of three men led by a Sergeant Kelly, had left the railway near Kanburi [in Malaya]. The two officers got quite far, but they would have had to walk through rough limestone country, stumbling over creepers, dense rough grass and thickets of bamboo. They probably did not have even a map as good as mine: what chance did they ever have?
>
> Sergeant Kelly's group was the first to be recaptured, followed by Howard and Pomeroy. All six officers and men were then murdered, without any form of trial or court martial. We heard that they had been shot out of hand; we heard that they had been killed slowly, bayoneted to death one by one after being made to dig their own graves. No-one knew what to believe.

It's a mixture of accurate-sounding details—the men's names, the landscape—and actions that would sound like a propagandist's invented atrocity if it came from some other theater of war, but here seem likely enough, given the known cruelty of the Japanese. What was the truth? Nobody knew.

Prisoners heard escape stories like this one, and they heard atrocity stories, like the one about the Australian nurses, which apparently originated with POWs brought to Malaya from Sumatra. The nurses were fleeing Singapore on a ship headed for Java, when the ship was sunk and the nurses were cast ashore on a small island. A Japanese landing party found them there. They were ordered to walk to the beach, and were machine-gunned. Twenty-one nurses died. The story is told in several personal narratives from Malayan prison camps. I don't know if it is true; but it is a part of the tale.

Rumors like these were all the news prisoners in the camps had. The Japanese were determined to prevent access to any news source that might report how the war was going; possession of a radio in one Malayan camp was punished by crippling beatings and harsh prison terms. The Germans tried to achieve the same news blackout but were not very successful: Europe leaked news. The Japanese did better; narratives of life in their prison camps agree that prisoners there knew nothing about events in the world. Being completely cut off from the news of the war was especially hard. The war was the cause for which they were imprisoned; not to know how it was going was to be ignorant of whether their sufferings had meaning or were simply a waste of their lives.

In the soldiers' tale of the war in Asia and the Pacific, two POW stories are as memorable and bitter as any battle. Both begin with a humiliating defeat and surrender—of British and Commonwealth troops at Singapore, of Americans at Bataan—and move on, one to Changi jail and the Burma-Siam railway, the other to the Death March and Bilibid prison. Those stories contain the war's extreme brutalities; together they are testimony and proof of Japanese inhumanity to their military prisoners, as the rape of Nanking is the testimony of their inhumanity to civilians.

The fall of Singapore was the worst defeat in the British Army's history. The story is one of history's epic disasters, a bit of common knowledge, like the sinking of the *Titanic*. We all know how it goes: how the great British guns pointed south, to defend against an attack by sea that never came, while enemy forces streamed down from the north—on ten thousand bicycles, according to one story—and overwhelmed the city's defenders; how Singapore, the impregnable fortress city, fell in a few weeks and 130,000 troops surrendered.

Most of the men who tell the Singapore story were new civilian soldiers, rushed to the city by troopship and plane from England, South Africa, Bombay, Hong Kong, to arrive in time to defend it for a week or a month and then to surrender and so become nonsoldiers almost before they had learned what fighting was. Their stories begin and end with bitterness and anger, not against the war itself—nobody questioned its moral rightness—but against the men who commanded them so complacently and incompetently, the generals, the Blimps. "Our generalship," says one, "was almost always bad and wrong"; "the fault ... lies not with, but above, us," says another. That bitterness is part of the story and makes it different from narratives of other disasters, of Pearl Harbor, say, or Dunkirk. For this shameful defeat, and the years of suffering that followed, there were men to blame: not us, but those above us. This isn't a criticism of strategy; it's a moral judgment.

But the defense of Singapore is not the primary story; in most memoirs it occupies a couple of pages at most. The story is the long imprisonment. That story is focused on two centers: Changi jail, the island's principal prison, and the railroad that the Japanese determined to build into Burma. Changi became for the conquerors a storehouse of laborers, who could be sent "up the line" to work on the railroad. Prisoners were an energy supply, like the wood the locomotives burned; as one prisoner remarked, the railway was burning men. How many died building it is uncertain: thirteen or fourteen thousand British troops, plus an uncountable number of Asian laborers—perhaps a hundred thousand, perhaps twice that many.

Men died on the railway because their captors didn't care if they lived or not, because to the Japanese, men who had surrendered in war were not men. A survivor of that ordeal recalled that

> we were not, it appeared, recognized as conventional prisoners-of-war as established by well-meaning but misguided politicians, but as shameful captives. The traditional Japanese military philosophy allowing no alternative to victory but death, we were the dishonoured, the despised, the lowest of the low. Armbands were issued to this effect, to be worn by certain of the camp administration [that is, the prisoners' own leaders] bearing this inscription in Japanese: "One who has been captured in battle and is to be beheaded or castrated at the will of the Emperor."

The Japanese who ran the camps were careless with their human fuel; they starved and beat their prisoners, let their diseases go untreated, worked them until they died and then brought more men up the line to replace them. And the prisoners? They endured, or they died; what else could they do? Again and again their memoirs pose the rhetorical question: where could they go? They were as much prisoners of the jungle as of the Japanese.

What was it like to be a prisoner in that awful place? There are two personal narratives that are classic answers to that question. One is the work of a man who was not really a writer but a visual artist of great gifts. Ronald Searle was a nineteen-year-old art student in Cambridge when he was called up for service in September 1939. His regiment was sent to Singapore at the end of 1941; he arrived in the city in January 1942 and surrendered a month later, without having fired a single shot. The story of his fighting war takes up a single page in his book.

Searle was a prisoner for four years; he worked up the line, he suffered the illnesses and infections that they all suffered, he endured the hardships of Changi. And he survived. He survived, I think, because he opposed his captors in the only way he could: he drew what he saw. There is a passage in Bruno Bettelheim's account of his imprisonment in Dachau that is pertinent to this point. Bettelheim is writing of his own survival:

> To observe and try to make sense out of what I saw was a device that spontaneously suggested itself to me as a way of convincing myself that my own life was still of some value, that I had not yet lost all the interests that had once given me self-respect. This, in turn, helped me to endure life in the camps.

Bettelheim used his skills as a psychologist to bear witness and to survive. Searle used his art. "During my captivity," he wrote,

> I had, in a somewhat unimaginative and already ambitious way, convinced myself that my mission was to emerge from the various camps, the jungle and finally prison, with a "significant" pictorial record that would reveal to the world something of what happened during those lost and more or less unphotographed years.

He would record in drawings what was done to him and to his fellow prisoners. And by recording, he would oppose.

It was a commitment of extraordinary courage and persistence. He had no drawing materials and had to scrounge for paper and pens. And what he was doing was forbidden, something for which he could have been killed. He had to make his drawings secretly and keep them always hidden from the guards; sometimes he concealed them on the bodies of men who were dying of cholera, where the Japanese were not inclined to search.

Searle's book is titled *To the Kwai—and Back: War Drawings 1939–1945*, which makes the text seem ancillary to the pictures. But it has its own narrative power, beyond what the drawings by their very nature can have. It tells of powerlessness and great suffering, from hunger, disease, overwork, and torture. But not *passive suffering.* Searle and his fellow prisoners steal from their captors, share what they have, nurse each other, and so remain a "we" at war with a "them." I don't want to romanticize and exaggerate their opposing actions; they were men weak to the point of death, continually guarded by brutal, armed soldiers, and without any weapons of their own. There was not much they could do. They didn't manage anything as dramatic as sabotaging the bridge they were building (that only happened in Pierre Boulle's novel), or any other successful act of direct defiance. But they opposed, and so preserved some fragment of their freedom and their humanity.

Their story, as Searle tells it, is more often grotesque than heroic, because survival under extreme conditions *is* grotesque. Their bodies were disgusting, their clothes were rags, the places where they slept were wretched beyond what we would call endurable. The food they were given would not sustain life, and they had to supplement it with whatever passed by—a boa constrictor or, one Christmas, two Burmese kittens ("rather like baby rabbit," Searle says, "but more delicate and sweeter. Delectable.").

The tone of that remark—objective, ironic, a little amused—is the tone of Searle's narrative. It's a retrospective tone: Searle wrote his story in the mid-1980s, some forty years after the events, and though his memories of suffering are still vivid, they are distanced, like a nightmare remembered in daylight. If you compare that ironic tone to other Second War narratives—to Keith Douglas's or Farley Mowat's—you'll see that Searle manages to speak with the war's characteristic voice: not that of a victim but of an ironic survivor.

There is another story in Searle's book, which is not retrospective but immediate—the story told in the drawings. Page after page, they assault the reader's eye and overpower the written text. Together they amount to a diary in images of

Searle's entire war, from the troopship that brought him to Singapore, into Changi jail, up the line in a railway work party and back again, to the day when Changi was liberated. They are the witness that Searle swore to record and bring out of the jungle and the prison—the story of what it was like there, *as it happened.* Words won't convey their disturbing power, but some of the titles and subjects will suggest the story they tell: "Chinese cleaning up bodies from the streets after Singapore's capitulation"; "Heads of executed Malay 'underground' workers exhibited as a warning by Japs" (similar instances of heads on stakes occur in other narratives by prisoners of the Japanese); "Man dying of cholera"; "Man dead of cholera"; "Man sick with tropical ulcers and fever, three days before death"; "Limbless Prisoners of War"; "Hungry prisoner." As you turn the pages, the men become more emaciated, more glassy-eyed and staring; by the middle of the book, in 1943, every man is a skeleton. There are no images of escapers, or of any prisoners *acting* at all; only the Japanese guards act—they beat, they torture, they decapitate. Looking at those images, we know about life at Changi—the punishment, the suffering, the death, and the cruelty, cruelty, cruelty.

Some of Searle's drawings are portraits, both of captives and of their captors. It's the captors that interest me most; looking at their images, I think: This is what hate looks like—not *their* hate, but the hate of the man who drew their faces. In our peaceable, liberal hearts we all believe, or try to believe, that hatred is a destructive emotion; but in extreme situations it is clearly a source of strength and a nourishment for the soul. Searle got through four years of imprisonment by hating: it's all there in his drawings.

The other classic narrative of the POW war in Southeast Asia is even more distantly retrospective than Searle's written text. Eric Lomax began writing *The Railway Man* in the mid-1980s and published it in 1995, fifty years after the end of his experiences as a prisoner. Like Searle, Lomax was captured at

Singapore, was held in Changi, and worked and suffered on the railway. His narrative confirms some essential truths about that experience. One is the way the geography of their situation affected them:

> It gradually dawned on us that the boundary keeping us in was as much psychological as it was physical; that we could walk for miles in the pineapple plantations around Kranji [where he was on a working party] without seeing a single Japanese, that we could sell stolen Japanese equipment to the local Chinese traders, but there was nowhere to go to: north of us was the long peninsula, separated from Burma and therefore from India by high mountains choked with forest; south or west were the occupied Dutch colonies of Java and Sumatra; east, nothing but the sea.

"There was nowhere to go to": that makes an essential distinction between the Japanese POWs' story and the European one; if there is nowhere to go, how can one be an agent in one's own imprisoned life?

Yet it was necessary to oppose, somehow. That stolen equipment Lomax mentions was one way of doing it. The prisoner who steals from his captors acts against them and so reclaims a fragment of his free identity, if only momentarily. Airey Neave saw this necessity too. "The prisoner of war," he wrote, "is not a criminal, yet he must employ all the criminal's ingenuity and cunning." Lomax says, with evident satisfaction, that in the camps he learned the arts of subterfuge and quiet resistance and became a competent thief.

Not quite competent enough, though. He was one of the men I mentioned who tried to breach their isolation by constructing a radio and were caught. Lomax's account of his punishment for that crime answers another, and most harrowing, question about that life: What was it like to be tortured? It was like this:

I was called forward. I stood to attention. They stood facing me, breathing heavily. There was a pause. It seemed to drag on for minutes. Then I went down with a blow that shook every bone, and which released a sense of scorching liquid pain which seared through my entire body. Sudden blows struck me all over. I felt myself plunging downwards into an abyss with tremendous flashes of solid light which burned and agonized. I could identify the periodic stamping of boots on the back of my head, crunching my face into the gravel; the crack of bones snapping; my teeth breaking; and my own involuntary attempts to respond to deep vicious kicks and to regain an upright position, only to be thrown to the ground once more.

At one point I realized that my hips were being damaged and I remember looking up and seeing the pick-helves coming down towards my hips, and putting my arms in the way to deflect the blows. This seemed only to focus the clubs on my arms and hands. I remember the actual blow that broke my wrist. It fell right across it, with a terrible pain of delicate bones being crushed. Yet the worst pain came from the pounding on my pelvic bones and the base of my spine. I think they tried to smash my hips. My whole trunk was brutally defined for me, like having my skeleton etched out in pain.

It went on and on. I could not measure the time it took. There are some things that you cannot measure in time, and this is one of them. Absurdly, the comparison that often comes to my mind is that torture was indeed like an awful job interview: it compresses time strangely, and at the end of it you cannot tell whether it has lasted five minutes or an hour.

I do not know that I thought I was dying. I have never forgotten, from that moment onwards, crying out "Jesus," crying out for help, the utter despair of helplessness. I rolled into a deep ditch of stagnant water which, in the

second or two before consciousness was finally extinguished, flowed over me with the freshness of a pure and
sweet spring.

This is Battlefield Gothic without a battlefield—or a battle. It
makes excruciatingly vivid what war may become when absolute
power confronts absolute powerlessness. We will confront this
situation again, in other narratives of other sufferers.

Searle and Lomax tell essentially one story, of men pushed
to the edge of what is endurable, and beyond, and left there
year after year. It's a story of pure inhumanity—or almost. For in
both narratives there are Japanese who draw back, if only ever
so slightly, from that edge. Searle meets an officer, Captain
Takahashi, who studied art in Paris before the war; he gives
Searle paper and colored pencils and once, taking up Searle's
sketchbook, he makes a delicate line drawing of a mother and
child. Then he reverts to his role as prison administrator, and
Searle goes on hating him. Lomax recalls that "always, whether
on the railway or in the camps, there were people who were
humane enough to take risks to help us," though his example of
that humanity is a thin one: "Some of the Japanese prison staff
tried to do nothing to add to our squalor and unhappiness."
These exceptions don't really alter the brutal world of the narratives; they only remind us that *absolute* brutality is impossible to
achieve when many individuals are involved.

Both of these memoirists looked back on their years of
imprisonment over intervening decades. Can we infer, from
their examples, the effects of introspection? On clarity of recollection there seems to be no effect at all: how could Lomax's
memory of his beating be clearer? Or Searle's memory of the
taste of kittens? But if they didn't forget, could they forgive?
Here their stories differ. Searle's prose narratives suggests a
recovered calm and an ironic distancing from the events; but
though the hatred cooled, a cold hatred can be as fierce and
lasting as a hot one, and there is no forgiveness in his story. In

Lomax's story there is. In the early Nineties he learned the whereabouts of the Japanese who served as interpreter at the interrogation in which he was so savagely beaten, and learned also that the man had spent his postwar life in remorseful penance. A meeting was arranged, and they met—appropriately, at the Kwai bridge—and made peace. "Sometime," the book ends, "the hating has to stop."

These two memoirs tell the up-the-line story, in all its brutality. Other survivors of the Singapore surrender tell other, less terrible stories. Robert Hardie, for example, was a British military doctor who served at camps along the railway; his story has nothing to do with brutality or executions, everything to do with disease, overwork, and starvation. What it was like, for him, was this:

> The sickness in 16 Battalion in these six weeks has become alarming—240 out of 400 are unable to work now. Many are desperately ill with dysentery, beriberi and pellagra, malaria and exhaustion.... We are having about four deaths a day at present. Desperately sick men are brought in from time to time from neighbouring small camps where there are no British medical officers or orderlies. These men have been kept without attention for so long that when they get here there is nothing to be done except see them die—they are so far gone that there is nothing to work on in attempting to save them.

That's the doctor's story. There is also a bureaucrat's story. David Nelson had been a civil servant in Singapore. At Changi he set up a Bureau of Records of Enquiry, which he said, proudly, was "the only general record and information centre operating behind the lines in the whole of what was known by Japan as the Greater East Asia Co-Prosperity Sphere." Nelson's bureau sounds slightly ridiculous, after Hardie's pained account; but it, too, performed necessary and valuable services. Nelson kept track of the thousands of prisoners who came to Changi;

he saw that their mail was delivered and that their pay records were kept; and when they died he recorded that too. In other prison camps, men died anonymously and were forgotten. Nelson gave the dead back their names.

Hardie and Nelson were officers and were billeted with other officers, and that made a difference in prisons, both German and Japanese. Hardie could leave the camp and go to a nearby town to buy supplies and have a pleasant meal at "a new eating place by the town gate," as he might have done at any peacetime posting, and when he changed camps he joined a new officers' mess, and found the officers there "an extremely pleasant crowd." And Nelson noted in his diary for June 2, 1943:

> I went with Captain Burnet to dine at Southern Area H.Q. and sat with the Commander, Lt. Co. Tawney. After a good "dinner" everyone went to *Smoky Joe's*, now the area's cabaret and night club; it is a great effort and was crowded. There is an orchestra with cabaret turns, and drinks are available.

Here, too, the life seems grotesquely to mimic peacetime. It wasn't just that these men were officers, though that helped; Lomax and Tom Henling Wade were officer-prisoners too, and were starved and beaten. Still, the odds seemed to favor men with commissions, and the higher the better. Armies are class systems, as both the Germans and the Japanese recognized.

But it's also true that life for all ranks in the camps (as distinct from up the line) was not all suffering, that men created societies there that imitated societies they had known before. As narrators describe them, they often seem grotesque parodies of British middle-class life, modeled perhaps on some suburban golf club, or an expatriate community like the one in Forster's *A Passage to India*. There were lectures and language courses, and at Changi even a university; there were concerts and endless theatricals: a play by Shaw, Maugham's *The Circle, The Chocolate Soldier, Night Must Fall, Babes in Toyland,* a Christmas pantomime. Books were read and exchanged: one prisoner noted in his diary that he had read *Waverley*, Churchill's *World Crisis*, *Pickwick Papers*, *David Copperfield*, *The Return of the Native*, *Pride and Prejudice*, and Bridges's *The Testament of Beauty*. It's all so predictable. And I suppose that's the point; they made the strangeness of imprisonment endurable by giving it a familiar facade. Not that it wasn't bad; it was terrible: *Babes in Toyland* and *Pride and Prejudice* don't work like aspirin. But one must conclude that for some men, in some places in Malaya, life was endurable.

Of the other core story of Asian captivity—the story of Bataan and Bilibid—perhaps less needs to be said. The Japanese were the same and behaved in the same way: they cut off heads and stuck them on poles, they starved and beat and overworked their prisoners. And the prison was much the same too: I can't see much difference between conditions in Changi and conditions in Bilibid.

There are many narratives to tell us what it was like to be a prisoner in the Philippines, narratives by both officers and men of the U.S. Army, Navy, and Marines. The best, to my mind, the most affecting and particular, is the diary of Commander Thomas Hayes, a regular Navy doctor who was stationed in Manila when the Japanese came in December 1941. With other American forces, he retreated along the Bataan peninsula and then to the island of Corregidor (an "impregnable island fortress," like Singapore) and there surrendered, after a four-month siege. He spent two and a half years in Bilibid, first as chief of surgery for the prisoners and then as senior medical officer. In December 1944 he was put aboard a Japanese transport for transfer to Japan. The ship was attacked by American planes and sunk. He survived and was moved to another ship, which was also attacked; this time he was killed.

Like Searle's drawings, Hayes's diary was a secret, forbidden record. He kept it hidden while he was in Bilibid and, when he left, entrusted it to a fellow prisoner, who divided it and buried parts in scattered places around the prison. Some parts have been discovered, but some are lost—perhaps still buried in the prison yard. Because it is a diary, it has no retrospection about it, no calm after the storm, and no forgiveness—neither of the Japanese nor of his fellow prisoners. For Hayes was an angry man, and a good hater. He hated the Japanese, but he also hated the U.S. Army and its doctors (who sold their medicines to their patients, he said, and charged them for treatment). He complained of inter-service politics and corruption and of theft among the prisoners, and he despised and resented other American officers.

That may not sound like the portrait of a hero, but there wasn't much scope for heroism in a Japanese prison. Hayes did what he could; he maintained an espionage link with Filipinos outside the walls, and he treated the patients who were brought to him as well as he was able. But most of all, like Searle he *testified* in the only way he could, and so made the unimaginable squalor of Bilibid imaginable.

One theme recurs in Hayes's diary that is troubling, because it appears in the narratives of other prisoners: isolation, and the inability to establish bonds with other men. "Times like these," he writes, "tend to produce comradeships of strong ties and deep feelings. It hasn't done so for me." He expresses no warm human feelings, either for the men around him or for friends or family at home; prison, it seems, had frozen his heart. The same coldness is in other memoirs of that place: an army sergeant wrote of his first day in prison: "I damn sure didn't aim to get too well acquainted with anyone. Right now, I owed allegiance to no one and I expected none from anybody around me." You wouldn't expect such hostile, self-regarding men to create societies in their camps, as the British did; and indeed they don't seem to have done so. At least the memoirs don't mention any lectures, or theatrical productions, or concerts, or camp magazines. The camps are unalleviated imprisonment. What are we to think about that? That the loss of comradeship is the price of survival if the conditions are grim enough? Or that Americans respond to hardship in self-regarding ways? Not the latter, I hope; but I can find no comparable confessions in British POW memoirs.

From the copious records that exist of the lives of prisoners of war one might extract some basic principles of how to survive in that state. First and most obvious: be a prisoner in Europe. Second: be an officer. Third: construct a prison society; model it on the army or on an English public school, or choose some other institution—a monastery or a trade union, but give your collective existence form and familiarity. But not all of those rules are real options, and in the end perhaps the only useful rule is the "old sweats" philosophy that Tom Wade, a prisoner at Changi, learned:

> Each one of us had to come to terms with our despondency and gloom. Prison camp was going to be about survival: one could not afford to mope about a failure; one had to be forward-looking, optimistic, a cheerful comrade to one's fellows in order to survive this ordeal. I noticed how most of the old soldiers in our barrack were cheerful, practical and almost "at home" in their new surroundings. To them it was just a rather bad army posting; you simply had to make the best of it, did the most you could with what was available, had a laugh, made a joke and "carried on regardless." They were right, the old sweats. Learn from them. Smile, be brave, be optimistic. Be ready to take anything the Japs might throw at you—and *survive.*

Prisoner-of-war stories can be exciting, violent, terrible, heroic: but are they *war* stories? Surely a soldier's story ends when his opposition ends; when one side has seized all the power and the other is reduced to utter powerlessness, the story becomes something else. War, as we have seen it in other soldiers' stories, is about killing one's enemies by fighting, on battlefields; but in POWs' narratives men die of their captors'

indifference or malevolence, of disease and exhaustion and
starvation and neglect, and even the killings are indifferent
murders.

But in fact opposition didn't end with surrender, though it
took furtive courses. Imprisoned men went on opposing, in such
ways as were possible: by sabotaging the work they were
assigned to do; by working slowly and "stealing time"; by
stealing anything else they could lay their hands on; by reaching
out for news of the continuing war; by mocking their captors;
and by surviving, remembering, and testifying. Those who
didn't oppose (and there were many) didn't tell their stories;
they had no war stories to tell, because they had quit their war.
They were no longer soldiers and weren't yet civilians; they
must have seemed to themselves to be in a state of suspended
animation, between one self and another. But those who did
oppose—the ones who survived—preserved both self and story:
of how they continued to be agents in their own lives, however
confined, of how they went on being soldiers, opponents, enemies. Their stories, however burdened with suffering, are not
victims' narratives. Not quite.

The story of the sufferings of prisoners of war is a terrible one;
but it isn't new. There have always been prisoners, and often
they have been cruelly mistreated: the American Confederacy's
Andersonville Prison was not all that different from Changi, and
there were British concentration camps in South Africa during the Boer War. Up to 1945, such stories, and the stories of
peoples massacred and towns destroyed, were what the world
knew about atrocious war.

But in 1945 two things happened that changed human
understanding of what men could do to other human beings if
they wished to: the German death camps were liberated; and
the first atomic bomb was detonated over Hiroshima. These two
events give a disturbing, dissonant tone to the end of the
Second World War. There in the last months, when the war was

won in Europe and as good as won in the Pacific, humankind learned two unwelcome truths: that in Europe a greater evil had been done than we had imagined possible in our world; and that in the Pacific our side, the *good* side, had introduced an instrument of destruction so powerful it might annihilate all life on earth. So both wars ended with a kind of stunned shock. Victory had not cleared the air; there would be worse wars to come.

The death camps and Hiroshima have this in common, that though both are essential parts of the war, neither belongs to the narratives of the *agents*. They are sufferers' tales. They have something else in common: these were events that had not been imagined before—had not had to be imagined, because they had not been possible. The senior medical officer with the British troops that liberated Belsen told reporters: "Anything you have ever read, heard or seen does not begin the story"; and a witness at Hiroshima wrote: "No one ... can talk about it ... it eludes words." There were no words for those new realities, but words would have to be found and the stories told so that we, all the citizens of the world who were not there, could imagine what was unimaginable. Over years, and with difficulty, the stories were told. They are the most original and important narratives to come out of the war—war-narratives at the edge, extreme cases of what is possible in war, now.

It may seem wrong to some readers that I should treat the bombing of Hiroshima and the Holocaust as comparable. To do so, the argument goes, is to "normalize" the Nazi atrocities, by implying that they were simply another extreme act of war. I understand the concern in that argument: we all want to preserve our sense that human behavior has limits, and that the extermination of death-camp prisoners went beyond humanity, and in a unique way. But the Holocaust, like the atom bomb, happened in history; like the bomb, it is now among human possibilities. Not, God help us, *normalized*; but possible. "It is a grave error," that wise critic Irving Howe wrote, to make, or "elevate," the Holocaust into an occurrence outside history, a sort of diabolic visitation, for then we tacitly absolve its human agents of their responsibility.... The Holocaust was long prepared for in the history of Western civilization, though not all those who engaged in the preparation knew what they were doing or would have welcomed the outcome.

The moral force of extermination of those millions was that it was *not* unique, that human beings have always destroyed other human beings for ethnic, ideological, and religious reasons (and out of pure sadism too). The history of the world since the Holocaust has proved that point over and over; in Cambodia, Uganda, Bosnia, Rwanda. Murder is human: surely we all know that.

Still, this is a book about war narratives. Was the Holocaust a war? Many who should know have thought it was. Lucy Davidowicz thought so, when she titled her great study of the Holocaust *The War Against the Jews.* Primo Levi thought so, when he wrote of his Auschwitz existence: "This life is war." The Nazis thought so: the Wansee Conference document that promulgated the Final Solution to the "Jewish problem" called it "the struggle ... against this enemy" (what is a struggle against an enemy if it isn't a war?). So yes, the Holocaust was a war; though the Nazis had redefined the term to include a vast action in which only one side was organized as an army, armed, and aggressive, in which one side did all the killing and the other side did all the dying. It was a technological war of extermination, imposed on helpless, innocent people: on Gypsies, socialists, Jehovah's Witnesses, the physically unfit, but systematically on European Jews. And in the case of the Jews, with a war aim of absolute clarity: total extermination.

It was a war; and existence in the camps was in some ways like military life as soldiers have recorded it. The camps were run in an authoritarian, regimented way that aimed at the suppression of individuality and will, that blunted the senses and tortured the bodies of the persons subject to it. Life there was lived in the constant presence of violent death, and survival became the only value. That isn't an *exact* description of a soldier's life as most men-at-arms have known it, but it resembles that life in the way the grotesque resembles the real. It was a life such as soldiers might invent for their enemies, in a war world where everything was allowed.

The stories of that life are war narratives, though the term must be extended: "the man who was there" must be stretched to include the old and the sick, women, children—all of humanity except the powerful. Their stories will be war stories; they'll deal with the central questions that war narratives ask and answer: What happened? What was it like? (Not what was the Holocaust like? but what was it like *there*, at Dachau or Belsen? What was one prisoner's life like?) And they'll add another question, a question for victims: What suffering was inflicted on you, and on others like you?

Holocaust narratives answer those questions by reconstructing intolerable existences, particular by particular and day by day. I've quoted before Pasternak's remark that "life is always deep in details"; these narratives are like that, and must be, if they are to make horror believable and belief unavoidable. So they move through details, from barracks to formation to work to food to barracks again. They describe the daily life of bargaining and trading to survive, the thieving, the betrayals. They show us the gas chambers and the ovens, the smoking chimneys and the gallows, the dead. *Deep* in details, strung along a narrative line that is the struggle to survive, seen at a more elemental level than any of us will ever know (though some of the men up the line in Malaya knew something like it and would understand). And out of those details and that narrative the tellers accomplish what literature always accomplishes, if it is literature: they make what we have not experienced, and cannot imagine, imaginable.

But there is one hard question to be confronted about this Holocaust war. In wars men die for a cause; whether they believe in it or not, the force they march with is moved by motives and reasons, by declarations and decisions. What were those death-camp prisoners dying for? One answer is: *for nothing*. Here is the British historian Ian Buruma, reviewing a recent book on Holocaust memorials:

> And yet, and yet ... I cannot help feeling that with all the talk of martyrdom and common remembrance, too much meaning is heaped upon the millions of victims. For the awful truth is that the Jews who were exterminated, as though they were vermin (Himmler's phrase), died for nothing. There was no higher meaning attached to their deaths. They were killed, because they were denied the right to live. And that was all.

That is nearly true. But "nearly" makes a great human difference. From the Nazi point of view, the Jews had no cause, and did not fight, and died like animals. But war creates its causes, and there is more than extermination in the narratives of the survivors.

One of the most moving, terrible, and intelligent of Holocaust memoirs is Primo Levi's. Levi was an Italian Jew who had been a chemist in Turin. (One must begin examination of Holocaust narratives by looking first at the prior life, to fix a human frame for the inhumanity that will follow.) He joined a Resistance group in the Italian mountains in 1943, and so for a time he was a soldier on the same side and in the same place as other tale tellers that we have been considering—Calvino and Mowat and Bowlby and Trevelyan. But not for long. At the end of that year he was captured by Fascist militia, and when he identified himself as a Jew he was transported with other Jews to Auschwitz.

Levi was a scientist, and he brought a scientific objectivity to his narrative of Auschwitz existence. Like an anthropologist observing some remote savage tribe, he made the life there—the patterns of behavior, the customs, the rituals—his subject, as Bettelheim and Searle made their imprisonments their subjects. I don't mean that he was cold or detached from the sufferings around him, or felt them less. Rather the opposite, for his scientist's ethic required him to accept the truth of what he observed and to describe it without self-deception, like an actual Dante in an actual hell (an analogy that runs through his book).

In some fundamental ways Levi's hell resembles the world of the POWs, and especially the Japanese camps. At Auschwitz, as at Changi, prisoners were an expendable energy source, like coal or wood, to be used up and replaced. Like POWs, they were condemned to suffer punishment for no crime. Like them, they created in their camps parodic societies in which prisoners with nothing nevertheless carried on commercial dealings; like them, they stole from their captors and from each other; like them, they were motivated by the will to survive. Some of them, who had special skills or attractions—doctors, tailors, musicians, young homosexuals—or were pitiless and inhuman enough to betray their fellow prisoners, aligned themselves with their oppressors and became *Prominenten,* privileged persons in the camp. Their opposites, the weakest ones, lost hope and faded until they died: *Muselmänner,* they were called; they were living, but they were already dead. There were men of both those kinds in Bilibid and Changi too.

But there was one deep difference between the Japanese POW camps and the German concentration camps. The Japanese killed their prisoners, as Lomax said, out of carelessness, out of indifference to their humanity. The Germans acted with the intention, based on ideology, of destroying Jews and other "inferior" beings, but, as Levi put it, "to annihilate us first as men in order to kill us more slowly afterwards." That intention is in the title of Levi's book: *Se questo è un uomo—If This Is a Man.*

Man/Humankind/Humanity: that is the subject. Is the humanity in a human being eradicable? Can it be extinguished by force and privation? Levi says yes, it can.

Consider his second chapter, titled "On the Bottom," in which he describes arriving at Auschwitz. Stripped of their clothes, their hair and beards, tattooed with numbers that will henceforth be their names, the prisoners stand together like miserable and sordid puppets:

> Then for the first time we became aware that our language lacks words to express this offence, the demolition of a man. In a moment, with almost prophetic intuition, the reality was revealed to us: we had reached the bottom. It is not possible to sink lower than this; no human condition is more miserable than this, nor could conceivably be so. Nothing belongs to us any more; they have taken away our clothes, our shoes, even our hair; if we speak, they will not listen to us, and if they listen, they will not understand. They will even take away our name.

Levi the meticulous scientist observed and analyzed the elements of this nether world, and so determined the natural laws of hell. Here is an example:

> Driven by thirst, I eyed a fine icicle outside the window, within hand's reach. I opened the window and broke off the icicle but at once a large, heavy guard prowling outside brutally snatched it away from me. *"Warum?"* I asked him in my poor German. *"Hier ist kein warum"* (there is no why here), he replied, pushing me inside with a shove.
>   The explanation is repugnant but simple: in this place everything is forbidden, not for hidden reasons, but because the camp has been created for that purpose.

For a scientist like Levi, that incident is in itself a definition of hell: hell is a place without *why. Why* leads to reason and to civilization; there will be none of that here. This is life on the bottom—utterly helpless, degraded, outside human history and below the level of mankind. Levi's answer to the question Is humanity eradicable? is as clear and as necessary as a syllogism, or the result of a careful laboratory experiment: inhumanity, when it is driven by absolute power, *can* destroy humanity.

Eli Wiesel's *Night* tells essentially the same story, but in a different voice and from a different prior life. Wiesel begins as a young, believing Jew in a Hungarian community of believers, a small, personal world defined by customs, beliefs and the rituals of those beliefs, by modest possessions, by kinship bonds. All these defining, human things are stripped from the prisoners as they move to and within Auschwitz. And so, Wiesel says, as Levi said, "we had ceased to be men." But for Wiesel, there is one other, terrible loss: the Nazis have murdered God, or have driven Him out from their inhuman world. "It's the end," a rabbi says. "God is no longer with us."

Levi's telling of the Holocaust story is coolly analytical; Wiesel's is burning and passionate, as deep in details as Levi's but with details that are monstrous and are told as events beyond possibility, yet true: bodies of children are burned in a bonfire like autumn leaves; two prisoners help their oppressors to hang a man, in return for a plate of soup; a son kills his father for a piece of bread. These are parables of atrocity, more like Greek tragedies or the Book of Job than like any war narrative that we have known. Deep in details, yes: but if the details are all of suffering, if every detail is an atrocity? This, surely, is the ultimate victim narrative, the point at which the story of war goes beyond, or below, the soldiers' tale.

If This Is a Man and *Night* are narratives of a one-sided war waged by inhumanity against humanity—a war that humanity lost, some have said, because it did not fight. It was a war in which virtually none of the casualties rebelled against their oppressors, or resisted, or uttered one word of defiance on the way to the gas chambers; on the contrary, we are told, prisoners were obedient, cooperated with their enemies, volunteered even to operate the crematories, and accepted their terrible destinies passively.

It was this passivity that Bruno Bettelheim found so unbearable. "Why then," he asked, "—and this is the question that haunts all who study the extermination camps—why then did millions walk quietly, without resistance, to their death?" Not all did, of course, and Bettelheim was aware of the exceptions—the eight hundred men of the twelfth Sonderkommando, who revolted against their impending deaths, and killed seventy SS troops before they were annihilated, the brave men and women who rose in the Warsaw ghetto to fight a military action, armed only with a few rifles and homemade bombs against the tanks, artillery, and flamethrowers of the Wehrmacht. But they were so few, out of so many millions.

Bettelheim wanted the prisoners to be agents in their lives, not sufferers; he wanted the victims to be human. If they had to die, regardless of their actions, then they should have died like soldiers in a war, to whom the old words of war—courage, heroism—could be applied with meaning. He was not asking his question out of ignorance; he had been in Dachau and Buchenwald in 1938–39. He had not been in the extermination camps during the war years, though; he didn't know the worst.

Yet there *was* opposition in those camps. Simply to continue to live was a kind of opposing, given the conditions of existence and the intentions of the captors. And there were other, more active gestures of resistance—small, confined, and of doubtful consequence, but nonetheless individual willed acts, done for the self's preservation and against the enemy. They were much like what the POWs did: pilfering food, stealing almost anything belonging to Germans, avoiding hard labor or doing it slowly. None was a heroic or even very significant act, but each was a small affirmation of self and of the will to live. They form an important part of what might be called (in a cruel oxymoron) *ordinary* Holocaust lives.

Take, as an example, *Breathe Deeply, My Son,* the narrative of

Henry Wermuth. Wermuth was a fifteen-year-old boy in Frank-
furt am Main in 1938, when he and his family were driven out
of Germany. They crossed the border into Poland and after the
German invasion were separated; mother and daughter disappeared and were presumably murdered by the Nazis; father and
son were moved from one concentration camp to another, and
eventually to Auschwitz. They survived there until early 1945,
when the Germans evacuated their prisoners westward, ahead
of the advancing Russians. In that move, the father died. Wermuth was liberated by the Americans two weeks later.

A story like that tells us what "ordinary" means in the collective tale that we call the Holocaust. Wermuth tells it with what
seems a total recall of details. But his narrative is more than
remembered particulars: it is shaped by the problem that
troubled Bettelheim: the problem of action in extreme circumstances. As Wermuth recalls his life as a prisoner, he creates a
young self who is aware of the importance of action and under-
stands that to stay alive he must be alert, cunning, and un-
scrupulous. He remembers the occasions when he did manage
to act—when he changed his position in a column of prisoners,
when he chose one group rather than another, the moment in a
freight car when he faced up to his guards—and so perhaps
affected his fate and his father's. But there were other times, the
moments for a large and desperate action, when he might have
escaped, or defied his captors, but did nothing. Why did he fail
then? Why did he choose certain suffering over possible
freedom? Why did prisoners not act courageously together
when their only alternative was certain eventual death? These
are Bettelheim's questions; but the asker in this case is a man
who was there.

Wermuth's answer is in this passage, describing two hangings at Plaszów camp:

> Two hangings! Must I feel ashamed that, when I saw the
> gallows, my survival instinct signalled a message of relief

through my system? Two poor wretches were going to die—but it wasn't me.

Curiosity took over and then a flash of hot anger. Here we stood, in a ratio of perhaps 100 to one against them, hopeless, helpless. My eyes wandered. Was there not one of those classical heroes among us who, by sheer personality, would unite us in an instant by moving forward and giving the command—"Attack!" We could crash into them, take their weapons, kill them. I was almost willing it to happen—I would certainly join. After a spontaneous move by a determined smaller group, the rest would surely follow, if only because there was no alternative—kill, or be killed.

Alas, there was no such person or organised group. Ten thousand frightened people had to watch, in powerless misery, the hanging of two of their brethren. Seething, but frightened like the rest, I stood and watched in silence.

What Wermuth describes here is a failure to act. But is it a failure of *courage*? Of *heroism*? Surely those concepts depend on some element of power in the agent; and these people have been reduced to powerless misery. It is a stage in the process that Levi wrote about: the annihilation of the humanity in men, before the other dying happens.

In this war against the powerless, the terms of war—courage, heroism, cowardice—take on new meanings. And so do the dead. Writing about other wars, I have taken the presence of dead soldiers, and narrators' awareness of them, to be an inevitable and defining element in the soldiers' tale. The Holocaust tells a version of the story that is different in this respect as in others, and, as in others, worse. The dead appear continually in the narratives—skeletal, anonymous, and without dignity. Wermuth's last vision of dead prisoners is a memorable example. It is May 1945, and he has just learned that he has been liberated. He steps from his prison barracks for the first time, into the bright, free sunlight, and sees two, very large, pyramids of corpses in varying states of decay. Grotesquely grinning, twisted faces looking at me and through me into nowhere. Faces distorted by pain and suffering, even in death. Layer upon layer, arms, legs, bodies entangled in all directions like discarded rubbish. Most of them were naked.

What is there about these dead that makes them so different from, say, the burned Frenchman that Rifleman Harris saw, or Sassoon's two dead Germans, or the corpses Keith Douglas found in the Italian tank? It's that they didn't die *for* anything, that they were not even the victims of any particular violent intention; they were simply prisoners among the millions, who stopped living before liberation came and were piled in a heap to be discarded. Like garbage, not like human beings. But aren't the others, the battlefield dead, like that? No, they aren't. Not quite.

Reading in the narratives of that war against humanity, we must accept Levi's image: when we enter there, we go to the bottom. Down there we learn that elements of our nature as human beings that we thought were immutable can be diminished or destroyed, and that the human heart may be colder and crueler than our experience has shown us. The process of disillusionment with progress and civilization reached its lowest depth there, in those camps designed by reason and by science for the efficient destruction of human lives.

If there is nevertheless some affirmation in these dark books, it must be this: that in this brutal world of powerless suffering it was possible, just possible, to be an agent—by small assertions of the will in opposing actions and, afterward, by telling. Because remembering is an action; to bear witness is to oppose. If you make the truth survive, however terrible it is, you are retaliating against inhumanity, in the only way the powerless have. So, in the Warsaw ghetto during the war, Michael Zylberberg began a diary:

The idea of creating a permanent record of what has happened came to me at the end of 1942, when of a Jewish
population of half a million some three hundred thousand
had already been exterminated. Among those killed were
my parents and three younger brothers, and my wife's parents and three younger sisters. I had the feeling that there
would be no one left to tell of the tragedy which ravages
the largest Jewish community in Europe.

No one left to tell: that must have seemed likely to many of
those victims. Yet the telling survives. And because it does,
we can believe that humankind is not completely powerless so
long as it has a voice. Humanity has not been abolished if the
stories live.

Our subject here is war against the helpless—victim war—and for
a last instance we must turn away from the terrible darkness of
the Holocaust to an instant of terrible light: the detonation of
the atomic bomb over Hiroshima. It was an act of war, clearly,
involving two belligerent nations, each with its armed forces in
action. And although it was an attack not on a specific military
target but on a city, that was not new in August 1945; many
cities were in ashes by then. But it was a strange, unique act of
war: an action without a battle, without armies, without a visible
enemy, in which neither courage nor cowardice mattered; an
action for which there was no possible retaliation; an action so
far outside the capabilities of armies up to then that it seemed
like some catastrophic natural disaster—only it was *un*natural.
That was what was most disturbing about it, and still is. Just as
what troubles us most about the death camps is that in them
human beings acted without humanity, as though the limits of
human behavior had been annulled, so at Hiroshima natural law
seemed to have been altered and a new kind of disaster added.
    There were other strangenesses. The action at Hiroshima

was an action without duration: in its story everything is aftermath. And everyone was a victim. Nobody resisted. So it was
different from the other bombed, burned-out cities, where there
were guns and fighter planes to oppose the attack. Different,
too, from Vietnam, with its multitudes of victims. There the
dead children were *mistakes;* here they were simply part of the
target (three-quarters of all the thirteen-year-olds in Hiroshima
were killed, according to one source, because their school class
happened to be working out of doors that morning). It is more
entirely a victim war even than Auschwitz, where resistance was
just barely possible and survival might be an act of will; more
than the prisoner-of-war camps, helpless though those captives
sometimes were. It was a unique event in the history of man's
capacity to destroy his species.

Tellers of the Hiroshima story speak neither with soldiers'
nor with civilians' voices but with the voices of victims. Their
accounts gather around two passive-victims' themes: the paralyzing strangeness of what happened, and the suffering. The
strangeness was in the explosion itself, which was over before it
could be observed. Here is a schoolboy's effort to describe that
instant:

> To say that I saw it at that instant is not quite accurate. The
> phenomenon that occurred at that instant registered on my
> eyeballs, but I had no way of knowing what it was. And
> whatever it was, it came and went with extraordinary
> speed. At first I thought it was something I had dreamed.
>
> The open space in front of the factory that was visible
> beyond the glass windows was filled with flames. But it
> was not that the ground was on fire and sending up flames.
> So I suppose I'd have to say that the flames were spewed
> down from the sky and were licking at the earth.
>
> But then with astonishing speed the instant came to an
> end and reality returned. Only it was a kind of stunned
> reality, full of terrible contradictions.

It's all there in that passage: the event of no duration, the strange manifestations of the bomb's power, the new and contradictory reality afterward. In that new reality, other testimonies tell us, nothing natural behaved naturally: trees were torn apart in midair, a tide rose and did not recede, tornadoes swirled out of nowhere, and black rain fell.

The victims, too, were strange. Another young man testifies:

> There was a schoolboy, stretched out on a straw mat. He kept whimpering for his mother, until his little close cropped head rolled over and he became very still. I saw a young girl with grossly swollen lips: "Water—please," were the only words she could force from her throat. There was a woman, stark naked. Her face was a featureless pulp of flesh. I saw a young man whose skin had burnt off to expose dark reddish muscles. An elderly man lay limp on a bridge. Blood kept oozing out of his head.
>
> There was nothing to be done.

Casualties like these, in other wars, I've called Battlefield Gothic and have cited as examples of the truth that in modern war most dying is grotesque. But at Hiroshima all of the victims, both the living and the dead, were grotesque: Battlefield Gothic was as commonplace as pain.

Of the personal memoirs of Hiroshima that I know—which are those that have been translated from the Japanese—all but one have this in common, that they are gatherings of images rather than continuous narratives. And one can see why this might be the form those memories would take. These books are by men and women who were there, under that burst of apocalyptic light and heat, and who witnessed the utter strangeness of the event and its aftermath. They looked on a scene more radically unfamiliar and more desolate than any battlefield: the dead more hideous, the surface of the earth more utterly devastated. Nothing was recognizable, neither persons nor places: children did not recognize their parents, people returning to their neighborhoods couldn't find where their own houses had stood, or even their streets. As for the order in time that continuity in a story implies, where was it? What could be expected or predicted in this annihilated place? How could there be a tomorrow?

Even the one continuous narrative, Dr. Michihiko Hachiya's *Hiroshima Diary,* has this quality of radical strangeness; it is a diary, a day-to-day report of a life, yet it has no sense of dailiness about it, none of the familiarities and repetitions by which ordinary life (even in a prison, even in Auschwitz) goes on. Dr. Hachiya's days pass without coherence, in a town that no longer exists, in a time that is out of time. The strangeness is in the first entry, dated August 6, 1945—the day of the bomb. It is morning; Dr. Hachiya is sprawled on his living room floor, dressed only in his underwear, exhausted by a night of air-raid-warden duty.

Suddenly, a strong flash of light startled me—and then another. So well does one recall little things that I remember vividly how a stone lantern in the garden became brilliantly lit.... Garden shadows disappeared. The view where a moment before all had been so bright and sunny was now dark and hazy. Through swirling dust I could barely discern a wooden column that had supported one corner of my house. It was leaning crazily and the roof sagged dangerously.

Moving instinctively, I tried to escape, but rubble and fallen timbers barred the way. By picking my way cautiously I managed to reach the *roka* [a sort of gallery around the house] and stepped into my garden. A profound weakness overcame me, so I stopped to regain my strength. To my surprise I discovered that I was completely naked. How odd! Where were my vest and pants?

What had happened?

All over the right side of my body I was cut and bleeding. A large splinter was protruding from a mangled wound in my thigh, and something warm trickled into my mouth. My cheek was torn, I discovered as I felt it gingerly, with the lower lip laid wide open. Embedded in my neck was a sizeable fragment of glass which I matter-of-factly dislodged, and with the detachment of one stunned and shocked I studied it and my blood-stained hand.

The note through the entry is of stunned astonishment; a man of science finds himself in a new world of events without causes.

The dead and dying that he sees around him are part of that terrible strangeness. Shadowy burned figures pass him, like walking ghosts; a naked woman appears carrying a naked baby; the river is full of corpses, and soldiers are seen who have no faces: "their eyes, noses and mouths had been burned away, and it looked like their ears had melted off. It was hard to tell front from back." Confronted by these damaged people, the doctor cannot comprehend the causes of their injuries; and later, when radiation-sickness cases begin to appear, he can neither diagnose nor treat their illness: "there was not one with symptoms typical of anything we knew." He doesn't even have a medical language for what he sees; he speaks more like a survivor of some primal catastrophe, like Noah after the flood, than like a doctor.

Helplessness is a condition of victim literature, perhaps the definitive condition. So long as you can *do* something, oppose your enemy somehow, you are not entirely a victim. But here, as the schoolboy said, there was nothing to be done, and the doctors felt that as much as anyone. "There is nothing I can do," a fellow doctor tells Dr. Hachiya; "nothing anybody can do." But there is something they can do; they can testify, as scientists, to what has happened. "We had no microscope, no laboratory reagents, and no laboratory, but what history and clinical findings we could record might one day be important. Nowhere before in the history of the world had a people been subjected to the devastating effects of an atomic bomb." And so the helpless man opposes, by bearing witness.

For the winners of the Pacific war—Americans and their allies—the detonation of the atomic bomb at Hiroshima was the final curtain of the war. It was over; we could all get up and go home. But losing is a different, longer story. For the Japanese, the bomb was only the beginning of the last act of their tragedy; it was followed by political conflict within the government, the Emperor's speech of capitulation, formal surrender, and the occupation of Japan by American forces. All of these events are in Dr. Hachiya's narrative; while he struggles in his hospital with a new kind of dying, the order and discipline of the wartime nation unravels, like another slow, strange death.

Dr. Hachiya expresses no bitterness or hatred for the invaders who have destroyed his city, slaughtered his people, and humbled his nation; his anger, when it appears, is against the military leaders who led his country to defeat. "I ... found myself hating the military authorities with whom I had been in sympathy," he writes. "They had betrayed the Emperor and the people of Japan." And again: "You can understand our contempt, indeed, hatred for the army leaders. Their ruthlessness and stupidity knew no bounds." Such feelings are not surprising; every defeat is a betrayal, to the people who suffer it, and every defeated leader is culpable. Except the Emperor of Japan; his divinity protected him from blame.

Doctors are by their calling agents in catastrophes; but there were other narrators of the Hiroshima bomb who were pure sufferers. They were the *hibakusha,* the persons who were there and survived, to live on as pariahs, scarred and deformed by keloids, weakened by radiation sickness, feeling somehow guilty among the healthy, the untouched. In some ways the *hibakusha* were like those war victims in the worst of the camps—in Changi and Bilibid, Auschwitz and Treblinka—who expected to die but were determined that their stories should somehow live. Also they were in a way like those veterans of the Vietnam War who carried home with them the trauma that would endure in their lives and cripple them as men. But still, the *hibakusha* were different; in their bodies, the instant of fire at Hiroshima burned on and would continue until it claimed them as its casualties. In them, the atomic holocaust went on happening. And they felt an obligation to humanity to testify, and to go on testifying against war's worst weapon.

But how is one to tell a story so strange and so absolute in its annihilations? If something has happened to you that you didn't see and can't comprehend, followed by helpless, incoherent suffering and chaos, what can you *tell*? The most that survivors of that day could recover, it seems, were terrible images of death by fire. Yet, like the man in the Warsaw ghetto, they felt compelled to record what they remembered. "I must set these things down in writing," one memoirist wrote; and another: "It has to be written."

Life is always deep in details; and so is death. The details in these visions of the bombed city are unforgettable: the burned bodies, with skins that peeled off like the skin of an overripe peach; the bloated masses of dark-reddish flesh bobbing in the river like rafts; the quiet wounded waiting so patiently; the silence. Unforgettable; and yet the most powerful effect of the bomb on our imaginations was not those images of what had happened but images generated by that event, of what would happen in the fire next time that would be the Third World War. In the years after the bomb a new era began—the Era of Nuclear Terror—in which men and women lived in fear of their own technology, and waited for a war that might use nuclear power to destroy all humankind. The mood of that time is palpable in this passage from an essay by the biologist Lewis Thomas:

> I cannot listen to the last movement of the Mahler Ninth without the door-smashing intrusion of a huge new thought: death everywhere, the dying of everything, the end of humanity. The easy sadness expressed with such gentleness and delicacy by that repeated phrase on faded

strings, over and over again, no longer comes to me as old, familiar news of the cycle of living and dying. All through the last notes my mind swarms with images of a world in which the thermonuclear bombs have begun to explode, in New York and San Francisco, in Moscow and Leningrad, in Paris, in Paris, in Paris. In Oxford and Cambridge, in Edinburgh. I cannot push away the thought of a cloud of radioactivity drifting along the Engadin, from the Moloja Pass to Ftan, killing off the part of the earth I love more than any other part.

This is not an apocalyptic fantasy, it is a scientist's image of the war that *could* come, an elegy for the future. A war in which every living thing on earth might be a victim was now possible, and therefore imaginable; it was the new war-in-the-head.

Sufferers' stories of the Holocaust and the bomb, and a vision of the end of humanity, close the soldiers' tale of our century: not because they stand at the chronological end of modern war narratives (wars and their stories go on, as I write, as you read) but because they mark the extreme edge of military destructiveness in our time—as far as humankind has been able to extend the idea of war toward pure victimhood, beyond imaginable conflicts of armies to mass annihilation of the helpless and the innocent, and the end of war stories.

An Epilogue on Epilogues

A ll war narratives—even the most immediate forms, the diaries and journals and letters—are in a sense epilogues to the wars they record. Men who were there recall the extraordinary events in their (mostly) ordinary lives and record what it was like to be there: after the actions, the stories. Some narrators add to that retrospection another; having looked back in their narrative, they look back again on the story they have told, and put their last thoughts on their wars in an epilogue or a postscript. What they say partly depends on the war they were in and the role they played there; but there are certain things that recur, and they are worth noting here.

What those narratives tell us can perhaps best be expressed in a collage of their concluding retrospective remarks, with some comments following.

From the First World War:

> My attitude is that war is one of the characteristic pursuits of the crowd, with which I would not attempt to interfere, only deprecating it in so far as it interfered with me and failed to make the pleasurable most of itself.... Fighting in man is as ineradicable an instinct as love, with which of course it has much in common: the chief common quality being romanticism. (Robert Graves)

279

Sometimes [back in England in the summer of 1918] I longed poignantly to be back with my old comrades in the regiment, or in the squadron (but nearly all were gone by the time the Hindenburg Line was broken in October 1918); and at other times dread and terror would break into my rest at night. All men who went through the war will understand this. (D. H. Bell)

Those who have not known passionate love or passionate religion are generally unable to appreciate them and sometimes doubt their existence; but lovers or religious mystics feel for one another. They have inner life in common. In the same way, though in a lesser degree, soldiers who have fought side by side are conscious of being initiated: they are "illuminati." It is important, too, to remember that not only unpleasant emotions have thus been shared. If we have known fear and discomfort we have also felt courage and comfort well up in our hearts, springing from the crowd-emotion of our company, for even Active Service brings moments of intense happiness. (Charles Carrington)

From the Second World War:

Let it be said then that I wrote this book in the absolute conviction that there never has been, nor ever can be a "good" or worthwhile war. Mine was one of the better ones (as such calamities are measured), but still, a bloody awful thing it was. So awful that through three decades I kept the deeper agonies of it wrapped in the cotton-wool of protective forgetfulness, and would have been well content to leave them buried so forever ... but could not, because the Old Lie—temporarily discredited by the Vietnam debacle—is once more gaining credence; a whisper which soon may become another strident shout urging us on to mayhem. (Farley Mowat)

I wrote the first draft of the book in 1947. By 1954 I'd written five or six others. None of them was much good. The sentences were strung together and I couldn't remember any dialogue. In 1955 I had a breakdown. I "heard" shells screaming past my earhole. 88s, by the sound of them. Just like old times. As my world broke up I turned to the one thing I had left to hang on to—my book. I tried another draft. The dialogue came back. I saw the words in my head, just as they'd been spoken. As I scribbled them down I thought of the dead. I owed them so much. I was writing the book for them, for those who were there, and for those who wanted to know what it was like—in that order. At the same time I was trying to forget the dead, to get shot of them. You can't grieve forever. You can't bottle it up either. (Alex Bowlby)

It was a great campaign. (Bernard Fergusson)

During all these years the war has, though obviously not forgotten, seemed far away. But it was always there in the background, and in the depths of my mind the war has remained the defining experience of my life.... (Alvin Kernan)

I have spent the whole day going through these notes, changing a word here, a phrase there, excising sentences, making paragraph divisions, or just staring at the silent world behind the typescript, and the room is filled with ghosts. It all seems a long way off, yet strangely and intolerably close at hand, like the memory of an early dream, or the bright scenes reflected in the surface of Christmas tree ornaments, except that my left index finger still carries the mark where a tiny shell-fragment entered it once, back there one raving afternoon. (Donald Pearce)

From Hiroshima:

> When I think of the kindness of these people [American doctors], I think one can overlook thoughts of revenge; and, even at this moment, I feel something warm in my heart when I recall those days and those friends. (Michihiko Hachiya)

From the concentration camps:

> What will future historians make of these incomparable events which still cause their victims nightmares and whose perpetrators largely managed to escape to foreign lands and punishment: events that are harrowing the innermost being of grieving and frustrated survivors, haunted by unparalleled memories to their dying moment—yet are beyond the most eminent writer to convey and impossible for non-participants to apprehend? (Henry Wermuth)

> [A Jewish woman, a survivor of Auschwitz, meeting a group of German tourists in Paris in 1975]: Isabella took several steps, paused, and then in a rising crescendo of pain began to scream, "Murderers! Murderers! Murderers!" (Isabella Leitner)

From Vietnam:

> My mind shot back a decade, to that day we had marched into Vietnam, swaggering, confident, and full of idealism. We believed we were there for a high moral purpose. But somehow our idealism was lost, our morals corrupted, and the purpose forgotten. (Philip Caputo)

In these passages are all the contradictions that together constitute the soldiers' tale of modern war. War persists in the minds of those who have fought or suffered, a gallery of unforgettable ghosts—yet men try to suppress their memories. War is a world so different from ordinary life as to seem, in recollection, like a dream; yet it makes that ordinary life feel somehow unreal. War is a source of pain and grief and sometimes of shame; yet it may also offer satisfactions—excitement, comradeship, pride—such as peacetime cannot equal. War is a human institution, and an instinct as deep as love; yet so terrible in its human costs that no rational man could wish it on his people or his descendants. War is unimaginable for those who have not experienced it; yet men and women tell their war stories. War's crimes are unforgivable; yet war's crimes may be forgiven.

Does the sum of all such contradictory witnesses amount to the one huge and coherent story of men at war that I imagined, at the beginning of this book? Not entirely: how could it, when so many voices remain silent, so many memories untold? But it comes as near as we can ever get to a full answer to our urgent human question: *what is it like, in war?* In the telling of a story so huge, so various, and so complex in its particulars, there will be many dissonances: old soldiers will dispute what happened in the whirl and muddle of action, the voices of winners and losers, agents and sufferers, the living and the dead, will utter their discordances. But together they will make real the experience of war—not war-in-the-head, but war understood with the flesh, as the French soldier put it.

That compound story will answer our question about how war feels to those who are in it, but it will settle no moral issues and reach no plain conclusions, because, like the experience itself, it will contain contradictions. Soldiers in their narratives demonstrate again and again the contradictory nature of war—that grievous trial, which yet they would not have missed. The most self-aware of them make the point explicitly. Here, as an example, is that fine writer, Tim O'Brien:

> I would wish this book could take the form of a plea for everlasting peace, a plea from one who knows, from one who's been there and come back, an old soldier looking back at a dying war.

That would be good. It would be fine to integrate it all to persuade my younger brother and perhaps some others to say no to wars and other battles.

Or it would be fine to confirm the odd beliefs about war: it's horrible, but it's a crucible of men and events and, in the end, it makes more of a man out of you.

But, still, none of these notions seems right. Men are killed, dead human beings are heavy and awkward to carry, things smell different in Vietnam, soldiers are afraid and often brave, drill sergeants are boors, some men think the war is proper and just and others don't and most don't care. Is that the stuff for a morality lesson, even for a theme?

Do dreams offer lessons? Do nightmares have themes, do we awaken and analyze them and live our lives and advise others as a result? Can the foot soldier teach anything important about war, merely for having been there? I think not. He can tell war stories.

The whole point is in the two opposing verbs there at the end: soldiers can't *teach;* they can *tell.* Their tellings are our soldiers' tale.

In the first chapter of this book, I said that storytelling is a primal need. I think that need encompasses both the teller and the listener. For the teller of a war story, the telling gives disordered experience order and therefore meaning; in the telling he finds the man he was and the war he fought, and how he was changed, and why. For the listener, the story makes huge and terrible events in history assume human faces and human voices, turning the suffering and the excitement and the anonymous numbers of the dead into *this* soldier, at *this* place, feeling *this.*

What the narrators of war stories tell us is what they learned: what war is like, how it feels, how it affects men and women. But can such knowledge really be transmitted to those who did not suffer to learn it? Tellers of war stories, beginning with the

Roland poet, have said No, emphatically and sometimes very bitterly. "Too many people," Guy Sajer wrote in *The Forgotten Soldier*,

> learn about war with no inconvenience to themselves. They read about Verdun or Stalingrad without comprehension, sitting in a comfortable armchair, with their feet beside the fire, preparing to go about their business the next day, as usual. One should really read such accounts under compulsion, in discomfort, considering oneself fortunate not to be describing the events in a letter home, writing from a hole in the mud. One should read about war in the worst circumstances, when everything is going badly, remembering that the torments of peace are trivial, and not worth any white hairs.

That's *us* he's talking about, with our feet beside the fire, eternally barred from understanding by our comforts and our ignorance.

But we must reject that severe exclusion; we must believe that human beings can learn from the testimonies of others (or what are libraries for?). Because wars exist in history, personal narratives of war must add to our historical knowledge. But war exists also in our imaginations—like love, as both Graves and Partridge observed; and it is there that we can gain most, altering our understandings of war and bringing our wars-in-the-head closer to the truth of human experience, by engaging vicariously in other persons' wars.

Notes on Sources

References are to first editions, unless otherwise indicated. Where two dates of publication are given, the second is a re-issue which is the source of the quotation.

PROLOGUE: THE ACTUAL KILLING

PAGE

xi "War always": Tolstoy, "The Raid," in *Tales of Army Life*, Centenary Edition, vol. IV (London: 1933), p. 3.
"the history of mankind": Lt. Col. C. à Court Repington, *The First World War 1914–1918*, vol. II, p. 391.

xv "sane, low-toned": T. E. Lawrence, Letter to F. V. Morley dated July 29, 1929; in the R. Norris Williams Collection, Van Pelt Library, University of Pennsylvania.

xvi "already seems": Aharon Appelfeld, quoted in Lawrence L. Langer, *Holocaust Testimonies: The Ruins of Memory* (New Haven: 1991), epigraph.

CHAPTER ONE

1 "The geste": David Jones, *In Parenthesis* (London: 1937), p. 187. The marks of elision are in Jones's text.
"How can they judge": Marcel Fourier, *Avec les chars d'assaut* (Paris: 1919), p. 117; quoted in Jean Norton Cru, *War Books* (San Diego: 1988), epigraph.

2 "The man who": Jean Bernier, *La parcée* (Paris: 1920), p. 68; quoted in Cru, epigraph.
"You have to": Eric Lomax, *The Railway Man* (London: 1995), p. 202.

"Those who haven't": Guy Sajer, *The Forgotten Soldier* (London: 1971), p. 68.

3 "July 1st 1916": Lt. P. Howe, M.C., quoted in Martin Middlebrooke, *The First Day of the Somme* (London: 1971), p. 316.

"This book": Philip Caputo, *A Rumor of War* (New York: 1977), p. xi.

5 "Throughout Europe": Charles Edmonds [C.E. Carrington], *A Subaltern's War* (New York: 1930), p. 192.

7 "I can still": Rudolph Binding, *A Fatalist at War* (London: 1929), pp. 216–7.

"When I got back": Byron R. Abernethy, ed., *Private Elisha Stockwell Jr. Sees the Civil War* (Norman, Okla.: 1958), p. 46.

8 "the rather romantic tone": Edmonds/Carrington, *A Subaltern's War*, p. 8.

"As I look back": Elmer Bendiner, *The Fall of Fortresses* (New York: 1980), p. 108.

"The damnable truth": Farley Mowat, *And No Birds Sang* (Boston and Toronto: 1979), p. 205.

9 "this body of men": Guy Chapman, *A Passionate Prodigality* (London: 1933), p. 339.

"I was afraid": Alex Bowlby, *The Recollections of Rifleman Bowlby* (London: 1969/1989), p. 89.

"Although I knew": Mowat, *And No Birds Sang*, p. 123.

10 "He was lying": John Harris, *Recollections of Rifleman Harris* (London: 1848/Hamden, Conn.: 1970), p. 49.

12 "very local": Edmund Blunden, *Undertones of War* (London: 1928), p. vii.

"I do not pretend": Harris, *Recollections*, pp. 19–20, 27.

"Shell-hole": Ernst Jünger, *Copse 125: A Chronicle from the Trench Warfare of 1918* (London: 1930), pp. 263–4.

"Today near": anon. [D. H. Bell], *A Soldier's Diary of the Great War* (London: 1929), p. 166.

13 "One morning": A.P. Thornton, "A Summer Crossing," *Queen's Quarterly*, vol. 101 (Fall 1994), 661.

"We actually": Franklyn A. Johnson, *One More Hill* (New York: 1949), p. 39.

"From the air": Hamilton Coolidge, *Letters of an American Airman* (Boston: 1919), pp. 160–1.

14 "A battalion's field": Rudyard Kipling, *The Irish Guards in the Great War* (London: 1923), vol. 1, pp. v–vi.

16 "It was practically": Robert Graves, *But It Still Goes On* (New York: 1931), p. 33.

17 "the scum": Philip Henry, 5th Earl Stanhope, *Notes of Conversations with the Duke of Wellington* (London: 1888), p. 14.

18 "Max Plowman": Mark Seven [Max Plowman], *A Subaltern on the Somme* (London: 1927), p. 30; see also Robert Graves, *Good-bye to All That* (London: 1929), p. 226.
19 "Just past": Edwin Campion Vaughan, *Some Desperate Glory* (New York: 1982), p. 134.
20 "We had just passed": Sajer, *The Forgotten Soldier*, p. 106.
"A man saw": Caputo, *A Rumor of War*, p. 4.
"Eventually": Anita Lasker-Wallfisch, *Inherit the Truth 1939–1945* (London: 1996), p. 92.
"I shot at him": Thomas Hardy, "The Man He Killed," in *Time's Laughingstocks* (London: 1909), p. 186.
21 "What I felt": R. H. Tawney, "The Attack," in *The Attack and Other Papers* (London: 1953), p. 18.
"The lull came": Raleigh Trevelyan, *The Fortress* (London: 1956/1985), p. 209.
22 "For my own part": Harris, *Recollections*, p. 106.
"It was": Lance Corporal Francis Ledwidge, Royal Inniskilling Fusiliers, quoted in Martin Gilbert, *The First World War* (New York: 1994), p. 189.
"So much noise": William E. Merritt, *Where the Rivers Ran Backward* (Athens, Ga.: 1989), p. 289.
23 "What I would": Italo Calvino, *The Road to San Giovanni* (New York: 1993), pp. 84–5.
26 "I have tried": Hervey Allen, *Toward the Flame* (New York: 1926), p. vii.
27 "what fear feels like": Caputo, *A Rumor of War*, p. 95.
"anyone who fought": *A Rumor of War*, p. xv.
29 "The early-winter": Eric Partridge in R. H. Mottram, John Easton and Partridge, *Three Personal Records of the War* (London: 1929), p. 280.
"the war, old chap": Guy Chapman, *A Passionate Prodigality* (New York: 1966), p. [7]. The quotation, from a new "Author's Preface," is not in earlier editions.

CHAPTER TWO

32 "it is still": T. E. Lawrence, *Seven Pillars of Wisdom* (London: 1935), p. 6.
33 "We all know": Major-General M. F. Rimington, *Our Cavalry* (London: 1912), pp. 154, 158–9, 165.
35 "Francis and Rivy": John Buchan, *Francis and Riverdale Grenfell* (London: 1920), pp. 191–2.
"We had simply": diary, quoted in Buchan, p. 195.
36 "That charge": Buchan, p. 194.

"It was not": quoted in Buchan, pp. 196–7.

38　"What a bloody": quoted in Buchan, p. 231.

39　"Then I got leave": quoted in Nicholas Mosley, *Julian Grenfell* (New York: 1976), pp. 238–9.

40　"I went out": quoted in Mosley, p. 242.

43　"the uncleanness": Graves, *Good-bye to All That*, p. 163.

44　"It was a new": Chapman, *A Passionate Prodigality*, pp. 5–6.

45　"I was at Harlech": *Good-bye to All That*, p. 99.
　　"I had recently": T. C. Owtram, "Some Personal Memories of the 1914–18 War," unpublished manuscript, Imperial War Museum, London, p. 2.

46　"As I approached": Vaughan, *Some Desperate Glory*, p. 133.

47　"I had expected": *Some Desperate Glory*, p. 1.

48　"By now": Chapman, *A Passionate Prodigality*, p. 32.
　　"Bethune!": Partridge, in *Three Personal Records of the War*, p. 210.
　　"The Lys": Duncan Grinnell-Milne, *Wind in the Wires* (London: 1933/1971), p. 57.

49　"I began to think": "Ex-Private X" [A. M. Burrage], *War Is War* (London: 1930), p. 12.

50　"As yet he had": Partridge, in *Three Personal Records of the War*, pp. 278–9.

51　"People will think": Carroll Carstairs, *A Generation Missing* (New York: 1930), p. 16.
　　"I was not": Edmund Blunden, *Undertones of War*, p. 1.
　　"I was loath": *A Passionate Prodigality*, p. 13.

52　"After a meal": *Good-bye to All That*, pp. 132–3.

53　"The country": Mark Seven [Plowman], *A Subaltern on the Somme*, pp. 41–2.

54　"We are marching": Plowman, *Subaltern on the Somme*, p. 24.

55　"the war was still": Edmonds/Carrington, *A Subaltern's War*, p. 21.
　　"Certain general factors": J. H. Boraston, ed., *Sir Douglas Haig's Despatches* (London: 1919), p. 324.

56　"In the face": C. R. M. F. Cruttwell, *History of the Great War* (London: 1934), pp. 153–4.

57　"Captain Pryce": Carstairs, *A Generation Missing*, pp. 201–2; the official account, as told in Sir John Smyth, *The Story of the Victoria Cross*, is essentially the same.

58　"Military courage": Marc Bloch, *Memoirs of War, 1914–15* (Ithaca, N.Y.: 1980) p. 166.

59　"The misery": *Good-bye to All That*, p. 302.
　　"My God! I understand": *A Subaltern on the Somme*, p. 123.
　　"Perhaps those": *A Passionate Prodigality*, pp. 122–3.

60　"He had gone": *Three Personal Records*, p. 373.

61　"Finally Wood": *Some Desperate Glory*, pp. 224–5.

62 "windy ... helpless with fear": *Some Desperate Glory*, pp. 210–2, 218, 222.
63 "The first result": W. H. R. Rivers, *Instinct and the Unconscious*, 2nd ed. (Cambridge: 1922), pp. 4–5.
"Fear and its expression": *Instinct and the Unconscious*, p. 209.
66 "On coming": *Three Personal Records*, p. 337.
67 "Among others": Ernst Jünger, *The Storm of Steel* (London: 1929), p. 23.
68 "It gave me": Siegfried Sassoon, *Memoirs of an Infantry Officer* (London: 1930), pp. 81–2.
"we were so": Jünger, *Storm of Steel*, p. 23.
69 "Some parts": Frank Richards, *Old Soldiers Never Die* (London: 1933), p. 199.
70 "In this sunshine": *A Subaltern on the Somme*, p. 172.
"terror and death": *Some Desperate Glory*, p. 199.
71 "My nerves are under control": anon. [D. H. Bell], *A Soldier's Diary of the Great War*, p. 152.
"my nerves are in perfect order": Harold Owen and John Bell, eds., *Wilfred Owen: Collected Letters* (London: 1967), p. 580.
"To get a cushy one": *Good-bye to All That*, p. 151.
72 "After about five": Edward G. D. Liveing, *Attack* (New York: 1918), p. 63.
73 "In the beginning": *A Generation Missing*, p. 206.

CHAPTER THREE

77 "Nasir screamed": *Seven Pillars*, p. 304.
78 "Tallal had seen": *Seven Pillars*, p. 632.
79 "Among the Arabs": *Seven Pillars*, p. 549.
80 "Ah, I wish to hell": Lord Cranworthy, Foreword to Capt. Angus Buchanan, *Three Years of War in East Africa* (London: 1919), p. vii.
81 "One talks": H. G. Wells, "Looking Ahead. The Most Splendid Fighting in the World," *Daily Chronicle*, Sept. 9, 1914, p. 4.
82 "I begin to realize": *A Soldier's Diary of the Great War*, p. 178.
"I turned south": Cecil Lewis, *Sagittarius Rising* (London: 1936), p. 57.
84 "Wilhelm grabbed": Grinnell-Milne, *Wind in the Wires*, p. 87.
85 "There must": L. A. Strange, *Recollections of an Airman* (London: 1933), p. 218.
86 "May 2nd, 1917": quoted in Jacques Mortane, *Guynemer, The Ace of Aces* (New York: 1918), p. 230.
86 "*der Spitze*": Manfred Frhr. von Richthofen, *Der rote Kampfflieger* (Berlin: 1917), p. 106.
"Had a splendid": *The Personal Diary of Major Edward "Mick" Mannock* (London: 1966), pp. 127–9.

"from the first": *Sagittarius Rising*, p. 45.

87 "he asked us all": James Byford McCudden, *Flying Fury* (London: 1930), p. 196.

89 "It seems": *Flying Fury*, p. 173.

"I hate": *Flying Fury*, p. 236.

"We were always": *Sagittarius Rising*, pp. 60–1.

90 "a sort of plodding": *Sagittarius Rising*, p. 60.

91 "At once a little trickle": *Flying Fury*, p. 170.

92 "I can't prevent": D. H. Bell, *A Diary of the Great War*, p. 240.

"Mannock ... McCudden": anon., *War Birds* (New York: 1926), pp. 233, 236.

93 "The annals of war": Haig, *Despatches*, p. 299.

95 "Standing near": *Some Desperate Glory*, p. 232.

97 "Suddenly": *Toward the Flame*, p. 246.

99 "So it was over": *Sagittarius Rising*, p. 255.

"To throw": Edmonds [Carrington], *Subaltern's War*, p. 190.

100 "Funny, after": *Wind in the Wires*, pp. 216–7.

101 "a generation": Samuel Hynes, *A War Imagined* (New York: 1991), p. xii.

102 "when we achieved": "The Suppressed Introductory Chapter for *Seven Pillars of Wisdom*," in A. W. Lawrence, ed., *Oriental Assembly* (London: 1939), pp. 142–3.

"War is a horrible thing": *War Birds*, p. 268.

103 "England": V. M. Yeates, *Winged Victory* (London: 1934), pp. 149–50.

"My knight-errantry": Siegfried Sassoon, *Sherston's Progress* (London: 1936), p. 278.

104 "Loath to speak": *Subaltern's War*, pp. 192–3.

"I was surprised": Robert Graves, *But It Still Goes On* (New York: 1931), pp. 6–7.

106 "Never such": Philip Larkin, "MCMXIV," *The Whitsun Weddings* (London: 1964), p. 28.

CHAPTER FOUR

109 "If war began": Edward Blishen, *A Cackhanded War* (London: 1972), p. 13.

110 "it seems to me": Philip Toynbee, *Friends Apart* (London: 1954), p. 91.

112 "We knew": Richard Hillary, *The Last Enemy* (London: 1942), p. 17.

"Like the rites": Patrick Davis, *A Child at Arms* (London: 1970/1985), p. 1.

"I never lost": Keith Douglas, *Alamein to Zem Zem* (London: 1946), p. 7.

"prompted by": Eugene Sledge, *With the Old Breed at Peleliu and Okinawa* (New York: 1981/1990), p. 5.

"Seventeen years old.": Alvin Kernan, *Crossing the Line* (Annapolis: 1994), p. 6.

112 "This war, at least": John Updike, "Books: Michel Tournier," *The New Yorker*, July 10, 1989, 96.

114 "When it's all over": quoted in Martin Blumenson, *Patton: The Man Behind the Legend* (New York: 1985), p. 223.

115 "the first in": Robert Sherwood, quoted in Paul Fussell, ed., *The Norton Book of War* (New York: 1991), p. 312.

117 "The dismal work": Christopher Seton-Watson, *Dunkirk-Alamein-Bologna* (London: 1993), p. 37.

118 "In the early stages": *Dunkirk-Alamein-Bologna*, p. 145.

120 "A general": John Verney, *Going to the Wars* (London: 1955), p. 147.

"What did": Bernard Fergusson, *Beyond the Chindwin* (London: 1945), p. 241.

121 "to exorcise": *Beyond the Chindwin*, p. 16.

122 "If we were eager": *Going to the Wars*, p. 148.

"We have been": Field Marshal Earl Wavell, "Foreword" to F. Spencer Chapman, *The Jungle is Neutral* (London: 1949), p. vi.

123 "All my very rosiest": W. Stanley Moss, *Ill Met by Moonlight* (London: 1950), p. 135.

124 "I was in": D. M. Crook, *Spitfire Pilot* (London: 1942), p. 28.

126 "In a fighter": Hillary, *Last Enemy*, p. 21.

"My first emotion": *Last Enemy*, p. 137.

128 "I'm not": Antoine de Saint-Exupéry, *Wartime Writings 1939–1944* (New York: 1982), p. 121.

130 "the last": *Last Enemy*, p. 231.

"I was the only": *Spitfire Pilot*, p. 72.

132 "Far ahead": John Muirhead, *Those Who Fall* (New York: 1986), pp. 139–40.

133 "We were somewhere": Elmer Bendiner, *The Fall of Fortresses* (New York: 1980), pp. 171–2.

134 "I saw death": *The Fall of Fortresses*, p. 101.

136 "I like you, sir": Douglas, *Alamein to Zem Zem*, p. 9.

"I am not writing": *Alamein to Zem Zem*, p. 7.

137 "But it is exciting": *Alamein to Zem Zem*, p. 8.

"Outside the wagon": Neil McCallum, *Journey with a Pistol* (London: 1959), p. 37.

138 "jagged brown peaks": John Guest, *Broken Images: A Journal* (London: 1949), p. 105.

"The desert": R. L. Crimp, *Diary of a Desert Rat* (London: 1971), p. 29.

"The other day": Guest, *Broken Images*, p. 116.

139 "The eastern mountains": *Diary of a Desert Rat*, pp. 181–2.
"There is satisfaction": *Dunkirk-Alamein-Bologna*, p. 93.

140 "The greatest joy": *Dunkirk-Alamein-Bologna*, p. 145.
"apparently": *Diary of a Desert Rat*, p. 52.

141 "Gradually": *Alamein to Zem Zem*, pp. 56–7.

142 "He was fantastically": *Alamein to Zem Zem*, p. 80.

143 "gentle obsolescent breed": "I Think I Am Becoming a God," *Alamein to Zem Zem*, p. viii.

144 "We repeated": *Alamein to Zem Zem*, pp. 140–1.

146 "Such was our": Mowat, *And No Birds Sang*, pp. 61–2.

148 "I had scarcely": *And No Birds Sang*, pp. 115–6.

150 "I was woken": Bowlby, *The Recollections of Rifleman Bowlby*, p. 98.

151 "Keep your nut": *Recollections*, p. 26.
"I don't know": Trevelyan, *The Fortress*, p. 124.

152 "When a citizen Army": *Parliamentary Debates* (Commons), vol. 410, col. 629 (April 20, 1945).
"an enormous armada"/"the airspace": Douglas Sutherland, *Sutherland's War* (London: 1984), pp. 114 and 128.

153 "like large ripe": Donald R. Burgett, *Currahee!* (Boston: 1967), p. 85.
"abandoned": Charles Cawthon, *Other Clay* (Niwot, Col.: 1990), p. 54.
"the first assault": *Other Clay*, p. 54.
"Mine is an account": *Other Clay*, p. 62.

154 "Small private wars": *Currahee!*, pp. 86–7.
"There is a dreadful": *Other Clay*, p. 71.

155 "country fought over": Ken Tout, *Tank!* (London: 1985), p. 53.

156 "a relaxed air": *Other Clay*, p. 168.

157 "Today": Donald Pearce, *Journal of a War* (Toronto: 1965), p. 125.

158 "It was": *Sutherland's War*, p. 183.
"We were still": *Other Clay*, p. 172.

160 "A destroyed city": *Journal of a War*, p. 151.

161 "As far as I could see": *With the Old Breed at Peleliu and Okinawa*, p. 252.

162 "The attitudes": *With the Old Breed*, p. 34.

163 "As we moved": *With the Old Breed*, p. 148.

164 "Putting/No one/As to the Japanese": George MacDonald Fraser, *Quartered Safe Out Here* (London: 1992/1993), pp. 86, 96, 125.

167 "In the ordnance shack": Alvin Kernan, *Crossing the Line* pp. 69–70.

168 "It had already": *Crossing the Line*, p. 72.

169 "Among the burning": *Crossing the Line*, p. 72.

170 "exploding planes": James J. Fahey, *Pacific War Diary 1942–1945* (Boston: 1963), pp. 229–30.

"Parts of destroyed": *Pacific War Diary*, p. 231.

173   "Well, this may be hell": Fergusson, *Beyond the Chindwin*, p. 181.

"Glad I was there": *Quartered Safe Out Here*, p. 222.

174   "Until the millennium": *With the Old Breed*, p. 315.

"The two world wars": Freeman Dyson, *Weapons and Hope* (New York: 1984), p. 134.

CHAPTER FIVE

177   "I enlisted": Frederick Downs, *The Killing Zone* (New York: 1978/1993), p. 189.

"we believed": Caputo, *A Rumor of War*, p. xii.

"I wanted": Tobias Wolff, *In Pharaoh's Army* (New York: 1994), p. 46.

178   "When I saw": in Timothy J. Lomperis, *Reading the Wind* (Durham, N.C.: 1987), p. 30.

180   "In the fall of 1968": Downs, *The Killing Zone*, p. 11.

"It didn't help": Robert Mason, *Chickenhawk* (New York: 1983), pp. 107–8.

182   "As far as I": William E. Merritt, personal letter, April 4, 1994.

183   "Category four": "The General at Ease," interview with General William C. Westmoreland, *MHQ: The Quarterly Journal of Military History*, vol. 1 (Autumn 1988), 34.

188   "we walk through": Tim O'Brien, *If I Die in a Combat Zone* (London: 1973), p. 124.

"In effect": Caputo, *A Rumor of War*, p. 95.

"Of course": Downs, *The Killing Zone*, p. 188.

189   "The place": Wolff, *In Pharaoh's Army*, p. 139.

190   "I lay there": Rod Kane, *Veteran's Day* (New York: 1990), pp. 145–6.

191   "There were three": Downs, *The Killing Zone*, p. 71.

"It looked": *Killing Zone*, pp. 71–2.

192   "Jap skull": *Life*, May 22, 1944, 34–5. The item is headlined: "Arizona war worker writes her Navy boyfriend a thank-you note for the Jap skull he sent her." The accompanying descriptive note explains: "When he said goodby two years ago to Natalie Nickerson, 20, a war worker of Phoenix, Ariz., a big handsome Navy lieutenant promised her a Jap. Last week Natalie received a human skull, autographed by her lieutenant and 13 friends, and inscribed: 'This is a good Jap—a dead one picked up on the New Guinea beach.' Natalie, surprised at the gift, named it Tojo. The armed forces disapprove strongly of this sort of thing."

"Lieutenant": *A Rumor of War*, p. xvii.

"Before you leave": *A Rumor of War*, p. 137.

"Why did we want": *The Killing Zone*, pp. 148–9.

194 "Maybe I was": David Donovan, *Once a Warrior King* (London: 1986), p. 224.

195 "It was a little": Specialist 4 Richard J. Ford III, in Wallace Terry, *Bloods: An Oral History of the Vietnam War by Black Veterans* (New York: 1984), p. 44.

"All the empty huts": Matthew Brennan, *Brennan's War* (Novato, Calif.: 1985), p. 32.

196 "I examined": Mason, *Chickenhawk*, p. 209.

197 "I did another": Edward G. Briscoe, *Diary of a Short-Timer in Vietnam* (New York: 1970), pp. 15, 16, 27.

198 "In Nam": Ronald J. Glasser, *365 Days* (New York: 1971), p. 9.

"I knew only": Lewis B. Puller, Jr., *Fortunate Son* (New York: 1991), pp. 156–7.

202 "doped to": Michael Herr, *Dispatches* (New York: 1977/1978), p. 120.

"psychotic": *Dispatches*, p. 229.

"I keep thinking": *Dispatches*, p. 223.

203 "the best book"; "the best book": quoted on front cover of Avon paperback.

204 "We'd camped": Merritt, *Where the Rivers Ran Backward*, p. 100.

"Sitting in Saigon": *Dispatches*, p. 44.

"At the bottom": *Dispatches*, p. 45.

205 "I was there": *Dispatches*, p. 20.

208 "It's like": Kane, *Veteran's Day*, p. 288.

"And I finally": Donovan, *Once a Warrior King*, p. 312.

211 "The camera": Merritt, *Where the Rivers Ran Backward*, pp. 42, 44.

213 "We split a beer": Caputo, *A Rumor of War*, pp. 193–4.

214 "Out on the patrol": *A Rumor of War*, pp. 193–4.

"They gave": *A Rumor of War*, p. 194.

215 "You can't hit": Downs, *The Killing Zone*, p. 55.

"I don't want": *A Rumor of War*, p. 46.

"He saw where": Terry, *Bloods*, p. 25.

"I didn't see": Mark Baker, *Nam: The Vietnam War in the Words of the Men Who Fought There* (New York: 1981), p. 50.

217 "The little fellow": John Ketwig, ... *and a hard rain fell* (New York: 1985), p. 147.

"I think": Ron Kovic, *Born on the Fourth of July* (New York: 1976), p. 9.

219 "Mr. Kane": Kane, *Veteran's Day*, p. 203.

220 "I haven't really": quoted in Jonathan Shay, *Achilles in Vietnam* (New York: 1994), p. xiv.

"Bob, a Texan"; "Tom remembers": quoted in Chaim F. Shatan, "The Grief of Soldiers: Vietnam Combat Veterans' Self-Help Movement," *American Journal of Orthopsychiatry*, 43 (4) (July 1973), 642.

221 "they have been compared": Shatan, "The Grief of Soldiers," 640.

222 "A 1980 Veterans Administration": Stanley Karnow, *Vietnam: a History* (London: 1983/1991), p. 480.

CHAPTER SIX

224 "Doesn't anyone": Kane, *Veteran's Day*, pp. 99–100.

226 "Atrocities": Graves, *Good-bye to All That*, pp. 234–5.
"For instance,": *Good-bye to All That*, pp. 234–5.

228 "Stephen Spender": "The background to this war, corresponding to the Western Front in the last war, is the bombed city . . ." Spender, Introduction to *Air Raids: War Pictures by British Artists*, Second Series, No. 4 (London: 1943), p. 6.

230 "At first": Marie Vassiltchikov, *The Berlin Diaries 1940–45* (London: 1985) pp. 109–10.
"A few scenes": Elena Skrjabina, *Siege and Survival* (Carbondale, Ill.: 1971), pp. 26–7.

231 "I've a sick shadow": Nella Last, *Nella Last's War* (London: 1981/1983), p. 138.

232 "a nightmare": *Nella Last's War*, p. 284.
"The members": Tom Henling Wade, *Prisoner of the Japanese* (Kenthurst, Australia: 1994), p. 41.

233 "A defeated Army": Eric Lomax, *The Railway Man* (London: 1995), pp. 71–2.
"Such imprisonment": Airey Neave, *They Have Their Exits* (London: 1953), p. 22.

237 "Herr Leutnant": Neave, *They Have Their Exits*, p. 53.
"He is a soldier": Cyril Rofe, *Against the Wind* (London: 1956), p. 14.
"We were fed": Esmond Lynn-Allen, "Four July Suns," in D. Guy Adams, ed., *Backwater: Oflag IX A/H Lower Camp* (London: 1944) pp. 13, 15.

239 "With the approach": Rofe, *Against the Wind*, p. 33.
"For me": Neave, *They Have Their Exits*, p. 71.
"keys, wires": *They Have Their Exits*, p. 63.

240 "the poetic justice": *They Have Their Exits*, p. 189.

241 "Most escapers": Rofe, *Against the Wind*, p. 103.

242 "joining the fight": Neave, *They Have Their Exits*, p. 154.
"I would not": *Against the Wind*, p. 316.

"One prisoner in four": the figures are quoted in John W. Dower, *War Without Mercy: Race and Power in the Pacific War* (London: 1986), p. 48.

243   "In February": Lomax, *The Railway Man*, p. 112.

245   "Our generalship": Wade, *Prisoner of the Japanese*, p. 39.

      "the fault": Terence O'Brien, *Chasing After Danger* (London: 1990), p. 207.

246   "we were not": Ronald Searle, *To the Kwai—and Back* (London: 1986), p. 80.

247   "To observe": Bruno Bettelheim, *The Informed Heart* (London: 1960), p. 111.

      "During my captivity": Searle, *To the Kwai*, p. 9.

248   "rather like baby": *To the Kwai*, p. 158.

250   "It gradually": Lomax, *Railway Man*, p. 77.

      "The prisoner": Neave, *They Have Their Exits*, p. 192.

251   "I was called": Lomax, *Railway Man*, pp. 119–20.

252   "always": *Railway Man*, p. 164.

253   "Sometime": *Railway Man*, p. 276.

      "The sickness": Robert Hardie, *The Burma-Siam Railway* (London: 1983), p. 91.

      "the only general": David Nelson, *The Story of Changi, Singapore* (West Perth, Australia: 1973), p. 29.

254   "a new eating"; "an extremely": Hardie, *Burma-Siam Railway*, pp. 59, 65.

      "I went": Nelson, *Story of Changi*, p. 98.

256   "Times like these": Thomas Hayes, *Bilibid Diary* (Hamden, Conn.: 1987), p. 30.

      "I damn sure": Dick Bilyeu, *Lost in Action* (Jefferson, N. C.: 1991), p. 103.

257   "Each of us": Wade, *Prisoner of the Japanese*, p. 43.

259   "Anything you": "30,000 Died in Nazi Prison Camp at Belsen," *Daily Telegraph* (London), April 19, 1945, 5.

      "No one": Kazuo Chujo, *The Nuclear Holocaust* (Tokyo: 1983), p. 33.

      "It is a grave": Irving Howe, "Writing and the Holocaust," *New Republic*, October 27, 1986, 27.

260   "This life": Primo Levi, *If This Is a Man* (London: 1960/1987), p. 63.

262   "And yet": Ian Buruma, "The Memory Tourist," *Times Literary Supplement*, July 30, 1993, 5.

263   "to annihilate us": Levi, *If This Is a Man*, p. 57.

264   "Then for the first": *If This Is a Man*, pp. 32–3.

      "Driven by thirst": *If This Is a Man*, p. 35.

265   "we had ceased": Elie Wiesel, *Night* (London: 1981) p. 48.

      "It's the end": *Night*, p. 88.

266   "Why": Bruno Bettelheim, *The Informed Heart* (London: 1960), p. 264.

267 "Two hangings": Henry Wermuth, *Breathe Deeply My Son* (London: 1993), p. 90.
269 "two, very large": *Breathe Deeply*, pp. 198–9.
270 "The idea": Michael Zylberberg, *A Warsaw Diary* (London: 1969), p. 9.
271 "To say that": Katsuzo Oda, "Human Ash," in Kenzaburo Oe, ed., *The Crazy Iris* (New York: 1985). pp. 68–9.
272 "There was a schoolboy": Kazuo Chujo, *The Nuclear Holocaust* (Tokyo: 1983), p. 7.
273 "Suddenly": Michihiko Hachiya, *Hiroshima Diary* (London: 1955), pp. 13–14.
274 "their eyes": *Hiroshima Diary*, p. 28.
"there was not one": *Hiroshima Diary*, p. 51.
"There is nothing": *Hiroshima Diary*, p. 34.
"We had no microscope": *Hiroshima Diary*, pp. 102–3.
275 "I . . . found": *Hiroshima Diary*, p. 104.
"You can understand": *Hiroshima Diary*, p. 121.
276 "I must set"; "It has to be": Hara Tamiki and Ota Yoko, in Richard H. Minear, ed., *Hiroshima: Three Witnesses* (Princeton: 1990), pp. 30, 136.
"I cannot listen": Lewis Thomas, *Late Night Thoughts on Listening to Mahler's Ninth Symphony* (New York: 1984), pp. 164–5.

EPILOGUE

279 "My attitude": Graves, *But It Still Goes On*, p. 38.
280 "Sometimes": anon. [D. H. Bell], *A Soldier's Diary of the Great War*, pp. 251–2.
"Those who": Edmonds [Carrington], *A Subaltern's War*, p. 194.
"Let it be said": Mowat, *And No Birds Sang*, pp. 218–9.
281 "I wrote": Bowlby, *Recollections of Rifleman Bowlby*, p. 222.
"It was": Fergusson, *Beyond the Chindwin*, p. 241.
"During all these years": Kernan, *Crossing the Line*, p. 165.
"I have spent": Pearce, *Journal of a War*, p. 185.
282 "When I think": Hachiya, *Hiroshima Diary*, p. 252.
"What will": Wermuth, *Breathe Deeply*, p. 208.
"Isabella took": Epilogue by Irving A. Leitner to Isabella Leitner, *Fragments of Isabella* (New York: 1978), p. 109.
"My mind shot back": Caputo, *Rumor of War*, p. 345.
283 "I would wish": Tim O'Brien, *If I Die in a Combat Zone*, pp. 22–3.
285 "Too many people": Sajer, *The Forgotten Soldier*, p. 223.

Personal Narratives of Modern War:
A Selected List

THE FIRST WORLD WAR

The Western Front:

British and Commonwealth
Adams, Bernard. *Nothing of Importance: A Record of Eight Months at the Front with a Welsh Battalion, October, 1915, to June, 1916* (London: 1917)

Anon. [Douglas H. Bell]. *A Soldier's Diary of the Great War* (London: 1929)

Blunden, Edmund. *Undertones of War* (London: 1928)

Carstairs, Carroll. *A Generation Missing* (New York: 1930)

Chapman, Guy. *A Passionate Prodigality: Fragments of Autobiography* (London: 1933)

Edmonds, Charles [Charles Carrington]. *A Subaltern's War* (London: 1929)

Ex-Private X [A. M. Burrage]. *War Is War* (London: 1930)

Graves, Robert. *Good-bye to All That* (London: 1929)

Hamilton, the Hon. R. G. A. *The War Diary of the Master of Belhaven* (London: 1924)

Jones, David. *In Parenthesis* (London: 1937)

Liveing, Edward G. D. *Attack: An Infantry Subaltern's Impressions of July 1st 1916* (London: 1918)

Mark Seven [Max Plowman]. *A Subaltern on the Somme* (London: 1927)

Mottram, R. H., John Easton, and Eric Partridge. *Three Personal Records of the War* (London: 1929)

Read, Herbert. *In Retreat* (London: 1925)

Richards, Frank. *Old Soldiers Never Die* (London: 1933)

Sassoon, Siegfried. *Memoirs of a Fox-Hunting Man* (London: 1928); *Memoirs of an Infantry Officer* (London: 1930); *Sherston's Progress* (London: 1936)

Tawney, R. H. *The Attack and Other Papers* (London: 1953)

Vaughan, Edwin Campion. *Some Desperate Glory* (London: 1981)

American
Allen, Hervey. *Toward the Flame* (New York: 1926)

French
Bloch, Marc. *Memoirs of War, 1914–15* (Ithaca, N.Y.: 1980)
Lintier, Paul. *My Seventy-Five* (London: 1917)

German
Binding, Rudolph. *A Fatalist at War* (London: 1929)
Jünger, Ernst. *Copse 125: A Chronicle from the Trench Warfare of 1918* (London: 1930)
———. *The Storm of Steel* (London: 1929)

Mediterranean and the Middle East:

British and Commonwealth
Black, Donald. *Red Dust: An Australian Trooper in Palestine* (London: 1931)
Lawrence, T. E. *Seven Pillars of Wisdom* (London: 1935)
Partridge, Eric. In Mottram, R.H., et al., *Three Personal Records of the War* (London: 1929) [the Dardanelles]

Africa:

British and Commonwealth
Buchanan, Angus. *Three Years of War in East Africa* (London: 1919)
Meinertzhagen, Richard. *Army Diary 1899–1926* (Edinburgh/London: 1960)
Young, Francis Brett. *Marching on Tanga* (London: 1917)

War in the Air:

British and Commonwealth
Benn, Wedgwood. *In the Side Shows* (London: 1919) [Middle East]
Grinnell-Milne, Duncan. *Wind in the Wires* (London: 1933)
Lewis, Cecil. *Sagittarius Rising* (London: 1936)
Mannock, Edward. *The Personal Diary of Major Edward "Mick" Mannock* (London: 1966)
McCudden, James. *Flying Fury* (London: 1930) [first published in 1918 as *Five Years in the Royal Flying Corps*]
Strange, L. A. *Recollections of an Airman* (London: 1933)
Yeates, V. M. *Winged Victory* (London: 1934)

American
Anon. [Grider, John McGavock]. *War Birds: Diary of an Unknown Aviator* (New York: 1926)
Coolidge, Hamilton. *Letters of an American Airman* (Boston: 1919)
Rickenbacker, Edward V. *Fighting the Flying Circus* (New York: 1919)

French
Villars, Jean Beraud. *Notes of a Lost Pilot* (Hamden, Conn.: 1975)

German
von Richthofen, Manfred. *The Red Battle Flyer* (New York: 1918) [in Germany *Der rote Kampfflieger* (Berlin: 1917)]

Women's War:

British and Commonwealth
Asquith, Cynthia. *Diary 1915–1918* (London: 1968)
Bagnold, Enid. *A Diary Without Dates* (London: 1918)
Farmborough, Florence. *A Nurse at the Russian Front: A Diary 1914–18* (London: 1974)
Luard, K. E. *Unknown Warriors: Extracts from the Letters of K. E. Luard, R.R.C., Nursing Sister in France 1914–1918* (London: 1930)
Sinclair, May. *A Journal of Impressions in Belgium* (London: 1915) [with an English ambulance unit]

American
Aldrich, Mildred. *A Hilltop on the Marne* (London: 1915); *On the Edge of the War Zone* (London: 1917); *The Peak of the Load* (London: 1918)

Prisoners of War:

British and Commonwealth
Green, Arthur. *The Story of a Prisoner of War* (London: 1916)
Waugh, Alec. *The Prisoners of Mainz* (London: 1919)

THE SECOND WORLD WAR

Dunkirk and the Fall of France:

British
Bartlett, Sir Basil. *My First War: An Army Officer's Journal for May 1940* (London: 1940)
Seton-Watson, Christopher. *Dunkirk-Alamein-Bologna* (London: 1993) [includes also North African and Italian campaigns]

French
Habe, Hans. *A Thousand Shall Fall* (London: 1942)

Southeast Asia:

British and Commonwealth
Chapman, F. Spencer. *The Jungle Is Neutral* (London: 1949)
Davis, Patrick. *A Child at Arms* (London: 1970)
Ferguson, Bernard. *Beyond the Chindwin* (London: 1945)

Fraser, George MacDonald. *Quartered Safe Out Here: A Recollection of the War in Burma* (London: 1993)
Masters, John. *The Road Past Mandalay* (New York: 1961)

North Africa:

British and Commonwealth

Crimp, R. L. *Diary of a Desert Rat* (London: 1971)
Douglas, Keith. *Alamein to ZemZem* (London: 1946)
Guest, John. *Broken Images: A Journal* (London: 1949)
McCallum, Neil. *Journey with a Pistol* (London: 1959)

American

Johnson, Franklyn. *One More Hill* (New York: 1949)

German

Schmidt, Heinz Werner. *With Rommel in the Desert* (London: 1951)

Italy:

British and Commonwealth

Bowlby, Alex. *Recollections of Rifleman Bowlby* (London: 1969)
Mowat, Farley. *And No Birds Sang* (Boston/Toronto: 1979)
Trevelyan, Raleigh. *The Fortress* (London: 1956)

American

Bassett, John T. *War Journal of an Innocent Soldier* (Hamden, Conn.: 1989)

The Eastern Front:

German

Fuchs, Karl. *Sieg Heil! War Letters of Tank Gunner Karl Fuchs, 1937–1941* (Hamden, Conn.: 1987)
Kern, Ernst. *War Diary 1941–45* (New York: 1993)
Pabst, Helmut. *The Outermost Frontier* (London: 1957)
Pöppel, Martin. *Heaven and Hell: The War Diary of a German Paratrooper* (Royal Tunbridge Wells: 1989) [includes operations in Holland, Poland, Crete, the Russian Front, Sicily, Normandy]
Sajer, Guy. *The Forgotten Soldier* (New York: 1971)
Zieser, Benno. *In Their Shallow Graves* (London: 1956)

Northwest Europe:

British and Commonwealth

Pearce, Donald. *Journal of a War—North-west Europe 1944–45* (Toronto: 1965)
Sutherland, Douglas. *Sutherland's War* (London: 1984)
Tout, Ken. *Tank! 40 Hours of Battle, August 1944* (London: 1985); *Tanks Advance!* (London: 1987)

American

Burgett, Donald R. *Currahee!* (Boston: 1967)
Cawton, C. R. *Other Clay* (Niwot, Colo: 1990)
Spencer, Henry C. *Nineteen Days in June 1944* (Kansas City: 1984)
Standifer, Leon C. *Not in Vain* (Baton Rouge, La.: 1992)

Pacific Islands:

American

Kahn, Sy M. *Between Tedium and Terror* (Champaign, Ill.: 1993)
Sledge, E. B. *With the Old Breed at Peleliu and Okinawa* (Novato, Calif.: 1981)

Japanese

Ogawa, Tetsuro. *Terraced Hell* (Rutland, Vt.: 1972)

Special Operations:

British and Commonwealth

Dormer, Hugh. *Hugh Dormer's Diaries* (London: 1947)
Millar, George. *Maquis* (London: 1945); *Horned Pigeon* (London: 1946)
Moss, W. Stanley. *Ill Met by Moonlight* (London: 1950)
Verney, John. *Going to the Wars* (London: 1955)

War in the Air:

British and Commonwealth

Anon. [Paul Richey]. *Fighter Pilot: A Personal Record of the Campaign in France, Sept. '39–June '40* (London: 1941)
Bailey, Jim. *The Sky Suspended* (London: 1965)
Crook, D. M. *Spitfire Pilot* (London: 1942)
Hillary, Richard. *The Last Enemy* (London: 1942) [in U.S.: *Falling Through Space* (New York: 1942)]
Hough, Richard. *One Boy's War* (London: 1975)
Johnson, J. E. *Wing Leader* (New York: 1956)
Lamb, Charles. *War in a Stringbag* (London: 1977)
O'Brien, Terence. *Out of the Blue* (London: 1984); *The Moonlight War* (London: 1987); *Chasing After Danger* (London: 1990)
Peden, Murray. *A Thousand Shall Fall* (London: 1981)

American

Ardery, Philip. *Bomber Pilot* (Lexington, Ky.: 1978)
Arnold, Fredric. *Doorknob Five Two* (Los Angeles: 1984)
Bendiner, Elmer. *The Fall of Fortresses* (New York: 1980)
Boyington, Gregory (Pappy). *Baa baa Black Sheep* (New York: 1958)
Cubbins, William R. *The War of the Cottontails* (Chapel Hill, N.C.: 1989)
Muirhead, John. *Those Who Fall* (New York: 1986)

Newby, Leroy W. *Target Ploesti* (Novato, Calif.: 1983)
Park, Edwards. *Nanette* (New York: 1977)
Spencer, Otha C. *Flying the Hump* (College Station, Texas: 1992)
Stiles, Bert. *Serenade to the Big Bird* (New York: 1952)

French
Saint-Exupéry, Antoine de. *Flight to Arras* (New York: 1942)

German
Steinhoff, Johannes. *The Straits of Messina: Diary of a Fighter Commander* (London: 1971)

Japanese
Nagatsuka, Ryuji. *I Was a Kamikaze* (New York: 1974)

The Naval War:

British and Commonwealth
Ross, Alan. *Blindfold Games* (London: 1986)
Vian, Sir Philip. *Action This Day* (London: 1960)

American
Fahey, James J. *Pacific War Diary 1942–1945* (Boston: 1963)
Jernigan, Emory J. *Tin Can Man* (Arlington, Va.: 1993)
Kernan, Alvin. *Crossing the Line* (Annapolis: 1994)
O'Kane, Richard H. *Wahoo: The Patrols of America's Most Famous World War II Submarine* (Novato, Calif.: 1987)
Stafford, Edward P. *Little Ship, Big War* (New York: 1984)

Japanese
Hashimoto, Mochitsura. *Sunk: The Story of the Japanese Submarine Fleet, 1941–1945* (New York: 1954)
Yoshida, Mitsuru. *Requiem for the Battleship Yamato* (Seattle: 1985)

Prisoners of War:

British and Commonwealth
Coast, John. *Railroad of Death* (London: 1946)
Hardie, Robert. *The Burma Siam Railway* (London: 1983)
Kee, Robert. *A Crowd Is Not Company* (London: 1947)
Lomax, Eric. *The Railway Man* (London: 1995)
Neave, Airey. *They Have Their Exits* (London: 1953)
Newby, Eric. *Love and War in the Appenines* (London: 1971)
Rofe, Cyril. *Against the Wind* (London: 1956)
Searle, Ronald. *To the Kwai—and Back* (London: 1986)
Wade, Tom Henling. *Prisoner of the Japanese* (Kenthurst, Australia: 1994)

American
Bilyeu, Dick. *Lost in Action* (Jefferson, N.C.: 1991)

Hayes, Thomas. *The Secret Notebooks of Commander Thomas Hayes* (Hamden, Conn.: 1987)
Lawton, Manny. *Some Survived* (Chapel Hill, N.C.: 1984)
Westheimer, David. *Sitting It Out* (Houston: 1992)

Women's War:

British and Commonwealth
Borden, Mary. *Journey Down a Blind Alley* (London: 1946)
Last, Nella. *Nella Last's War: A Mother's Diary 1939–45* (London: 1981)
Origo, Iris. *War in Val d'Orcia* (London: 1947) [an Anglo-American in Tuscany]
Teissier du Cros, Janet. *Divided Loyalties: A Scotswoman in Occupied France* (Edinburgh: 1962)

American
Settle, Mary Lee. *All the Brave Promises* (London: 1966) [an American in the WAAF]

French
Aubrac, Lucie. *Outwitting the Gestapo* (Lincoln, Nebr.: 1993)

German
Vassiltchikov, Marie. *The Berlin Diaries 1940–1945* (London: 1985)

Russian
Skrjabina, Elena. *Siege and Survival* (Carbondale, Ill.: 1971); *After Leningrad* (Carbondale: 1978)

VIETNAM

Brennan, Matthew. *Brennan's War* (Novato, Calif.: 1985)
Briscoe, Edward G. *Diary of a Short-timer in Vietnam* (New York: 1970) [a doctor]
Caputo, Philip. *A Rumor of War* (New York: 1977)
Donovan, David. *Once a Warrior King* (New York: 1985)
Downs, Frederick. *The Killing Zone* (New York: 1978)
Glasser, Ronald J. *365 Days* (New York: 1971) [a doctor]
Harrison, Marshall. *A Lonely Kind of War* (Novato, Calif.: 1989)
Herr, Michael. *Dispatches* (New York: 1977)
Kane, Rod. *Veterans Day* (New York: 1990)
Ketwig, John. *... and a hard rain fell* (New York: 1985)
Kovic, Ron. *Born on the Fourth of July* (New York: 1976)
Mason, Robert. *Chickenhawk* (New York: 1983)
McDonough, James. *Platoon Leader* (Novato, Calif.: 1985)
McGrath, John Michael. *Prisoner of War* (Annapolis: 1975) [drawings, with commentary]

Merritt, William E. *Where the Rivers Ran Backward* (Athens, Ga.: 1989)
O'Brien, Tim. *If I Die in a Combat Zone* (New York: 1973)
Puller, Lewis B., Jr. *Fortunate Son* (New York: 1991)
Wolff, Tobias. *In Pharaoh's Army* (New York: 1994)

Oral Histories:

Baker, Mark. *Nam: The Vietnam War in the Words of the Men and Women Who Fought There* (New York: 1981)
Marshall, Kathryn. *In The Combat Zone: An Oral History of American Women in Vietnam* (Boston: 1987)
Terry, Wallace. *Bloods: An Oral History of the Vietnam War by Black Veterans* (New York: 1984)

THE WARS AGAINST CIVILIANS

The Holocaust:

The Persecuted

Borzykowski, Tuvia. *Between Tumbling Walls* (Tel Aviv: 1972) [Jewish Underground in Warsaw]
Hillesum, Etty. *An Interrupted Life: The Diaries of* (New York: 1985)
Kaplan, Chaim A. *Scroll of Agony: The Warsaw Diary of* (New York: 1965)
Klein, Gerda W. *All But My Life* (London: 1958)
Lasker-Wallfisch, Anita. *Inherit the Truth 1939–1945* (London: 1996)
Leitner, Isabella. *Fragments of Isabella: A Memoir of Auschwitz* (New York: 1978)
Lengyel, Olga. *Five Chimneys* (Chicago and New York: 1947)
Levi, Primo. *If This Is a Man* (London: 1960)
Lewin, Abraham. *A Cup of Tears: A Diary of the Warsaw Ghetto* (Oxford: 1988)
Nyiszli, Miklos. *Auschwitz: A Doctor's Eyewitness Account* (New York: 1960)
Orenstein, Henry. *I Shall Live: Surviving the Holocaust* (Oxford: 1988)
Szép, Ernö. *The Smell of Humans: A Memoir of the Holocaust in Hungary* (Budapest/London/New York: 1994)
Szmaglewska, Seweryna. *Smoke over Birkenau* (New York: 1947)
Tedeschi, Giuliana. *There Is a Place on Earth: A Woman in Birkenau* (London: 1993)
Topas, George. *The Iron Furnace: A Holocaust Survivor's Story* (Lexington, Ky.: 1990)
Wermuth, Henry. *Breathe Deeply My Son* (London: 1993)
Wiesel, Elie. *Night* (London: 1960)
Zylberberg, Michael. *A Warsaw Diary 1939–1945* (London: 1969)

The Persecutors

Browning, Christopher R. *Ordinary Men* (New York: 1992) [for the scattered testimonies of the German soldiers who were the executioners of the Final Solution]

Hoess, Rudolph. *Commandant of Auschwitz: The Autobiography of Rudolph Hoess* (Cleveland and New York: 1959)

The Atom Bombs:

Akizuki, Tatsuichiro. *Nagasaki 1945* (London: 1981) [a doctor]

Chujo, Kazuo. *The Nuclear Holocaust: A personal account* (Tokyo: 1983)

Hachiya, Michihiko. *Hiroshima Diary: The Journal of a Japanese Physician August 6–September 30, 1945* (London: 1955)

Katsuzo Oda. "Human Ashes," in Kenzaburō Ōe, ed., *The Crazy Iris* (New York: 1985) [in England *Fire from the Ashes* (London: 1985)]

Minear, Richard H., ed. *Hiroshima: Three Witnesses* (Princeton: 1990) [Hara Tamiki,Ōta Yōko, and Tōge Sankichi]

Index

311

316 **Index**

North Africa, WWII, 135–44, 159
Nostalgia for war, 101, 129
Nuclear terror, era of, 276–77

O'Brien, Terence, *Chasing After Danger*, 173
O'Brien, Tim, 211, 283–84
Officers, 33–34, 43, 63–64, 142–44, 205; as prisoners of war, 254
Okinawa, 160–62
Old Soldiers Never Die, Richards, 65
Once A Warrior King, Donovan, 205
Our Cavalry, Rimington, 33–34
Owen, Wilfred, 71

Pacific War Diary, Fahey, xv, 170–71
Partridge, Eric, 29, 60, 66–67
Passchendaele, 60–61, 94–95, 110
Passionate Prodigality, Chapman, 51, 98
Pasternak, Boris, 26, 261
Patriotism, British, 45
Patton, George Smith, 28, 114
Pearce, Donald, 155–57, 160, 281
Peleliu, battle of, 160–61
Personal narratives, xiv, 14–16, 25–26, 30; WWI, 58; WWII, 119–23
"Piccadilly Jim," 142–44
Pictures from Vietnam, 200–201
Pilots, 13–14, 82–93, 216; WWII, 124–26, 132–35, 166–67
Platoon Leader, McDonough, 205
Plowman, Max, 18, 59, 70, 94
Poetics, Aristotle, 223
Poison gas, first use, 56–57
Post-traumatic stress disorder (PTSD), 99, 219
Prisoner-of-war stories, 232–58
Professional soldiers, British, 33–34, 37, 42

Propaganda, 225–26
Pryce (Captain), 57–58, 78
Psychological effects of Vietnam War, 218–22
Psychology of war, 62–64
Puller, Lewis, Jr., 207; *Fortunate Son*, 198–99
Puritanism of war stories, 186

Quartered Safe Out Here, Fraser, 164–65

The Railway Man, Lomax, 249–53
Realism of war narratives, 26–27
Reasoner, Frank, 213–14
Recollections, Harris, 4, 18
The Recollections of Rifleman Bowlby, Bowlby, 149–50
Remembering, xiv, 23–24
Repington (British Colonel), xi
Requiem for the Battleship Yamato, Yoshida, 172
Richards, Frank, 69; *Old Soldiers Never Die*, 65
Richthofen, Manfred von, 83, 86, 94; toast to, 87
Rimington, M. F., *Our Cavalry*, 33–34
Rivers, W. H. R., 62–64, 65
Rofe, Cyril, 238–39, 241–42
Romance of war, 27, 30, 41, 47–48, 144; aviation, 81–82, 92, 125–26; civilian soldiers and, 43–44; desert warfare, 137, 141–42; machines and, 123–24; Vietnam, 215–16; WWI, 76–78, 110
A Rumor of War, Caputo, 3, 27, 213–14

Saint-Exupéry, Antoine de, 128
Sajer, Guy, *The Forgotten Soldier*, 285
Sassoon, Siegfried, 66–68, 94, 128; *Sherston's Progress*, xv, 103